SO-DFB-038

Evaluating
U.S. Foreign Policy

Evaluating
U.S. Foreign Policy

edited by

John A. Vasquez

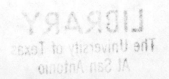

PRAEGER SPECIAL STUDIES • PRAEGER SCIENTIFIC

New York • Philadelphia • Eastbourne, UK
Toronto • Hong Kong • Tokyo • Sydney

Library of Congress Cataloging-in-Publication Data
Main entry under title:

Evaluating U.S. foreign policy.

   Includes index.
   1. United States--Foreign relations--1981-   --
Addresses, essays, lectures. 2. Reagan, Ronald--
Addresses, essays, lectures. I. Vasquez, John A.,
1945-   . II. Title: Evaluating United States
foreign policy.
E876.E92 1985   327.73   85-12212
ISBN 0-03-001967-2 (alk. paper)

Publis_ _d Distributed by the
Prae_ _blishers Division
(ISB_ _x 0-275)
of G_ _d Press, Inc.,
West_ _necticut

Published in 1986 by Praeger Publishers
CBS Educational and Professional Publishing, a Division of CBS Inc.
521 Fifth Avenue, New York, NY 10175 USA

© 1986 by Praeger Publishers

6789 052 987654321

Printed in the United States of America on acid-free paper

INTERNATIONAL OFFICES

Orders from outside the United States should be sent to the appropriate address listed below. Orders from
areas not listed below should be placed through CBS International Publishing, 383 Madison Ave., New York,
NY 10175 USA

Australia, New Zealand
Holt Saunders, Pty, Ltd., 9 Waltham St., Artarmon, N.S.W. 2064, Sydney, Australia

Canada
Holt, Rinehart & Winston of Canada, 55 Horner Ave., Toronto, Ontario, Canada M8Z 4X6

Europe, the Middle East, & Africa
Holt Saunders, Ltd., 1 St. Anne's Road, Eastbourne, East Sussex, England BN21 3UN

Japan
Holt Saunders, Ltd., Ichibancho Central Building, 22-1 Ichibancho, 3rd Floor, Chiyodaku, Tokyo, Japan

Hong Kong, Southeast Asia
Holt Saunders Asia, Ltd., 10 Fl, Intercontinental Plaza, 94 Granville Road, Tsim Sha Tsui East, Kowloon,
Hong Kong

**Manuscript submissions should be sent to the Editorial Director, Praeger Publishers, 521 Fifth Avenue,
New York, NY 10175 USA**

To My Sisters

Margie and Marie

PREFACE

I first conceived of preparing this book soon after Ronald Reagan assumed office and it became clear that he was resurrecting the Cold War. Not only was I opposed to this politically, in that I felt it unnecessary and damaging both domestically and internationally, but I felt that the assumptions underlying this shift to a hard-line stance were at variance with much of what we were beginning to learn as a community of scholars trying to create a scientific study of foreign policy and world politics. Most of the theoretical ferment within the international relations discipline and some of the quantitative research seriously question the validity of the realist or power politics assumptions that formed the bulwark of so much of the hard-liners' stance. Yet little of this academic work was able to permeate the main arena of political debate. Indeed, political debate seemed impervious to considerations of evidence, scientific inquiry, or the ambiguity of research findings. Thus, the fact that Carter pursued detente, got the Panama Canal treaty passed, could not prevent the invasion of Afghanistan, and could not obtain the release of the the U.S. hostages in Iran was taken by some as sufficient evidence that accommodation by soft-liners would not work, and that a return to a hard-line was essential. Now these people were in power. Although as a scientist my first temptation was to try to explain this shift and its implications for U.S. foreign policy, I could not help noting how small a role current inter-national relations theory and research or the spirit of scientific thinking about evidence was playing in these momentous decisions. I was also concerned that as a community of scholars we had not established more findings and that the findings we did have were not being communicated sufficiently well to policy makers, policy influencers, and the public as a whole. This seeming lack of progress in the cumulation of knowledge and establishing its relevancy to policy was widely perceived. This was leading some not only to abandon ship, but to join those who wanted to sink the scientific ship once and for all and get back to the art of diplomacy.

It was in this climate that I decided to ask a group of scholars, not all of them behavioralists, to try to review the theory and research in their area of specialization in order to apply its insights to evaluate some aspect of Reagan's foreign policy. This resulted in a panel on Reagan and the Cold War at the meeting of the American Political Science Association (APSA) in September 1982, which eventually gave rise to the analyses in Part II of this book. A follow-up panel was held at the International Studies Association (ISA) meeting in April 1983, where papers by Neil Richardson, Richard Ashley, and myself were presented. At this panel more attention was devoted to the philosophical and methodological questions that are raised by a group of scholars trying to evaluate foreign policy. In particular, I and the other members of the panel were concerned with the implications such an effort posed for the research agenda for the field, particularly comparative foreign policy. Finally, to insure that other salient aspects of Reagan's policy were included and to provide greater methodological diversity, I asked Thomas Rowe to prepare a chapter on Reagan's impact on human rights policy and Howard Zinn to assess the increasingly perilous situation in Central America. From the first, all participants knew that I was planning a volume that would not come out until 1986, so that a final draft of their papers would not be made until after the 1984 election. More importantly, they were told that their audience would be scholars and those concerned with making and influencing foreign policy. They were asked to write pieces that would be examples of foreign policy evaluation that attempted to make original contributions to knowledge rather than present a textbook overview of Reagan's policy. In this sense, none of the chapters try to give comprehensive assessments of Reagan's policy; rather, each only touches upon an aspect of that policy. In addition, since each chapter is intended as an example of how evaluation might be conducted, each offers only a preliminary assessment and not a definitive evaluation, which can only come years from now. Finally, an effort has been made to include pieces that would show how different techniques and modes of analysis can be employed in making evaluations.

Part I provides an introduction in which I discuss the need and importance of systematic foreign policy evaluation. I outline the ways in which it can be conducted and describe how each chapter illustrates the varieties of evaluation research. Part II evaluates Reagan's hard-line stance by assessing some of its assumptions and techniques in light of existing theory and research and certain normative concerns. A hard-liner may be defined as an individual who has a personal predisposition to adopt a foreign policy that is adamant in not compromising its goals and who believes in the efficacy and legitimacy of threats and force. Michael Wallace evaluates some of the hard-line assumptions underlying Reagan's defense policy, an area where Reagan has had a major impact. Russell Leng assesses the central tenet of any hard-line position, namely that "toughness works." Louis Beres critically examines what might be called nuclear hard-liners—those who believe that the United States should develop a strategy to win a nuclear war. Anatol Rapoport asks what factors make the war machine in the United States and the Soviet Union persist and discusses how behavioral theory must be extended to appreciate those factors and their dangers.

As one reads though these chapters, one cannot help but be struck by the disparity between the confidence with which hard-line positions are held and the dubious validity of some of their underlying assumptions. Even more portentous are the risks of war posed by this stance and the financial burden placed on the national (and global) economy to meet its requirements. All this is decided without much evidence, or research, or any thought to the fact that this might be a problem!

Part III looks at more specific actions that Reagan took in his first term. In each chapter it becomes clear that Reagan's hard-line stance has a measurable impact on the U.S. foreign policy, but that there is a continuity between his actions and those of some of his Democratic predecessors. Neil Richardson analyzes Reagan's use of economic incentives and sanctions to implement his Soviet policy. E. Thomas Rowe assesses some of the overlooked effects of Reagan's change in human rights policy. Howard Zinn looks at Reagan's policy toward Central America, an area that is a more critical test of U.S. policy toward revolution than was Grenada.

While these three chapters do not examine all Reagan's policies, they illustrate how Reagan's hard-line stance has had an impact on the U.S. foreign policy and how Reagan has dealt with some of the long-term problems that have faced the United States: trying to influence Soviet behavior, balancing idealism and morality with interest, and coming to terms with revolution. While each author reaches his own conclusion, it seems to me that Reagan's policies in each of these instances have not been very successful in handling—let alone resolving—some of these long-term problems. Furthermore, the hard-line stance has proved to be either irrelevant in achieving goals, as in human rights policy or changing Soviet behavior, or too risky, as in Central America.

Part IV looks at the future prospects of foreign policy evaluation and what must be done within the field to have a greater impact on foreign policy debate. Richard Ashley looks at some of the aspects of the scientific method that might have to be changed in order to engage in policy evaluation and make social science less tied to the status quo. In particular, he examines how the liberal positivist basis of the scientific study of foreign policy has made so much of its analyses irrelevant to policy questions or limited to technical matters. He argues in favor of adopting some of the insights of critical theory to broaden our methodology. In the final chapter, I look at how the scientific study of foreign policy might have to change its conceptualization of foreign policy in order to engage in policy evaluation. I see the need for us to try to explain actual foreign policies and not just isolated aspects of behavior. To do this scientifically, we must be able to classify different foreign policies, and I offer a taxonomy of foreign policies as a first step in this process. By making comparative *policy* analysis part of the research agenda of comparative foreign policy, we will help build a unified theory of foreign policy that not only explains but provides a foundation of knowledge upon which evaluation can be conducted.

The essays in this book are initial steps in an endeavor to make political science more sensitive to the need for foreign policy evaluation. They set an example of how the foreign policy of a current administration can be evaluated in a more scholarly and less journalistic fashion. Despite this common purpose, the views expressed by each author are his own and should not be attributed to the others. Similarly, my comments and concerns should not be construed as necessarily representing or agreeing with the views of the contributors. My thanks to each of the contributors for agreeing to participate in the project and to stay with it until after the 1984 election.

Harvey Starr, who served as discussant for the APSA panel, and Charles Hermann, who served as discussant for the ISA panel, provided comments that were not only valuable for the individual authors, but also aided my conceptualization of the entire enterprise. My thanks to Marie T. Henehan for helpful comments on the introduction and my own chapter. The Rutgers University Research Council and Faculty Academic Study Program provided financial support and released time that greatly aided the completion of the project. Finally, my thanks to Dorothy Breitbart and the editorial and production staff of Praeger for their assistance.

This book is dedicated to my sisters. Sisters are remarkable creatures who are usually underappreciated by brothers. I am grateful that my sisters have always been there and that they have been the kind of people they are.

February 1985
Block Island, Rhode Island

CONTENTS

Preface   vii

I

INTRODUCTION

1.   The Need for Foreign Policy Evaluation   3

     John A. Vasquez

II

EVALUATING REAGAN'S HARD-LINE STANCE

2.   Reagan and Vegetius: A Systematic Assessment
     of Some Assumptions of U.S. Defense Policy   19

     Michael D. Wallace

3.   Realism and Crisis Bargaining:
     A Report on Five Empirical Studies   39

     Russell J. Leng

4.   Flirtations with the Apocalypse:
     American Nuclear Strategy in Reagan II   59

     Louis René Beres

5.   Behavioral Theories and Global Strategies   73

     Anatol Rapoport

III

EVALUATING SPECIFIC POLICIES

6. **Reagan's Soviet Policy:
    Economic Linkage Unchained**   97

    Neil R. Richardson

7. **Human Rights: Assessing the Impact
    on Nongovernmental Organizations**   113

    E. Thomas Rowe

8. **Morality and National Interest:
    Vietnam and Central America**   135

    Howard Zinn

IV

THE FUTURE OF FOREIGN POLICY EVALUATION

9. **At the Impasse: Epistemology
    and the Scientific Evaluation of Foreign Policy**   159

    Richard K. Ashley

10. **Explaining and Evaluating Foreign Policy:
    A New Agenda for Comparative Foreign Policy**   205

    John A. Vasquez

Index   231

About the Editor and Contributors   239

I

INTRODUCTION

1

The Need
for Foreign Policy Evaluation

John A. Vasquez

In the United States the area of public policy that has potentially
the most widespread consequences is foreign policy. The sacrifice of
human life in war, the tremendous growth in military expenditures
since the beginning of the century, and the risk of nuclear
annihilation make this painfully obvious. Yet in no area of social
policy has systematic evaluation been avoided as it has in foreign
policy. Even the simplest review of policy that compares intentions
with consequences and sees whether means actually achieve goals
has been left undone. Instead, leaders and policy makers go blithely
forth commanding our loyalty, spending our money, and risking
our lives without so much as an effort at objective evaluation of the
major policies that have guided the state. This sad plight is made
even more disastrous by the fact that the conduct of foreign policy
by those with access to nuclear weapons may very well determine
whether Western civilization will survive.

What we do get are justifications and polemics that predict dire
consequences if this or that policy is not followed. These statements
rarely satisfy even the basic standards of scholarship, let alone
scientific rigor. Often they are no better than myth, distortion, and
sometimes outright lies.[1] There seem to be no judges or scientists
who seek the truth in the foreign policy establishment, but only
lawyers who seek to win. Thus, instead of evidence, we have

impression; instead of research, we have argument; instead of knowledge, we have myth.

If we know one thing about foreign policy as political scientists, it is that we know little about it, and those who conduct foreign policy know less because somehow this basic truth has eluded them. Little progress can be made until foreign policy makers and policy influencers at the highest levels admit that they have no idea whether their policies will work, or whether any beneficial consequences that do occur are due to their policies. Such an admission would be helpful, because it would make decision makers less prone to hubris and more open-minded, tolerant, tentative, and willing to encourage systematic research on the question.

Evaluation of foreign policy is based on the assumption that knowledge, in principle, is possible. We know from history that there are ways of regulating public health that are ineffectual and other ways that work and can actually extend life. We think we know that there are ignorant, knowledgeable, bad, and good ways of running the economy. The same is probably true of global relations, but since we have no knowledge about foreign policy effects, not even the crudest attempts at systematic trial and error, our conduct of foreign policy is mostly done in ignorance. The aim of foreign policy evaluation is to approach a level of knowledge that would make the scientific study of foreign policy at least as relevant to foreign policy as economics is to monetary policy. How should this be done, if it is possible? It is this question that will be addressed in this introduction.

Science can inform decision making in two ways. The first is by providing knowledge about how the world works and why it works the way it does. Until that knowledge is forthcoming, foreign policy makers are not going to be any more successful than were the forerunners of modern medical doctors in curing disease; which is to say, sometimes they will luck out, at other times they may stumble upon something significant, but usually they will be caught in a mire of ignorance. The scientific study of foreign policy is nowhere near providing the kind of knowledge the medical field has attained, but this may not be because it is inherently impossible. Other areas of international relations inquiry, namely the work on causes of war and on arms races, seem to be moving toward major breakthroughs (see Rummel, 1979; Singer, 1980; Wallace, 1982). Until such knowledge is attained, evaluation can proceed by an assessment of the accuracy of theoretical assumptions underlying a policy.

A second way that science can inform decision making, and which is more feasible for now, is to provide systematic feedback about the consequences—intended and unintended—of foreign policy. Although this is sometimes done intentionally by the government for more technically oriented policies, such as for foreign aid (or specific relief programs) or for weapons systems, it is not done for major policies. It is here where the most pressing need lies.

Evaluation research consists primarily of specifying criteria that a policy should satisfy and then doing careful unbiased research that meets the highest standards of scholarship and science to see whether the criteria have been satisfied. In everyday life we do something similar when we want to decide whether some object, such as a knife, is good. We begin by defining what we mean by "good" as precisely as possible (for a good knife we might mean: sharp enough to carve a rib roast and handsome enough to use in front of guests). We then apply these criteria to the knives under consideration (see Urmson, 1968). In the study of domestic public policy, evaluation research has been burgeoning (see *Policy Sciences, Public Policy, Evaluation Review, Evaluation News*), but it is only beginning to make an impact on foreign policy (see Bobrow and Stoker, 1981). Of course, evaluation of foreign policy occurs all the time, but it is rarely systematic, testable, or based on research.

At least two standard criteria can be employed in foreign policy evaluation research. The first criterion is that a policy should be based on an understanding of world politics that appears accurate. The policy task of the subfield should be to evaluate the underlying theory, assumptions, images, and myths of specific historical policies, such as the Truman Doctrine, then of more generic foreign policies, such as containment, and finally of general approaches to foreign policy, such as power politics. It is perhaps here that the most significant work can be done in the initial stages. So little has been done that just a systematic review of the evidence on the validity of underlying assumptions of foreign policies—like coercive diplomacy, balance of power, deterrence, and containment—would be enlightening. Those who have advocated these kinds of policies have often provided only the most impressionistic evidence, as Morgenthau's (1960:38) somewhat tautological remark: "All history shows that nations active in international politics are continuously preparing for, actively involved in, or recovering from organized violence in the form of war." Nevertheless, there has been some work done on alliances, power, and war (Singer and Small, 1974) and on deterrence (George and Smoke, 1974; Huth and Russett, 1984; Naroll et al., 1974). On the whole, this work is preliminary rather than definitive. Research needs to be more extensive, systematic, and couched within a policy evaluation framework. Likewise, work on specific policy assumptions such as the notorious domino theory would provide valuable information. Although traditional analysts have provided cogent criticism of specific policy proposals such as collective security and the United Nations, what is needed is criticism or justification that is grounded in empirical research. The initial result of such work will be to make evident how little support there is for the assumptions and theories that underlie dominant policy, and how little scientific investigation on them has actually occurred.

The analyses by Wallace and by Leng in Chapters 2 and 3 illustrate how significant evaluations of this type can be derived from quantitative research. Michael Wallace assesses the hard-line assumptions employed by Reagan and other members of his administration to justify their unprecedented peacetime military expenditures. He demonstrates that there is little empirical support for the notion of "peace through strength." Instead, the evidence strongly supports the idea that crises that occur in the presence of an ongoing arms race are much more apt to escalate to war than crises that occur during other times. He marshals evidence to question seriously the claim that the Soviet Union is ahead of the United States in strategic weapons and provides a statistical analysis to suggest that rather than responding to Soviet build-ups, the United States tends to initiate arms accelerations to which the Soviets then respond.

Russell Leng assesses some of the most fundamental realpolitik assumptions about bargaining that hard-liners, including Reagan, have adopted. In a review of five separate research studies he has conducted on the question, he finds that although decision makers often follow realist precepts in their bargaining, they are often not as prudent as realists advise. After quantitatively analyzing a number of crisis bargaining situations and conducting an in-depth review of U.S.–Soviet bargaining in the nuclear era, Leng finds that the use of a hard-line coercive strategy with an equal is more apt to result in defiance than in compliance and often ends in war. Even when it works in one crisis, it encourages the loser to be much more aggressive in the next dispute.

In addition to assumptions, evaluation research needs to examine the validity of images and myths guiding a foreign policy.

Images of human nature on which a policy is based may very well be archaic in light of scientific psychological research. More importantly, images of the other side, or of world politics generally, may be based on inappropriate analogies (Jervis, 1976; May, 1973). We need to explain not only why hard-liners or accommodationists have the images they do, but whether those images are valid and appropriate to the situation. There have been and continue to be those who have searched the past to learn from history. Their polemics and commitment to a particular policy too often biased their analyses and brought this form of inquiry into disrepute. Nevertheless, this effort suggests that we find it necessary to derive general lessons and patterns, and that we do learn from the past. We can continue to do it in a slip-shod primitive way, or we can be more rigorous in deriving lessons, testing the accuracy of images, and applying the best means of learning that we have—the scientific method.

An initial step is to compare official claims with the facts and the historical record (see Nielsen, 1974). This is a very useful way of testing the accuracy of images held by various political actors. In Chapter 8, Howard Zinn critically examines the self-image of the United States that its foreign policy is moral and in the national interest. He focuses on Reagan's policy in Central America and justifications of that policy by the Kissinger Commission and Jeane Kirkpatrick in light of the continuing debate over the lessons of Vietnam. He begins by stipulating what a moral foreign policy or one that is in the natonal interest might be reasonably expected to look like and then examines the record of the United States in Central America and Vietnam in light of these criteria. He finds a commonality in U.S. policy toward revolution that holds in both cases, and systematically refutes the various claims that have been made that U.S. policy is moral. He then examines whether U.S. policy in this area is in the national interest and finds no threat to the United States from the revolutionary movements in Central America. The Zinn analysis exemplifies a mode of foreign policy evaluation that examines decision makers' justifications and self-images of their policies to see whether their claims can stand careful scrunity; often they cannot. In the process, of course, Zinn derives his own lessons from history, which then form a foundation upon which to build a new and different policy.

While policy makers and polemicists are often important in creating images, academics and intellectuals are usually responsible for creating myths that are not valid. To a certain extent this is more insidious because myths are usually shrouded in the guise of scholarship and sometimes science. The most pernicious myth of our time was that of Aryan racial superiority. On a different level, the myth of the IQ and the use of testing to channel people point to the dangers that can accrue from misuses of science (see Gould, 1981). In our own day, the myth of coercive diplomacy led us to the brink of nuclear war in 1962 and proved to be an inappropriate strategy for fighting the Vietnam war. It is therefore important that myths be identified and evaluated for their validity.

An analysis of this type is presented in Chapter 4 by Louis René Beres, who challenges some of the myths that have surrounded U.S. nuclear strategy, with particular attention to the view expressed by some within the Reagan administration that the United States could survive and perhaps even win a nuclear war with the Soviet Union. He shows that the government has grossly underestimated the effects of a nuclear war on the United States and the world and has therefore underestimated the peril posed by current nuclear strategy. His analysis points out the important role myths can play in the making of crucial decisions and the need to assess their validity carefully.

In the absence of theoretical knowledge, one way of assessing current policy assumptions, images, and myths is to see how similar policies have fared in the past. Did they work or seem to have a chance of working? If they succeeded or if they failed, was it because of the assumptions, images, or myths—or some other factor? Were the indicators of success or failure internal to the policy, or did they reside in domestic or global factors? Are the conditions of success or failure that were present then also present now? While the number of such cases may prove too small for statistical inferences, systematic comparisons cannot help but improve the intellectual foundation upon which decisions are made and policy debated. Indeed, a small investment of this kind of research conducted by independent scholars outside the government would have a much greater impact and benefit than the effort placed on training area experts.

Likewise, a better understanding of the constellation of domestic and global factors that produce a generic policy will help us understand why an opponent or ally may be expected to disagree, and the extent to which change on their part or ours is possible. The analysis by Anatol Rapoport in Chapter 5 is written in this vein, providing an example of how empirical and evaluation research can work hand-in-hand. He tries to explain why the United States and the Soviet Union continue in an arms race that risks nuclear war and why it is so difficult to end the Cold War. He suggests that the reasons lie with the artifical needs of the "defense communities" of both the United States and the Soviet Union rather than with the needs of normal human beings. He then examines the implications of this view for both understanding and evaluating the foreign policies of the superpowers.

A second criterion for evaluation research is that a policy should accomplish what it was intended to do, and that unintended consequences should not outweigh the benefits of the policy. Clearly, one of the ways of applying this criterion is to examine the domestic and global reactions to the policy. Unlike the previously discussed evaluation research, this research need not await the development of any scientific theory or the cumulation of any great body of knowledge. It is fairly simple and straightforward and would seem to be *de rigueur* for any organization that takes itself seriously. Yet there are important bureaucratic and political reasons why that evaluation does not occur. In the foreign policy area, very little has been done along these lines; but there are some notable exceptions, particularly on foreign aid, that illustrate how such work could be conducted (see Sylvan, 1976).

The most pressing task of foreign policy evaluation would be to examine whether the anticipated consequences did occur.[2] Often debate on foreign policy is not so much over goals but over whether the policy will actually bring about the consequences its advocates say it will. Differences over the likely effects could serve as a guide to research. Here some of the advances in methodology and statistical analysis may aid in making inferences.

In Chapter 6 Neil Richardson follows this kind of research design to assess the attempts by the United States to affect Soviet behavior by offering or withdrawing certain economic benefits. He finds some empirical support for Kissinger's strategy of linkage and shows that Reagan's attempt to halt the construction of a natural gas pipeline between the Soviet Union and Western Europe was doomed to failure because it disregarded some essential conditions necessary for linkage to be a success. Instead, U.S. actions degenerated into economic sanctions, which usually do not work to change the behavior of the other side, although they express one's own displeasure. Richardson reviews the literature to outline what role economic linkage can play in superpower relations. His analysis shows how evaluation research can provide important feedback to policy makers.

Of equal importance for evaluation is research that delineates the unintended or unanticipated consequences of a policy. In particular, it is important to delineate the effect of the policy on other issues and on nontargets. In drug research, most of the effort is devoted to side-effects, yet in public policy research, analysts pay insufficient attention to this problem. Nowhere is this more evident than in the decision to go to total war, where utopian consequences are expected from victory and nothing but evil is assumed to result from the failure to fight, when in reality little is really known (see Braybrook and Lindblom, 1963).

In Chapter 7, E. Thomas Rowe examines the various effects, intended or not, of Reagan's change in America's human rights policy on organizations promoting the protection of human rights. Employing survey research, Rowe finds that most human rights organizations perceived Reagan as having a large impact on their ability to promote human rights. With the exception of those organizations concerned with the Soviet Union and Eastern Europe, the impact was seen as negative. Rowe details problems some of the organizations have had in working with the Reagan administration and outlines measures any administration could take to make these organizations' efforts more effective. Rowe's study shows how evaluation research can measure some of the secondary effects of major changes in foreign policy, in this case the impact on nongovernmental organizations.

Evaluation research that examines consequences can also be conducted on more general or generic foreign policies, such as balance of power (see Vasquez, Chapter 10), so that we get a sense of the usual results of these policies. The way to do this is to employ a quasi-experimental design where one instance of a generic foreign policy would be compared to other cases that would act as controls. For example, the many instances of balance-of-power policy can be compared to see what consequences emerged and perhaps to discover why they emerged. Eventually a set of empirical generalizations might be established that would tell us that under conditions X, Y, Z this kind of policy will result in the following consequences—intended, unintended, domestic, global— with the following probabilities.

To this we would want to add an assessment of risks, based on risks that seemed to have been associated with previous imple- mentations of the policy. For instance, certain policies may embody a strategy that is more likely to risk war (see Leng, 1980 and Leng's analysis in Chapter 3). Likewise, policies that simultaneously encourage arms races and hard-line bargaining in a crisis may risk escalation to war (Wallace, 1982; see also Wallace's analysis in Chapter 2). On the other hand, policies such as appeasement may risk failure and possible defeat when promulgated in the wrong historical situation and toward a leader not susceptible to accommodation. Similarly, certain policies may produce self-fulfilling prophecies. Realpolitik policies, as well as policies that seek revenge (for example, the Versailles treaty), seem to be prone to these risks, as might policies on limited nuclear war (see Beres' analysis in Chapter 4). One of the benefits of evaluation research is that eventually we could get a sense not only of what works and what does not work, but of the risks involved.

Up to this point, much of the evaluation research that has been suggested has been fairly typical of the kind of policy evaluation in public policy (see Bobrow and Stoker, 1981; Hoole, 1977; Nachmias, 1980). In an effort to be objective and scientific, some of this kind of policy evaluation has sought to be apolitical. Consequently, it has not evaluated the goals of a policy, unless they are not feasible, nor has it sought to determine who benefits or pays for a policy. The result of this has been to make the evaluation somewhat incomplete, if not at times myopic. Nor has this resulted in being apolitical, since such evaluation has the effect of supporting the status quo. In the United States, because this tradition stems from the work of John Dewey and because of the liberal dominance of the government, this research has often been accused, with some justification, of being little better than liberal social engineering. In addition, those doing this sort of evaluation have usually abandoned the role of the intellectual as social critic and questioner of prevailing beliefs and truth in favor of the role of the expert, the consultant, and the bureaucrat.

The only way to avoid this is to engage in what might be called "grand policy evaluation," that is, evaluation that asks fundamental political and moral questions. This kind of evaluation must look at goals, see who benefits and who is hurt, question motives and interests, search for deceptions and distortions, and expose untruths. In various ways, the essays by Beres and Zinn approach this kind of evaluation, even though they do not systematically discuss the larger goals of Reagan's policy. A complete evaluation from this perspective would involve completing three tasks: the evaluation of policy goals, an exposure of disortion and lies used to justify a policy, and the creation of policies that work and serve an explicitly stated set of values and publics.

The way to evaluate policy goals is to examine the domestic and global consequences of attaining or trying to attain them. Along with this must be an assessment of who benefits and who is hurt by a policy. If possible, comparisons should be made either hypothetically or historically to rival policies. While criteria for measuring costs and benefits should be reliable and testable, this does not stand in the way of making ethical judgments, so long as the moral system being employed is made explicit. All too often the state and all its policies have served the few at the expense of the many. It is probably the illusion of our time to think that democratic, capitalist, socialist, or communist states might be different. At any rate, since this is an empirical question, it should be answered on the basis of the evidence. Only a set of evaluators not wedded to the government or its shadow opposition could hope to address such a question and its ethical implications.

Any evaluation worth its salt is inevitably going to come across lies, distortions, and other self-serving instruments that have been used in justifying a policy. What distinguishes grand policy evaluation from internal or narrow policy science evaluation is that it can confront these machinations forthrightly and without fear of financial or political retribution. In a sense, what we need is a Ralph Nader for foreign policy. As academics, we need to instill in policy makers and policy advocates a respect for the truth and a fear that distortions will be exposed. In this regard it is important that our scholarship be impeccable. Eventually the foreign-policy-attentive public(s) will come to respect our integrity and trust our information. It is important that the truth of information distributed by the government and private policy advocates be assessed. This is not only because the truth is a value in and of itself, but because distortions of this sort are probably one of the reasons why foreign policy so often results in disasters or in wars many people do not want. Ultimately, this will mean that our right to know must be pushed vigorously, but until grand policy evaluation can prove itself, it is probably better to concentrate on the past where access is more open, passion is less intrusive, and the product is less threatening. Once we have been successful, it will be necessary to move quickly to current matters.

The evaluation of goals can help the scientific study of foreign policy break out of the technical rationality that is part of the positivist legacy it inherited. In Chapter 9, Richard Ashley addresses this problem in some detail and points out why the positivist basis of much of the scientific study of world politics makes it difficult for foreign policy evaluation to break out of this technical rationality mode. While there will be disagreements over the extent to which the scientific method is inherently confined to a technical rationality, there is little disagreement that the practice of social science within the international relations discipline has tended to be confined to that sort of rationality. To break out of that mode, Ashley calls for the adoption of a critical–dialogical perspective, which would introduce the possibility of more radical analysis. This would involve going beyond the evaluation of goals to an assessment of the social world being produced and sustained by the dominant ideas of international relations theory (including its method), and then using these insights to illuminate the possibility for fundamental change. Ashley's recommendations have implications not only for evaluation, but for empirical analysis. He is interested in knowing by what practices social worlds are hegemonically secured and then finding out under what conditions and by what practices such structures might be transformed.

Ashley's analysis makes it clear that if evaluation is going to be taken seriously, then it cannot help but have an impact on the way we empirically study politics. In the closing chapter, I suggest we will have to change the way we study and explain foreign policy, if our work is to be more conducive to policy evaluation, and I outline how we might explain foreign policy so that it can give rise to significant evaluation research. While studying aspects of foreign policy behavior is fine, we also need to explain the actual substantive policies of global actors in a scientific manner. This can best be done by developing a taxonomy of the different kinds of foreign policies that have been adopted. This permits an empirical analysis of the historical and theoretical factors associated with the various policies and an evaluation of the means, goals, and social worlds associated with the policies.

In the end, if evaluation is to succeed, it is not enough simply to review past and current policies; these insights must be employed to develop policies that will work. But how does one determine what works? While this depends, in part, on what one wants to work, and hence involves political choice, there are limits to what is possible, and scientific analysis can help identify those limits and separate the social limits from the historical and physical. At the level of technical rationality, a policy works if it reaches its goal with minimal risks and costs. At the level of grand foreign-policy evaluation, what works depends on the desirability and feasibility of the goals. Finally, at a critical–dialogical level, what works depends on the overall value of the social world being sustained.

Regardless of the level at which evaluation occurs, the movement from criticism to construction of alternative policies raises the question of what is to prevent evaluators from becoming partisans. Partisanship is difficult to avoid, for two different reasons. First, as one moves from means to goals to social worlds, one touches upon questions that are more explicitly value-laden. Second, the movement from criticism to construction brings one deeper into the realm of practice, not only because it involves studying the whole rather than just a part, but because it requires some attention to be paid to how support for such recommendations can be generated.

It is a mistake, however, to think that all partisanship is the same, and that one is either partisan and biased, or neutral and objective. Rather, there are *degrees* of partisanship. The only thing that can prevent scientists and scholars from becoming completely partisan is their commitment to put their loyalty to the truth above their loyalty to their party, their class, their ideology, their church, or their country. As Mannheim (1936) points out, this professional ethic of an intelligentsia may permit an escape from the social relativity of knowledge (see also Nielsen, 1974). Even if it does not provide a complete escape, it is likely at least to guarantee a sufficient respect for the evidence to prevent the fraud, deception, and lies of the past. Policy evaluation will not replace politics, but it may make politics more successful and less costly in resources and lives by helping us to learn what the real consequences of our policies are and what kinds of actions may help bring about the kind of world most of us would value.

Such general concerns must eventually confront specific historical circumstances. Ultimately, it is unlikely that any real change can occur in the policy of a state simply through intellectual effort. Intellectual analysis, if it is to have that kind of impact, is likely to be tied to a larger political movement from which it derives problems to study and to which it will give conceptualizations and policy recommendations. In this way, abstract thought becomes directly relevant to the realm of practice. The result, however, has usually been the creation and refinement of ideology. Historically, this has been the typical fate of those who have studied international politics. As the scientific study of foreign policy moves toward policy evaluation, its greatest challenge will be to keep a self-critical perspective, even within action, in order to avoid that fate.

NOTES

[1]It seems that the more momentous the decision, the greater the tendency to distort. Examples of this include James Polk's deception of Congress about the incident that led to the Mexican War, Lyndon Johnson's description of the Gulf of

Tonkin incident, and, more recently, Reagan's misuse of statistics. Non-U.S. examples would include the Nazi arguments and "evidence" in favor of Ayran racial superiority and Kipling's white man's burden.

[2]Some may be concerned that evaluation of current foreign policy might not be feasible because there is insufficient information on the real goals and strategies of an administration or on exactly what options or rival policies exist. While this is certainly a problem with ongoing policies, especially as these are affected by covert or private actions, this becomes less of a problem once an administration has left office.

It must also be kept in mind that precise information on decision makers' goals and strategies does not affect all evaluations equally. It is still possible to evaluate a policy in terms of the consequences it produces, whether they were anticipated or not, the risks and costs of a policy, and whether the public justification of the policy are fulfilled.

REFERENCES

BOBROW, D., and R. STOKER (1981). "Evaluation of Foreign Policy." In P. T. Hopmann, D. Zinnes, and J. D. Singer (eds.), *Cumulation in International Relations Research,* Vol. 18/3 Monograph Series in World Affairs, Denver, Colorado. Pp. 99–132.

BRAYBROOKE, D., and C. E. LINDBLOM (1963). *A Strategy of Decision: Policy Evaluation as a Social Process.* New York: Free Press.

GEORGE, A. L., and R. SMOKE (1974). *Deterrence in American Foreign Policy: Theory and Practice.* New York: Columbia University Press.

GOULD, S. J. (1981). *The Mismeasure of Man.* New York: Norton.

HOOLE, F. W. (1977). "Evaluating the Impact of International Organizations," *International Organization,* 31:541–63.

HUTH, P., and B. RUSSETT (1984). "What Makes Deterrence Work? Cases from 1900 to 1980." *World Politics,* 36:496–526.

JERVIS, R. (1976). *Perception and Misperception in International Politics.* Princeton, N.J.: Princeton University Press.

LENG, R. J. (1980). "Influence Strategies and Interstate Conflict." In J. D. Singer (ed.), *Correlates of War: II.* New York: Free Press. Pp. 125–57.

MANNHEIM, K. (1936). *Ideology and Utopia.* New York: Harcourt, Brace.

MAY, E. R. (1973). *"Lessons" of the Past.* London: Oxford University Press.

MORGENTHAU, H. J. (1960). *Politics Among Nations,* 3rd ed. New York: Knopf.

NACHMIAS, D., ed. (1980). *The Practice of Policy Evaluation.* New York: St. Martin's Press.

NAROLL, R., V. L. BULLOUGH, and F. NAROLL (1974). *Military Deterrence in History: A Pilot Cross-Historical Survey.* Albany, N.Y.: State University of New York Press.

NIELSEN, K. (1974). "Social Science and American Foreign Policy." In V. Held, S. Morgenbesser, and T. Nagel (eds.), *Philosophy, Morality, and International Affairs.* New York: Oxford University Press. Pp. 286–319.

RUMMEL, R. J. (1979). *War, Power, Peace,* Vol. 4: *Understanding Conflict and War.* Beverly Hills, Calif.: Sage Publications.

SINGER, J. D., ed. (1980). *The Correlates of War: II.* New York: Free Press.

SINGER, J. D., and M. SMALL (1974). "Foreign Policy Indicators: Predictors of War in History and the State of the World Message." *Policy Sciences,* 5:271–96.

SYLVAN, D. (1976). "Consequences of Sharp Military Assistance Increases for International Conflict and Cooperation." *Journal of Conflict Resolution,* 20:609–36.

URMSON, J. C. (1968). *The Emotive Theory of Ethics.* New York: Oxford University Press.

WALLACE, M. (1982). "Armaments and Escalation: Two Competing Hypotheses." *International Studies Quarterly,* 26:37–56.

II

EVALUATING REAGAN'S HARD-LINE STANCE

2

Reagan and Vegetius:
A Systematic Assessment
of Some Assumptions
# of U.S. Defense Policy

Michael D. Wallace

INTRODUCTION

Upon taking office in 1981, the Reagan administration embarked upon a major expansion of U.S. military capability whose projected cost exceeds one trillion (10^{12}) dollars. Heavily emphasized in this expansion are strategic weapons systems designed to pursue a major conflict with the Soviet Union, including the Trident submarine program, the cruise missile, the Pershing II IRBM, the ERW (neutron bomb), the MX ICBM, a revived B-I bomber, and even a follow-on bomber, the so-called "Stealth." The Strategic Defense Initiative alone has a projected research cost of $26 billion for two fiscal years. These major programs are supplemented by others designed to improve the accuracy, reliability, and yield of strategic warheads and to improve guidance systems and anti-satellite weapons.

This major expansion of strategic military capability has been undertaken in the face of two important obstacles: First, it is clear that military expenditures of this magnitude create significant economic problems. Although some scholars have argued that military expenditures can be used to stimulate the economy during periods of slack (Nincic and Cusack, 1979), the current consensus appears to be that military expenditures of the present magnitude are having the reverse effect by contributing to budget deficits.

Over the longer term, while some claim that military spending stimulates the growth sectors of the U.S. economy (Reich, 1982), an equally plausible case can be made that the heavy military focus of U.S. research and development reduces the competitive advantage of the United States in civilian markets. Japan's continuing success in displacing the United States as the sole supplier of high-technology goods suggests strongly that the pessimistic interpretation is correct.

Second, in addition to the economic problems associated with large military expenditures, Reagan's armaments program has generated strenuous opposition from those who claim that the competitive acquisition of armaments by contending nations magnifies and exacerbates the quarrels among them, deepening their mutual suspicions and fears. According to this view, these insecurities stimulate in turn further competitive acquisitions, and the resulting "armaments–tension spiral" (Singer, 1958), if not checked, will provide the mise-en-scène for all-out nuclear war. No longer confined to a small body of academics and clerics, this perspective has formed the basis for the broadly based and rapidly growing nuclear freeze movement. The magnitude of this political challenge can be measured by the vote on the nuclear freeze resolution in the House of Representatives: despite intense administration lobbying, it lost by a mere two votes (The *New York Times,* August 7, 1982).

In short, the Reagan armaments program has created both economic and political liabilities for the administration. Yet there appears no sign that the president will be deflected from his chosen course (Second Inaugural Address, The *New York Times,* January 22, 1985).

Clearly, Reagan's military program does not originate from simple calculations of political advantage but rather is founded in some of the deepest convictions of the administration. Yet, despite their central importance to the current debate, and despite the awesome risks that are posed should they be ill-founded, these intellectual foundations of administration policy have been advocated and supported by evidence that is often partial and anecdotal, and sometimes questionable and controversial.

It is the purpose of this chapter to examine more rigorously some of the major arguments employed by the administration to justify its expansion of U.S. military capability, and more particularly of strategic nuclear capability. After setting forth the major propositions of the administration's case, the chapter will attempt to assess them in the light of some of the author's research findings, supplemented by additional systematically generated data.

THE ARGUMENTS FOR ARMAMENTS

The president and administration officials offered four main arguments to justify their military buildup:

(1) They argued that the Soviet Union was ahead in strategic nuclear weaponry. The famous 1980 campaign statement that the United States has moved from a ranking of "second to none" to a position of "second to one" was followed by numerous statements proclaiming Soviet strategic superiority. Even more alarmist opinions warned of a "window of vulnerability" to a disabling attack on U.S. land-based ICBMs which, it was alleged, could be mounted by the Soviets using only a small fraction of their own missiles (Kaplan, 1980). In the view of the administration the United States had to move rapidly to increase its strategic capabilities or suffer the political and security costs of inferiority.

(2) The second argument advanced by the administration was that U.S. strategic inferiority threatens not only her particular strategic interests, but global peace itself. The belief that U.S. superiority is necessary to protect the peace is not, of course, an invention of this administration; it has been asserted by every president since Truman. Its intellectual antecedents are far more ancient: the doctrine of "peace through strength" is first attributed to the fourth-century Roman general, Vegetius Flavius:

> (Qui) desiderat pacem, praeparat bellum ... nemo provocare, nemo audet offendere quem intelliget superiorem esse pugnaturum.[1]

Thus, only when the status quo power has achieved significant military superiority will revolutionary or revisionist powers be deterred from disturbing the peace.

(3) The third argument was the converse of the second and sought to quiet the fears of those who saw administration policy as triggering a dangerous arms race. According to this view, it is not the arms race per se that is dangerous to peace; rather, peace will be determined by the *outcome* of the arms race.[2] Only if the Soviet side retains or extends its lead is there a threat to the peace; if the United States prevails, all will be well.

(4) The fourth argument used by the administration was that U.S. strategic buildup would not, in all probability, result in an arms race in any case. Instead, it will be the likely prelude to a significant arms-control agreement. This is because the threat of further U.S. strategic acquisitions will encourage Soviet concessions in arms-control talks and induce them to limit the augmentation of their own arsenal. But if the United States does not proceed with its procurements, the Soviets will neither agree to balanced arms control, nor limit their own growth. In other words, in contradiction to the claims of the advocates of a nuclear freeze, the administration argues that its military program will check rather than stimulate increases in Soviet strategic might.

Thus the administration's defense of its military policy. How do these arguments fare in the light of systematic evidence?

ARMS RACES
AND PEACE THROUGH STRENGTH

Existing research findings permit us to cast doubt on at least one element of the administration's case. The belief that the arms race does not of itself threaten war appears contrary to fact. In a study that examined 99 serious disputes among great powers (Wallace, 1979), I found that the great majority of disputes preceded by an arms race escalated to war 23 out of 28 times, while disputes *not* preceded by an arms race resulted in war only 3 out of 71 times. This would seem to support the contention of the nuclear freeze advocates that the arms race is indeed a danger sui generis.

Moreover, in a later article I was able to dispute the belief that a relative weakness on the part of the status quo power led to dispute escalation (Wallace, 1982). In 28 cases, the revisionist power was at least 50% stronger prior to the dispute, and in only 9 of them did the dispute escalate to war. Only a slightly smaller proportion (17 out of 54) escalated when the revisionist power was not stronger; the relationship was not statistically significant.

The situation proved to be no different if one looked at those cases in which the revisionist power was both stronger *and* increasing in strength prior to the dispute. Only 11 of 36 of such "revisionist threat" cases escalated to war; by contrast, 15 out of 63 "no-threat" cases escalated; once again, this difference in proportion is not statistically significant.

In other words, a systematic examination of serious disputes between great powers from 1816 to 1965 showed two things clearly: first, that concerns about the war-provoking effects of the super-power arms race appear well founded in the light of historical evidence; second, that the "peace through strength" doctrine appears to have much less basis in historical fact.

These findings, of course, speak only to the historical record, and not to the existing situation between the superpowers. It could (and has) been argued that the length of this arms race, the existence of only two significant powers, and, above all, the sobering fact of the enormous nuclear arsenals possessed by both sides, makes it risky to generalize to the present situation from historical data. Even if this be legitimate, these findings do not deal with the other elements of the administration's case, namely: (1) the belief that the Soviet Union is ahead, and (2) the assertion that a U.S. arms buildup will deter rather than provoke further Soviet growth. It is to these points that we now turn.

Alternative Indices of Strategic Capability: Counterforce and Countervalue

There are any number of ways to construct an index to measure the relative military capabilities of the two superpowers. And, as the reader will doubtless be aware, a wide variety of alternatives has been proposed in governmental circles, the media, and in scholarly articles. It will also come as no surprise that these variegated efforts have produced an incredible range of assessments; at the one end of the spectrum, there are those who claim that the United States is much inferior militarily to the Soviet Union (Rummel, 1976); at the other end, it is argued that the United States is considerably superior to the Soviet Union (Kaplan, 1980).

But winnowing the wheat from the chaff is not as hard as it might seem at first, since many of these indices may be dismissed fairly readily. One example would be those indices based upon the relative *military expenditures* of the two superpowers. While useful for many theoretical purposes (Wallace, 1979), expenditure-based indices are not appropriate here because they measure military *effort* rather than military *capacity*. Mr. Reagan and his colleagues are far less concerned about the economic sacrifices the Soviet people must make to build their military machine than they are in the ability of that machine to inflict damage upon the United States (Taagepera, 1980). Moreover, comparing the expenditures of the two superpowers raises extraordinary problems of data generation. Not only is there the whole matter of "hidden" expenditures and the thorny problem of the ruble–dollar conversion ratio, but one can even question whether even approximate price and cost comparisons between such totally different economic systems have any real validity (Lee, 1977; SIPRI, 1981).

But confining ourselves to indices of actual fighting capacity does not end our problems. Many of these "hardware" indices proposed in the literature are of dubious validity. It is not clear, for example, what military advantage is conferred by the *number* of missiles alone, or the number of warheads or throw-weight (Kaplan, 1980). It would seem that many of these indices have been selected, and many comparisons made, without much regard for the central theoretical question at issue: what aspects of military capability are likely to affect each superpower's perception of the threat posed by the other side, and consequently influence their respective military aquisition policies.

It is surely evident that in the nuclear age no less than the historical past, the first and perhaps most important threat that every state responds to is the ability of an enemy to waste its blood and treasure. That this capacity has become ludicrously overabundant in the second half of the twentieth century has not made its aquisition any less rapid or competitive (Science, 1982a). And despite the almost comic levels of "overkill" built into contemporary targeting plans (leading, for example, to the designation of several warheads in the 100-kt range to a single unprotected building), the number and power of theater and strategic nuclear weapons has continued to increase relentlessly.

A second and perhaps even more important feature of military might is that emphasized by Clausewitz: the ability of one side to destroy the military capacity of the other. Although in the nuclear age this capacity no longer implies military victory in the traditional sense, it nevertheless continues to be the central focus of strategic planning of both an offensive and a defensive nature. Defensively, both sides take great pains to hide or otherwise shelter their most important weapons systems from destruction, and both fret privately and publicly (Soviet Ministry of Defense, 1982) lest these efforts not be successful. Offensively, even in the nuclear age, military planners have been unable to curb the temptation to plot the unilateral destruction of the other side's strategic weaponry (*Los Angeles Times*, August 14, 1982), which impression is further reinforced by the ever-increasing hard-target killing capabilities of modern strategic weapons systems.

Taken together, these two aspects of military ability, indelibly labeled in the strategic lexicon as "countervalue" and "counterforce" capabilities, are without question the most provocative and sensitive features of the superpowers' military machines, and the ones most likely to concentrate the other's attention and response. And regardless of how scholars and commentators evaluate their importance, it is clear that the Reagan administration sees them as central indicators of the military balance. Given countervalue and counterforce as our foci, how do we go about measuring the superpowers' relative capabilities with any degree of accuracy and reliability?

Calculating Countervalue

Any attempt at the mensuration of the destructive capability of nuclear weapons must overcome a fundamental intellectual obstacle: the scale of destruction resulting from their use in large numbers would be so vast that even its lower end-point is beyond historical experience and almost beyond comprehension. Its upper end-point, the climactic disruption and biospheric collapse referred to as "nuclear winter," reaches to the very limits of scientific speculation, and well beyond the reach of firm scientific knowledge. The task of constructing a quantitative indicator of nuclear capability thus carries with it an element of unreality.

Consequently, no claim can or will be made to measure the potential impact of nuclear destruction on human societies or biological systems. All that can be done is to measure their impact in the crudest physical terms. Although such crude physical indicators are scarcely valid measures of the actual destruction that would occur in a war, the use of these and similar indices by military planners and policy-makers renders them valid indicators in the context of accounting for state behavior.

The simplest of such physical indices is simply the total explosive force that could be produced by the detonation of each nation's total strategic nuclear arsenal, comprising the sum of the explosive yields of all the nuclear devices whose delivery vehicles permit them to be targeted on the territory of the opposing superpower. This "total megatonnage" represents the total destructive force each side can bring to bear against the other. Note that neither the speed nor accuracy of the delivery vehicle enters into this calculation; against soft and essentially immobile targets, these factors are assumed to be irrelevant.

Now it has been argued that this simple sum results in a distorted total; the physical impact of the detonation of a large number of thermonuclear weapons is not the same as that of a large number of smaller ones. The larger weapons emit more of their energies in the higher reaches of the elctromagnetic spectrum, reducing the blast effect. To compensate for this, strategists have devised the concept of "equivalent megatonnage." If we let MT equal the raw explosive yield of a device, EMT (equivalent megatonnage) is given as

$$EMT = MT^{2/3}$$

Table 2.1 shows calculated total megaton and equivalent megaton values for the United States and the Soviet Union at four-year intervals from 1972 to 1984, corresponding to the last year of the administration of each of the last four Presidents.

No sophisticated mathematical techniques are required to interpret these figures from the perspective of strategic policy. Two features stand out immediately. To begin with the most obvious, both sides have increased their destructive capacities considerably since 1972. Even though in that year the two superpowers signed the first of the SALT accords which had the putative object of slowing the arms race, both continued to add destructive capacity to their arsenals; the U.S. increased its theoretical destructive capacity by about 16%, and the Soviet Union no less than 64%.

A second clear inference from these figures is the shifting *relative* position of the two powers on the megaton and equivalent megaton scale. From a position of considerable inferiority in 1972, the Soviet Union has added relatively more to its total

Table 2.1

Countervalue Capability of the United States and the Soviet Union

	Raw megatonnage		Equivalent megatons	
	U.S.A.	USSR	U.S.A.	USSR
1972	3,872	3,430	2,538	1,917
1976	4,625	4,660	3,003	2,108
1980	4,531	5,889	2,921	2,906
1984	4,711	7,020	2,934	3,142

megatonnage. This growth is not so striking in equivalent megatons, as it consists chiefly of larger, relatively "inefficient" warheads. Nevertheless, it was enough to give the Soviet Union a position of rough equivalence or even a marginal superiority by the 1980s.

These two aspects of superpower destructive capacity frame the debate between the Reagan administration and its critics. The administration stresses the relative U.S. decline, its critics the relentless bilateral increase in destructive capability far beyond any conceivable level of assured destruction. But arguably these figures neither reflect the true relative strategic capabilities of the superpowers, nor do they illuminate the motives behind their strategic doctrines and arms acquisition policies. To do either of these things we must develop more sophisticated indices of military capacity which measure *counterforce lethality*: the ability of each superpower to destroy not the other side's cities, population, or economy, but its strategic retaliatory forces.

Calculating Counterforce

Attempting to assess the counterforce capabilities of the superpowers involves us immediately in a buzzing welter of technical complexity. Our task is made harder by the political and bureaucratic contentiousness of many of the issues involved, and by the fact that many writers on the subject base their estimates on material that is subject to security classification (Wohlstetter, 1969). Nevertheless, the basic strategy for the construction of a counterforce index seems clear enough: (1) identify those weapons systems that can be used in a strategic counterforce role; (2) identify the probable success that each weapon would have in destroying the strategic weapons of the other side; and (3) aggregate these to produce an index of "counterforce kill capacity."

The first step is relatively easy, because the identity and numbers of weapons with counterforce capabilities can be readily determined with reference to such standard sources as the SIPRI Yearbook and the Military Balance. An examination of these sources reveals that we need consider only ballistic missiles with nuclear warheads, since only these systems combine the speed, accuracy, and yield capable of destroying "hardened" targets. With the introduction of multiple-warhead missiles (MIRVs and MARVs), we need to count not the number of missiles, but the number of warheads on each.

The second step—that of assessing the lethality of each weapon—is rather more complex. Weapons scientists have developed sophisticated formulae expressing the probability that a weapons system will destroy a protected (hardened) target as a function of (1) the *yield* of a missile's warhead, (2) the *accuracy* of the warhead, (3) the degree of protection or *hardness* of the target, and (4) the reliability of the complete weapons system. The formula used here will be the best that is available from unclassified sources, that proposed by Davis and Schilling (1973). Although their formula may be subject to minor inaccuracies resulting from pulse duration, burst height, terrain, weather, and a host of other random factors, it seems a good compromise between simplicity and the desire to take account of as many as possible of the factors affecting weapons lethality. According to Davis and Schilling,

$$TKP = R(1 - 0.5^{8.41y^{2/3}/H^{0.7}(CEP)^2})$$

where *TKP* is the "terminal kill probability" of the weapon, *R* its overall reliability, *y* its yield in kilotons, *CEP* its accuracy expressed as the radius in nautical miles of a circle within which one-half of such weapons may be expected to strike, and *H* the hardness of its target expressed as the number of pounds per square inch of dynamic blasts overpressure that it can withstand. Now it is evident from this formula that kill probability is critically dependent upon the *accuracy* of the weapon in question, and to a lesser extent upon the yield and hardness factors. It is therefore unfortunate that estimates of accuracy, target hardness, yield, and reliability are shrouded in official secrecy, and that even unofficial estimates vary widely.

After much agonizing, the author decided that a single reliable estimate for these factors was an impractical goal. Instead, what was done was to calculate *multiple* estimates of *TKP* reflecting the variation in the published sources. This was done as follows: Approximately 12 sources were consulted, which were used to generate three separate estimates of the performance characteristics of each weapon based on its accuracy, yield, and reliability. The first two estimates were the *highest* and the *lowest TKP* values that could be calculated from the figures in any source. The third estimate was the *mean TKP* value calculated from the figures in all sources.

Multiple estimates were also used for the hardness of the target each weapon would be aimed at. Since there is no easy way of determining in advance which missiles are aimed at which targets, two estimates were used, representing the minimum and maximum hardness that a counterforce-targeted weapon would encounter.

Since we used three estimates of weapon performance and two estimates of target hardness, we therefore calculated *six* estimates of the *TKP* of each weapon. To arrive at a "counterforce lethality" for each superpower, the *TKP*s for all its weapons were summed. This simple procedure might be open to criticism, because it ignores the problem of modifying *TKP* when multiple warheads are aimed at the same target, the "fratricide" effect, and the modifications that must be made in reliability estimates when warheads can be reprogrammed. But since a thorough consideration of these matters involves military intelligence and scientific knowledge that, as far as we know, is nearly as opaque to the strategists as it is to us, the simpler aggregation procedure seemed a more judicious choice.

The aggregate values for each of the six estimates—a total of 12 for both superpowers—are displayed for the years 1972, 1976, 1980, and 1984[4] in Table 2.2. These figures represent the number of land-based enemy weapons systems that could theoretically be destroyed if *all* of each side's missiles were counterforce targeted. What does the table show us?

WHO'S AHEAD AND DOES IT MATTER

The first thing that strikes one about the figures in Table 2.2 is the wide range spanned by the six estimates. For any given year, they vary by more than a factor of two for the United States and more than a factor of seven for the Soviet Union. It is little wonder that scholars and policy makers—to say nothing of the general public— have been so confused by the debate over strategic superiority.

The second striking feature of Table 2.2 is the tremendous growth in counterforce capability during the past dozen years. Even though the 1972 SALT agreements were negotiated to reign in this dangerous capacity, U.S. counterforce capability had nearly doubled by 1980, and the Soviet counterforce capability had increased by a factor of three or four. These figures account for the growing dissatisfaction with the SALT agreements on all sides: the "doves" because they had clearly not resulted in meaningful arms control, the "hawks" because the United States had clearly lost some of its relative advantage during the course of the agreement. But it is

Table 2.2

Counterforce Capability of the United States and Soviet Union

Nation	Target hardness	Weapon performance	1972	1976	1980	1984
United States	Low	Low	1,470*	2,555	2,630	3,237
		High	1,834	3,252	3,404	4,159
		Mean	1,662	2,828	2,980	3,637
	High	Low	911	1,542	1,579	2,073
		High	1,354	2,399	2,531	3,286
		Mean	1,066	1,812	1,972	2,587
Soviet Union	Low	Low	233	319	633	789
		High	804	1,400	2,976	3,486
		Mean	499	884	1,905	2,236
	High	Low	114	168	404	566
		High	517	921	2,124	2,665
		Mean	306	533	1,193	1,510

*Number of land-based missiles that could be destroyed.

worth noting in passing that while the Soviets improved considerably between 1976 and 1980, U.S. capabilities had increased greatly between 1972 and 1976. This suggests that the Soviet growth may have been in part a response to earlier U.S. growth.

One crucial thing to emerge from Table 2.2 is that as of 1980 (the year in which Reagan proclaimed Soviet superiority), there appears to be little question that it is the United States that has been ahead. Regardless of whether we choose the highest or the lowest figures for target hardness, or the highest, lowest, or average figures for weapon performance, the U.S. counterforce capability is superior, in many cases strikingly so. Only if we compare the *most* favorable estimates for Soviet weaponry with the *least* favorable estimates for U.S. weapons can we contrive to have the balance tilt toward the Soviets. And, indeed, of the 36 possible pair comparisons that can be made between the 1980 figures for the United States and the Soviet Union, only seven, or less than 20%, are in the Soviets' favor. Of these, six are based on a single source, which gives extremely high figures for Soviet missile accuracy found nowhere else in the literature. It would be unreasonable then to conclude that the balance of evidence suggests at worst Soviet–U.S. parity, and at best a palpable advantage for the United States. This advantage has remained during the first Reagan term, as the 1984 figures clearly show.

But there is another and much more ominous conclusion that can be drawn from Table 2.2. The magnitude of the counterforce capability figures for *both* sides now represents at the very least a large fraction of the total number of land-based missiles possessed by each side and in some cases exceeds it. Thus, the specter of a counterforce attack against land-based missiles—so often raised by Reagan's officials—cannot be lightly dismissed. The irony is that the threat to the Soviets is, on balance, much greater, particularly as a much greater proportion of their strategic forces is land-based. It is little wonder, then, that they are agitated by U.S. plans to deploy still more weapons with counterforce capabilities.

This concluding point leads naturally to the last major question to be dealt with in this chapter: who leads whom in the arms race? Is it a case of mutual action–reaction, is one side clearly the initiator, with the other playing "catch-up"? Or are both sides merely responding to internal stimuli, there being no real "race" at all? (Organski and Kugler, 1980). Linked to this theoretical issue is the practical policy matter arising from the fourth major assumption of Reagan's policy: that the U.S. weapons program will constrain rather than stimulate the Soviets in their own acquisition of new weapons.

ISOLATING ARMS INTERACTION

Some Problems

Puzzling out the dynamics of the superpower arms race has preoccupied more scholars than virtually any other topic in the field of quantitative international relations.[5] It would be presumptuous to assert that a single additional study can treat all the issues raised in this voluminous literature, and no such claim is being made here. Nevertheless, it is worth noting that attempts to isolate and examine the competitive and interactive component of superpower arms acquisition often fall prey to one or more of four serious problems.

The first problem—alluded to earlier—is the tendency to view the arms race as a spending competition rather than a weapons-building competition. As noted above, this conception creates three difficulties: (1) the relationship between military *effort* and military *capability* is by no means an easy or an evident one; (2) obtaining reliable and comparable fiscal data for the two superpowers creates almost insuperable problems; and (3) military budgets are subject to all manner of extraneous external influences that are simply contaminating noise from the point of view of our central theoretical concerns.

A second problem with many arms race studies lies in their attempt to fit the empirical data at hand to a deterministic mathematical model. The problem with this strategy, as Busch (1970) pointed out over a decade ago, is that the relatively small number of data points, and the width of the error bands about them, allow us to obtain an equally good fit for a multiplicity of models, even if, following Richardson, only continuous linear equations are used. If discontinuous or nonlinear terms are introduced, the problem of model specification becomes nearly insuperable (Wallace and Wilson, 1978).

Many scholars have attempted to avoid the problems with constructing a deterministic model of the arms race by employing various empirical curve-fitting techniques (Ostrom, 1978; Organski and Kugler, 1980). However, almost all of these studies employ least-squares methods to estimate the parameters, and these have important weaknesses when used with time-series data of the sort that describe an arms race. Such data are typically characterized by complex autocorrelation and moving average processes, which produce enormous and often undetectable distortions in parameters estimated by least-squares methods (Malinvaud, 1970). As a result, it has proven difficult or impossible to separate out the competitive and the autochthonous components of superpower arms growth.

There have been techniques developed by statisticians to deal with such complex autocorrelation and moving average processes. Chief amongst these are the methods developed by Box and Jenkins (1976), who advocate the explicit modeling and subsequent removal of such contaminating processes, decomposing the raw data series to yield a "whitened" series. The transformed data can then be used in a regression equation without biasing the error terms and thus distorting the regression coefficients.

Unfortunately, there are good reasons to believe that even these techniques might not produce unbiased regression results in the case at hand, for two reasons. First, the number of data points is quite a bit below what is usually considered the minimum for the robust application of Box–Jenkins techniques; these assume the data have good large-sample properties, something that is very difficult to claim with an effective n of 24. Second, there is some reason to suppose a degree of spurious dependence between the figures for the two sides. It turns out that many of the estimates for missile accuracy and silo hardness often quoted for the Soviet Union are not independently generated data, but are calculated from U.S. test results. Since the hardness and accuracy values appear in the *exponent* of the 35TKP34 equation, the 35TKP34 values for the superpowers' various weapons systems may themselves not be mathematically independent. If the resulting aggregated series are then subjected to various nonlinear transformations, the likely result will be spurious *statistical* dependence.

But although it would be risky to apply sophisticated mathematical analysis to these data, all is not lost; simple inspection of Table 2.2 will go a long way to answering our question about the Soviet response to the U.S. buildup.

The Soviet Response

Even a cursory glance at Table 2.2 casts doubt on the claim that the U.S. buildup has led to any dampening of the rate of Soviet increase. From it we can learn two things: (1) that during the past half decade, the United States has increased its strategic weapons lethality at an almost unprecedented rate, and (2) that the Soviet Union has made an earnest effort to match the rate of increase. In the process, the "essential equivalence" of the 1980 balance has been preserved, but at a level 20–30% above 1980 levels. But we do not have to rely on these figures alone to evaluate the Soviet response to the Reagan administration's military buildup; there are several other Soviet actions and statements that act as confirming evidence.

To begin with, the Soviets seem intent on matching the U.S. buildup qualitatively as well as quantitatively. This was particularly evident in their response to the stationing of U.S. ground-launched cruise missiles (GLCMs) and Pershing II MRBMs in Western Europe. Although both the continental United States and Western Europe are already heavily targeted, the Soviets stationed additional Yankee-class SSBNs off the U.S. coasts, and moved short-range SS-22 and SS-23 missiles forward onto the territory of their Warsaw Pact allies, with the avowed aim of putting the NATO states in "equivalent peril."

In a similar vein, recent Soviet military testing programs suggest that their R&D efforts have been directed at matching U.S. strategic systems already deployed or in the development phase. The Soviets are currently testing air- and ground-launched cruise missiles, a large SSBN patterned after the Trident, various types of ASAT systems, and a new long-range strategic bomber. The obvious inference that the Soviets intend to match the recent and planned U.S. deployments is amply confirmed by the statements of military and political officials alike.

Thus it would seem that the administration has been mistaken in its view that the rapid increases in U.S. counterforce capability that will result from current procurement decisions will deter a Soviet response. The record clearly shows the contrary; such wholesale increases in U.S. capabilities will bring a strong Soviet response with as much speed as their planning process permits.[6]

CAVEATS AND CONCLUSIONS

No claim is being made that this study has disproven conclusively the major arguments used by the administration to support its program to acquire new strategic capacity. The very magnitude of the uncertainty about the data estimates, combined with the evolving nature of the superpower relationship, is more than ample reason for caution. But the study has shed some light on the four major administration claims outlined earlier. Let us summarize the evidence addressed here concerning these, ad seriatim:

1. The assertion that the Soviets are ahead in strategic counterforce capability appears very dubious indeed. Although the margin of possible error is indeed wide, on balance it appears that the United States holds the advantage. More important, both sides are now moving close to the ability to destroy each other's land-based missile forces, with all of the destabilizing consequences that this entails.
2. Historical evidence does not appear to support the administration view that military inferiority on the part of the status quo power endangers the peace. On the contrary, the evidence suggests that the probability of the escalation of a serious great power dispute into war is largely independent of the relative military capabilities of the two sides.
3. The evidence also suggests—even more strongly—that the prospect of an all-out superpower arms race is not to be taken

lightly. If a serious dispute were to break out in the course of such an arms race, the probability of its escalation to all-out war would be very high indeed if we judge by the historical record.

4. Finally, contrary to the administration view, the United States has consistently led the strategic arms race, and the Soviet Union has consistently and doggedly attempted to catch up. There is, therefore, no evidence for the belief that they will fail to do so in the present case. On the contrary, the evidence clearly suggests that they will respond strongly to current U.S. deployment decisions with sharp increases in their own counterforce capabilities and forward deployments.

All in all, the evidence presented here is rather more supportive of those who call for a moratorium on weapons development. If the United States has approximately equivalent strategic capacity, wherein lies the peril? And if the dangers to peace posed by an arms race are so much greater than the dangers of relative inferiority, the balance of risk tilts still further toward a moratorium.

Finally, since the Soviets have always responded to U.S. strategic buildups, it is reasonable to believe that they will respond to U.S. restraint as well. If such mutual restraint is verifiable, there would appear little reason for concern given past behavior.

NOTES

[1]He who desires peace, prepares for war ... nor does he provoke, nor dare to offend him whom he knows to be superior in fighting.

[2]This argument is implicit rather than explicit in many administration statements. But Weede (1980), who asserts this with clarity, shows how essential it is to the pro-armament position.

[3]While I am reluctant to use these words because of the intellectual baggage often associated with them, I confess to failure in my attempts to conjure an alternative. The reader should keep in mind throughout that "counterforce" and "countervalue" refer not to a policy or a strategy, but to *capabilities*.

[4]The reader will note that these correspond to the last four presidential election years.

[5]The literature on this topic has become too copious to cite in detail. For good critical summaries, see, inter alia, Busch (1970); Chaterjee (1975); Gillespie et al. (1977); Hollist and Guetzkow (1978); Luterbacher (1975).

[6]For additional evidence supporting this interpretation see Bundy et al. (1984/85).

REFERENCES

BOX, G. E. P., and G. M. JENKINS (1976). *Time Series Analysis: Forecasting and Control.* San Francisco, Calif.: Holden-Day.

BUNDY, M., G. KENNAN, R. McNAMARA, and G. SMITH (1984/85). "The President's Choice: Star Wars or Arms Control." *Foreign Affairs,* 63:264–78.

BUSCH, P.C. (1970). "Mathematical Models of Arms Races." In Bruce M. Russett (ed.), *What Price Vigilance?* New Haven, Conn.: Yale University Press.

CHATERJEE, P. (1975). *Arms, Alliances and Stability.* Delhi: Macmillan.

DAVIS, L. E., and W. R. SCHILLING (1973). "All You Ever Wanted to Know about MIRV and ICBM Calculations But Were Not Cleared to Ask." *Journal of Conflict Resolution,* 17(2):207–42.

GILLESPIE, J., D. ZINNES, P. SCHRODT, G. TAHIM, and R. RUBISON (1977). "An Optimal Control Model of Arms Races." *American Political Science Review,* 71:226–44.

HOLLIST, W. L., and H. GUETZKOW (1978). "Cumulative Research in International Relations: Empirical Analysis and Computer Simulation of Competitive Arms Processes." In W. L. Hollist, *Exploring Competitive Arms Processes.* New York: Marcel Dekker.

KAPLAN, F. (1980). *Dubious Specter: A Second Look at the Soviet Threat.* New York: Boxwood.

LEE, W. Y. (1977). *The Estimation of Soviet Defense Expenditures: An Unconventional Approach.* New York: Praeger.

LUTERBACHER, U. (1975). "Arms Race Models: Where Do We Stand?" *European Journal of Political Research,* 3:199–217.

MALINVAUD, E. (1970). *Statistical Methods of Econometrics.* Amsterdam: North Holland Publishing Co.

NINCIC, M., and T. R. CUSACK (1979). "The Political Economy of U.S. Military Spending." *Journal of Peace Research,* 16:101–15.

ORGANSKI, A. F. K., and J. KUGLER (1980). "Deterrence and the Arms Race: The Impotence of Power." *International Security,* 1:105–38.

OSTROM, C. (1978). "A Reactive Linkage Model of the U.S. Defense Expenditure Policy Making Process." *American Political Science Review,* 22:941–57.

REICH, R. B. (1982). "Playing Tag with Japan." *New York Review of Books,* 29(11):37–40.

RUMMEL, R. J. (1976). *Peace Endangered: The Reality of Detente.* Beverly Hills, Calif.: Sage Publications.

Science (1982a). "An Upheaval in U.S. Strategic Thought" (editorial), 216:30–34.

Science (1982b). "Reagan's Plan for MX Attracts Fire" (editorial), 216:150–53.

SINGER, J. D. (1958). "Threat-Perception and The Armament-Tension Dilemma." *Journal of Conflict Resolution,* 2(1):90–105.

SOVIET MINISTRY OF DEFENSE (1982). *From Whence the Threat to Peace.* Moscow.

STOCKHOLM INTERNATIONAL PEACE RESEARCH INSTITUTE [SIPRI] (1981). *World Armaments and Disarmament.* London: Taylor and Francis.

TAAGEPERA, R. (1980). "Stockpile–Budget Ratio Interactions Models for Arms Races." *Peace Science Society (International) Papers,* 29:67–78.

WALLACE, M. D. (1979). "Arms Races and Escalation." *Journal of Conflict Resolution,* 23(1):3–16.

WALLACE, M. D. (1980) "Some Persisting Findings: A Reply to Professor Weede." *Journal of Conflict Resolution,* 24(2):89–292.

WALLACE, M. D. (1982). "Armaments and Escalation: Two Competing Hypotheses." *International Studies Quarterly,* 26(1):37–51.

WALLACE, M. D., and J. WILSON (1978). "Non-Linear Arms Race Models: A Test of Some Alternatives." *Journal of Peace Research,* 15(2):175–92.

WEEDE, E. (1980). "Arms Races and Escalation: Some Persisting Doubts." *Journal of Conflict Resolution,* 24(2):285–87.

WOHLSTETTER, A. (1969). "The Case for Strategic Force Defense." In J. Holst and W. Schneider, *Why ABM?* Elmsford, N.Y.: Pergamon.

3

Realism and Crisis Bargaining: A Report on Five Empirical Studies

Russell J. Leng

INTRODUCTION

One of the most influential texts for American students of foreign policy in the four decades since World War II has been Hans Morgenthau's *Politics Among Nations* (1978), a modern exposition of a "realist" or *realpolitik* approach to foreign policy—a tradition whose origins can be found as early as Thucydides' Melian dialogue and extending through history to Machiavelli and Clausewitz.

According to Morgenthau, realism has always represented the practical, if unspoken, tradition that has guided the statesman's understanding of politics and courses of action. By understanding its precepts, he argues, we can think as the stateman does and "understand his thoughts and actions perhaps better than he, the actor on the political scene, does himself" (1978:5). A proper understanding or description of the nature of politics naturally leads to prescriptive rules.

In this chapter we will consider the validity of some of the precepts of political realism, and of its extension into prescriptions for conflict bargaining, by examining the findings from a series of empirical studies of the behavior of states engaged in militarized disputes or crises. Each of the five studies (Leng and Wheeler, 1979; Leng, 1980; Gochman and Leng, 1983; Leng, 1983; and Leng, 1984a) examines particular realist precepts. Taken together, the findings provide an overview of the realist approach as descriptive and prescriptive theory in situations where it would appear to be most applicable: conflicts in which the state's security is threatened directly and other political concerns are likely to be subordinated to the dispute at hand. Before turning to a discussion of the five studies and their findings, we should summarize the realist approach as it would be applied to the behavior of states in militarized disputes.

Political Realism

The essence of political realism may be summed up in Morgenthau's classic statement: "International politics, like all politics, is a struggle for power. Whatever the ultimate aims of international politics, power is always the immediate aim" (1978:29). Thus political realism posits three basic foreign policy objectives: expand power, maintain power, and demonstrate power. The modes of accomplishing these objectives determine the techniques of bargaining with other states.

Morgenthau argues that in a "world where power counts" the only restraint on state action is prudence—that is, a rational calculation of the limits of one's power and the consequences of political action (1978:8,11). In pursuing national interests, the prudent statesman "minimizes risks and maximizes benefits" to his own state (1978:8). Not all statesmen, of course, always act rationally, and, given the conflicting objectives of states, the exercise of prudence is dependent on balancing power with power and on seeking mutual accommodation through skillful diplomacy.

On the other hand, expanding, maintaining, and demonstrating power can place a high premium on bargaining strategies that demonstrate resolve and a willingness to accept the risk of war to achieve one's objectives. Because a crisis presents the supreme test of a state's power and resolve, from the perspective of a national leader, the line between prudence and what may be perceived as a failure of nerve is not easily drawn.

The realist admonition to demonstrate resolve had led a more recent generation of realists, or "conflict strategists," to view conflict bargaining as something akin to a contest in risk-taking. Perhaps the most explicit exposition of this view is Schelling's *Strategy of Conflict* (1960). Schelling contends that it is possible to develop a theory of "intelligent, sophisticated conflict behavior—of successful behavior" (1960:4) in a game-winning sense.

The key to success, according to Schelling, lies not only in applying the requisite power to induce the other side to comply with one's demands, but also in making any accompanying inducements *credible*. Credibility is a function not only of the actor's power to carry out its threats, but also of its *commitment* to take the action. The emphasis is on the "exploitation of potential force"—the use of credible threats and punishments to achieve compliance with one's demands (Schelling, 1960:69–78). The goal is to achieve the adversary's compliance short of the actual application of military force, although a physical demonstration of the use of that force is seen as an effective way to obtain credibility. The latter, in its more extreme forms, is what Schelling (1966) calls the "diplomacy of violence." The realist paradox is that one must prepare for war to maintain peace; the conflict strategists' extension of this is that one credibly demonstrate a willingness to go to war to avoid it.

Critics of this approach counter with the argument that in crises, statemen frequently do not behave in an entirely rational, calculating manner. They see strong psychological and social pressures on both parties to respond to threats with counterthreats and argue that such situations easily escalate to war. Studies by social psychologists (Brehm, 1960) suggest that when an individual's freedom or prestige is threatened, "psychological reactance" is aroused, creating a motivational state directed toward restoring the freedom with little regard for the potential costs and risks. In addition to these psychological pressures, which statesmen may identify with their role as guardians of national prestige, students of international politics have long been impressed by the domestic political pressures on statesmen to respond with toughness in the face of overt threats from other states (see Carr, 1939, for an early discussion).

Critics of the conflict strategists note also that their bargaining prescriptions are based on an unspoken assumption of asymmetry in the military capabilities and in the motivations of the two parties. When *both* parties to a dispute become intent on credibly demonstrating their resolve to accept the risk of war to achieve their conflicting objectives, the dispute bargaining is like that of a poker game where the sky is the limit and each player is determined to up the ante until the other drops out. As each player commits more of his resources and reputation for resolve to "winning," the costs of losing grow. The result is not just a stalemate, but a spiraling escalation of the conflict that stems from each side's determination to make its commitment to winning more credible. Rapoport (1960) has described this process of escalating threats and counterthreats as a "fight" model of conflict behavior.

The discussion of the findings from the five studies will focus on the validity of the realist precepts that we have described and contrast them with the warnings of the counterrealists. Do statemen embroiled in militarized disputes behave as the realists say they do? If so, are they more often guided by that aspect of realism that prescribes prudence, or by a willingness to accept high risks to demonstrate resolve? When statesmen do act according to the prescriptions of the realists and conflict strategists, are they more or less likely to achieve their objectives? The last of the five studies focuses on these questions with particular reference to Soviet–U.S. crisis bargaining.

METHODOLOGY

The Data

The works that produced the findings that we will discuss were all quantitative studies·employing events data—that is, data on the actions and interactions of the participants in militarized disputes occurring between 1900 and 1975. In the three studies employing random selections of disputes (Leng and Wheeler, 1979; Leng, 1980, and Gochman and Leng, 1983), the cases were selected from prepared lists of the population of militarized disputes, with the number of disputes sampled ranging from 12 (Leng, 1980) to 30 (Gochman and Leng, 1983). A full discussion of the criteria for selecting disputes appears in Gochman and Leng (1983:116–17).

The events data for each case were coded from the *New York Times* and at least two diplomatic histories. Verbal chronologies were generated from each source and then merged into a single chronology prior to coding the events according to the Behavioral Correlates of War (BCOW) coding scheme developed by Leng and Singer (1977). The BCOW typology is particularly well suited for a fine-screened analysis of conflict bargaining behavior. For a full discussion of the coding scheme and its uses see Leng and Singer (1977) or Leng (1984b).

Analytic Techniques

Throughout the five studies, the actions and interactions of the disputants have been analyzed from two perspectives. The first approach has been to examine bargaining behavior as a series of influence attempt–response sequences. An influence attempt consists of a demand that state A directs to state B, which is accompanied by one or more inducements in the form of threats and/or promises. The response is represented by the mix of actions by state B immediately following A's influence attempt. (See Leng, 1980:138–43, for a fuller description). This is essentially a stimulus–response model, where A's influence attempt stimulates B's response and B's response serves as feedback used in choosing A's next influence attempt. Influence attempt–response sequences are analyzed from two perspectives: (1) the types of responses associated with individual influence attempts, and (2) the effects of the overall influence strategies represented by the mix of influence attempts chosen by state A over the course of the dispute.

The second approach has been to treat the events data as a time series to describe patterns of escalation and deescalation of conflictive behavior over the course of the dispute. Salient events of interest, such as the first threat of force, are treated as interventions that may or may not lead to changes in the pattern of the series.

Some Caveats

Each of these techniques will be discussed more fully when we consider the findings from particular studies. Before doing so, it is important to offer a few caveats about the nature of those findings.

The research approach assumes that, to a large extent, the strongest influence on one party's behavior is likely to be the behavior of the other party. Other variables have been chosen as predictors when they have been consistent with a realist interpretation: the relative power of the adversaries, the issues at stake, the participation or absence of major powers, or the diplomatic era in which the dispute took place. Nevertheless, a number of variables that have been considered important by some researchers, such as the personalities of particular statemen or the bureaucratic politics within decision-making bodies, are not included in the studies.

The findings that are reported in this chapter are *statistically* significant; however, the techniques employed vary from study to study, as do the strengths of reported associations and differences. All of the statistical analysis is, at best, associational. No claim is made for empirical demonstrations of causal relationships. The causal statements that appear in the text represent inferences from the observed associations based on the author's understanding of international politics.

FINDINGS

The discussion of the findings from the five studies is organized according to five types of research questions: (1) It begins with an examination of the effects of particular types of influence attempts, or bargaining *tactics,* in achieving compliance or less desired responses. This provides a direct way of investigating the prescriptions of the realists and, particularly, the conflict strategists, as well as a means of describing the types of inducements most frequently employed by states in militarized disputes. (2) Then we turn to a similar examination of the overall combination of influence attempts, or influence *strategy,* chosen by each party in the course of the dispute. (3) Moving from influence attempt–response sequences to a pattern of conflictive and cooperative actions over the course of the dispute, we examine a number of behavioral and contextual variables, such as the types of inducements employed or the relative power of the adversaries, to examine their associations with dispute escalation or deescalation. This affords some interesting indicators of the descriptive validity of the realist view. (4) Then we turn to what lessons statesmen are likely to draw from one dispute experience to the next. Is there an association between the outcome of a previous dispute with the same adversary and the influence strategy chosen in the current dispute? Are any changes in influence strategies consistent with the precepts of political realism? (5) Finally, we take a close look at three post–World War II crises between the Soviet Union and the United States and ask whether they offer any lessons for U.S. policy in any future confrontations with the Soviets.

Bargaining Tactics

Each influence attempt is a combination of a demand and inducements in the form of threats and promises. We categorize the inducements according to *types* (threats or promises, punishments or rewards, military or other), the *conditions* under which the inducement would be carried out (action or inaction by the target, third-party actions, or unconditionally), and the *specificity* of the inducement (time for action specified or not, specific action specified or not). The combination of types gives us a rough measure of the severity of the inducement. The conditions for action and the specificity of the commitment to act, along with the power relationship between the parties, provide a measure of the credibility of the inducement. The adversaries' responses were classified along a continuum ranging from outright compliance with the demand to a defiant threat or counterthreat.

These measures were used to examine the influence attempt–response sequence in twelve 20th-century dyadic disputes (Leng, 1980). Following the realist perspective, we began with the general proposition that the degree of state *B*'s compliance with an influence attempt by state *A* will be positively associated with the degree of inducement employed by state *A* and the credibility of *A*'s communicated intention to carry out the inducement(s), minus the cost of compliance to state *B*. The "cost of compliance" was based on what *A* demanded of *B*.

We found that the variance in *what* is requested was a weaker predictor of compliance or noncompliance in these disputes, than *how* it was requested—that is, the nature of the accompanying inducements. In this respect, the realist, and particularly the conflict strategists' emphasis on the credibility of inducements, was supported by the findings. As threats became more specific, they became more effective, and, as one might guess, they were also more effective when the threatener enjoyed an advantage over the target in military capability. Credibility, in fact, was a better predictor to compliance than the severity of the action threatened.

On the other hand, as threats became more severe and more credibly communicated, they were more likely to be associated with defiance in the form of counterthreats. Threats were most likely to be linked to defiant responses when they were (1) highly specific, (2) accompanied by physical demonstrations of military force, and (3) issued by a state of comparable military capability. The last finding is especially interesting because in disputes among states of relatively equal military capabilities, the proportion of defiant responses to *other* types of inducements (promises or carrot-and-stick) declined.

What do these initial findings suggest about the validity of the realist perspective? First, the salience of both measures of credibility (the specificity of threats and the conditions for carrying them out, along with the relative power of the disputants) are consistent with the importance attached to this component of conflict bargaining by the conflict strategists. That the most severe and most credible threats had the highest rate of outright compliance and that they were most effective when the threatener enjoyed a power advantage is certainly consistent with the realist notion that "power counts" as well as the conflict strategists' emphasis on credibly demonstrating a willingness to use it.

On the other hand, the positive associations between highly severe and credible threats and *defiant* responses, particularly in disputes between states of comparable military capabilities, support the counterrealists' contention that the tactics suggested by the conflict strategists are highly dangerous in disputes where there is symmetry in the power and motivations of the antagonists. That is the dark side of the prescription to demonstrate resolve.

Influence Strategies

Examining only the immediate responses to individual influence attempts could be misleading. Statesmen might initially respond defiantly to coercive influence attempts in order to save face before their domestic audiences and then move to a more accommodative response when it becomes clear the adversary means business. Moreover, there is always a danger of obtaining misleading results when the individual actions from a variety of disputes are aggregated for statistical testing. Therefore, to obtain a broader perspective on the bargaining process over the full course of particular disputes, we chose 20 randomly selected disputes to examine the effectiveness of the *overall influence strategies* employed by the participants (Leng and Wheeler, 1979). These were all dyadic disputes that took place between 1900 and 1975.

The influence strategies were classified according to four basic types: (1) a purely coercive "bullying" strategy, (2) an essentially tit-for-tat "reciprocating" strategy, (3) a "trial-and-error" strategy, where inducements that produce positive responses are repeated and those that do not are changed, and (4) an "appeasing" strategy consisting almost solely of positive inducements (Leng and Wheeler, 1979:657–63). The determination of which influence strategy, or strategies, was consistent with a particular choice of influence attempt was based on the adjustments in inducements made by the actor following the target's response to the actor's last influence attempt. Assume, for example, that the target state had responded to an influence attempt containing a threat as inducement by offering a modest concession short of actual compliance. If the actor repeated the demand with an even stronger threat, the influence attempt would be consistent with a "bullying" influence strategy; if it repeated the demand, but with a carrot-and-stick inducement employing the same threat and an accompanying concession, it would be consistent with a "reciprocating" bargaining strategy, and so on. Identification of the actor's predominant influence strategy is determined by the aggregate of inducement choices over the course of the dispute (Leng and Wheeler, 1979:669–70).

The findings from this study supported the views of the counterrealists. We found a high association between the use of "bullying" strategies and war outcomes. A "reciprocating" strategy turned out to be the most effective means of achieving a successful outcome to the dispute without either going to war or yielding to the demands of the other side. The best approach was to offer an occasional accommodative initiative, but otherwise to respond in kind to the other party's influence attempts and responses. This "firm but fair" strategy was also the most effective one for dealing with an adversary initially bent on a bullying strategy.

It is interesting to note that the effectiveness of the reciprocating influence strategy, especially in disputes between relative equals, is consistent with both tenets of the traditional realist prescription—demonstrate resolve and exercise prudence. The actor employs a firm tit-for-tat response to attempts at coercion and thereby demonstrates its resolve; on the other hand, it prudently avoids actions that deliberately challenge the resolve of the other party, while indicating a willingness to move to a mutually accommodative settlement. The findings, nevertheless, depart from the extension of the realism that appears in the prescriptions of the conflict strategists with their emphasis on the "exploitation of potential force" and an acceptance of the risk of war to obtain the credibility necessary to achieve compliance with one's demands. Bullying influence strategies not only were highly associated with war outcomes; they were also less frequently associated with diplomatic victories or compromise settlements than were reciprocating strategies.

Contextual Variables

The next step was to move away from the influence tactics and strategies of the parties to examine the overall patterns of dispute behavior according to several dimensions of interest. We began with yet another typology, a classification of militarized disputes according to three dimensions of interest: the escalation of conflictive behavior, the militarization (threats or use of force) of behavior, and the degree of reciprocity in the mix of conflictive and cooperative actions by the disputants (Leng and Gochman, 1982). Eight ideal dispute types were obtained by combining the three dimensions.

Within a sample of 30 militarized disputes occurring between 1838 and 1971, we found that those disputes having high scores on all three measures, which we labelled "fights," had the highest association with war outcomes. The second most dangerous type, which we labelled "resistance," had high scores on militarization and escalation, but a low score on the reciprocity dimension. There was a steady decline in the association with war as we moved down the ladder to "prudence," a dispute type with low scores on all three measures. However, between the extremes of the "fight" and "prudence" categories, there was a considerable variance in the association with war *within* the particular categories. This led to the question of what, for example, accounted for the difference between those cases falling into the "resistance" category that led to war and those in the same category that did not. Once again we adopted a realist approach to exploring the question and took a closer look at the context within which the dispute behavior occurred (Gochman and Leng, 1983).

Along with two variables that proved to be salient in our earlier studies—the relative power of the disputants and the types of influence attempts employed—we added two others: the types of issues in contention and the types of states participating in the dispute. Political realism prescribes that statesmen should be willing to pursue more aggressive strategies and to assume higher risks of war when vital issues (national territory or political independence) are at stake. To obtain a rough test of this, we made a simple distinction between vital and nonvital issues and examined the reactions of states to attempts at coercion. Traditional realism also assumes that skillful diplomacy is the key to resolving conflicts short of war, and that such diplomacy is the responsibility of the major powers. To test this assumption, we distinguished between the presence or absence of major powers on both sides of the dispute, either as participants or as intervening third parties.

The findings supported the realist description. High escalation scores were positively associated with the presence of vital issues and with the use of physical threats of force. The latter finding was consistent with our earlier observation (Leng, 1980) of the high association between defiant responses and demands accompanied by demonstrations of military force. The presence of vital issues at stake, not surprisingly, was also positively associated with war outcomes. These findings are consistent with the traditional realist view of when statesmen are most likely to accept higher risks of war to achieve their objectives.

Perhaps the most interesting findings from this study, however, concerned the participation of major powers. Disputes in which major powers were involved, either as participants on both sides or as mediators, were less likely to end in war. As one would expect, major powers were most successful as mediators when the conflict did not involve vital issues and, perhaps most important, when the contending powers were evenly matched. This, of course, is perfectly logical. An outside mediator, major power or otherwise, is most likely to be successful when neither side really wants to fight a war. That is most likely to be the case when the issues do not represent stakes worthy of the high costs of war and when neither party is confident of an easy military victory.

The remarkable consistency that we have observed between the traditional realist *description* of conflict behavior and the actions of states in the disputes in our studies suggests that national leaders may behave more rationally under stress than one might think. On the other hand, the dangerous consequences of following the realist and conflict strategists' prescriptions for demonstrating power and the willingness to use it without heeding the warning to exercise prudence has also been demonstrated across the studies. The next study, which focuses on what lessons statesmen bring from one dispute experience to guide their actions in the next, presents a graphic illustration of the dark side of the realist perspective.

Learning from One Dispute to the Next

Given the outcome of one militarized dispute, what "lessons" are statesmen likely to carry over into another confrontation with the same adversary? To investigate this question, we chose six pairs of states, relatively evenly matched in military capabilities, that were engaged in three successive militarized disputes within a relatively short period of time in this century. The pairs were: Russia–

Austria–Hungary, 1908–1914; France–Germany, 1905–1914; Britain–Germany, 1936–1939; India–Pakistan, 1947–1971; Egypt–Israel, 1947–1967; and the United States–Soviet Union, 1948–1962.

Using the same approach to determining the predominant influence strategy that we employed in the Leng–Wheeler (1979) study and drawing from the work of Jervis (1976), we began by hypothesizing that statesmen would tend to repeat strategies that had led to successful outcomes in the previous disputes and change those that had been unsuccessful. Given what we had already found regarding the apparent salience of the perceived necessity to demonstrate resolve among national leaders engaged in militarized disputes, we hypothesized that these changes would lead to more aggressively coercive bargaining in the next dispute with the same adversary. The same realist impulse, we hypothesized, would lead the other party to adjust its strategy during the course of the dispute to reciprocate the more aggressive bargaining of its opponent. Thus, unless the parties were able to end the dispute with a mutually satisfactory compromise, each successive dispute between the pair of states should become increasingly conflictive.

With few exceptions, the behavior of the states in the sample followed the patterns predicted by the hypotheses. The diplomatic loser in the preceding dispute was the first to threaten the use of force in the next encounter. These states all adopted more coercive influence strategies, which, in most instances, were reciprocated by the other party. These findings provide added support for findings from earlier studies (Leng, 1980; Gochman and Leng, 1983) suggesting that the realist precept to demonstrate one's power and resolve takes precedence over the admonition to act with prudence and restraint, especially in a military confrontation with a status equal.

Three Soviet–U.S. Crises

With these findings in mind, we decided to take a closer look (Leng, 1984a) at U.S.–Soviet bargaining behavior in the three major confrontations between the superpowers in the post–World War II era: the Berlin crises of 1948 and 1961 and the Cuban Missile crisis of 1962.

We were encouraged to undertake this study because of the Reagan administration's strong emphasis on the importance of demonstrating U.S. military power and a willingness to use it in future dealings with the Soviet Union (Leng, 1984a:338–40). U.S.

attempts at accommodation, according to this logic, would be interpreted as signs of weakness and encourage even more belligerent Soviet behavior. We outlined a series of hypotheses contrasting the "bullying" influence strategy implied by the president's statements with the "reciprocating" strategy found most successful in the Leng–Wheeler (1979) study.

We began the analysis by examining the immediate Soviet responses to particular types of U.S. influence attempts in much the same manner as in our first study of influence tactics (Leng, 1980). The findings indicated that the Soviets, like the evenly matched states in the earlier study, tended to respond in kind to U.S. threats and physical demonstrations of force. We found no instances of actual Soviet compliance with threats presented without any accompanying accommodating promises, no matter how credibly the threats were communicated. The most successful influence attempts, as in the 1980 study, were carrot-and-stick inducements combining threats with positive concessions. We also found a high degree of reciprocity in the mix of conflictive and cooperative interactions between the two parties—more, in fact, than the mean for other disputes between major powers.

Taken alone, these results suggest that the Reagan administration has been wrong in assuming that the most successful way to deal with the Soviets in a future confrontation would be by simply asserting U.S. military might and resolve. They also suggest that U.S.–Soviet crises are more similar to those between other major powers than the administration would credit.

Nevertheless, it is possible that the immediate Soviet responses to U.S. threats and military demonstrations are deceiving. The initial Soviet counterthreats could represent no more than face-saving gestures, to be followed by a gradual retreat in the face of U.S. resolve. If this occurred in the three crises, the effectiveness of a coercive U.S. strategy—if the U.S. strategy was coercive—would be vindicated in gradually more accommodating behavior by the Soviets following the U.S. threats of force. To explore this possibility, we examined the patterns of cooperative and conflictive actions for each side over the course of the three disputes. We paid particular attention to U.S. threats of force and modeled any changes in Soviet behavior for an extended period following these acts. A Box–Jenkins (1976) approach to modeling a time series with inventions (the threats of force) was employed for this stage of the analysis.

The findings for the two Berlin crises differed from those for the Cuban Missile crisis. The behavior patterns in the Berlin crises fitted the dispute type described as a "stand-off" in the dispute typology developed in the Leng–Gochman (1982) study. In a stand-off, a threat of force by one side causes a step level change in the level of hostility by the other, but the dispute does not continue to escalate. Neither party is willing to back down from the confrontation, but neither is either party willing to accept the risk of further increasing the level of hostilities. The dispute reaches a prolonged stalemate at a new level of hostility without "locking in" to the pattern of escalating conflict associated with a "fight." The Soviets responded in kind to U.S. threats of force in the Berlin crises, but in a measured manner. By the same token, the United States responded with firmness to protect the status quo, but with prudence and a sense of proportion to avoid unnecessary provocation. The United States employed a reciprocating strategy to counter the Soviet attempt to change the status quo, albeit with greater success in the blockade crisis of 1948 than in the Berlin Wall crisis of 1961, which ended in a stalemate.

The Cuban Missile crisis presents a more ambiguous picture. President Kennedy's public challenge to the Soviets in his "quarantine" speech of October 22, 1962, has become a classic example of a highly credible compellant threat of force (see Schelling, 1966). But the time series of Soviet behavior following the October 22 threat indicates a dramatic escalation of conflictive Soviet actions in the first five days following the speech. Then, on October 27, Robert Kennedy delivered a carrot-and-stick ultimatum to the Soviets that combined another, privately communicated, threat of force with U.S. concessions in the form of a pledge not to invade Cuba in the future and to remove U.S. missiles in Turkey. This led to the Soviet agreement to remove the missiles in Cuba, and the crisis began to de-escalate. Clearly the United States took a very tough stand in the Cuban Missile crisis and the Soviets retreated, but that retreat did not come until after the United States had coupled its threats with face-saving concessions. Moreover, prior to the carrot-and-stick influence attempt of October 27th, the conflict was on the verge of spiraling out of control. All of this took place in a crisis where the United States enjoyed the motivational advantage of defending the status quo in the face of a perceived threat to its most vital security interests, as well as an advantage in military capability, both locally and strategically.

It has been argued that the dramatic challenge that President Kennedy presented to the Soviets over Cuba reflected his sense that he had unsuccessfully communicated his resolve during the Berlin crisis of 1961. If that is true, it is consistent with our findings regarding the "lessons" that national leaders bring from one dispute to the next. It also suggests that in the next confrontation, when the shoe is on the other foot, the United States would be accepting high risks in adopting a bullying strategy with the Soviets.

In sum, the three Soviet–U.S. crises illustrate patterns of behavior that are remarkably consistent with those that we have observed for other powers. That the two powers acted with restraint in the two Berlin crises is confirmation of the good sense of a realist approach that recognizes the need to act with prudence and give the other party its due. The Cuban Missile crisis, while an often-cited success for U.S. diplomacy, nevertheless demonstrates the dangers of attempting to employ a bullying strategy with an adversary of comparable military capability.

CONCLUSION

The Findings Summarized

As *descriptive* theorists, the realist and conflict strategists fare quite well in the findings from our five studies of crisis behavior. Considerations of power and credibility do appear to assume a central role in crisis bargaining. Statesmen were willing to assume higher risks when vital security interests were at stake, and states with an advantage in military strength were more successful in achieving compliance with their demands. The credibility of inducements was, as the conflict strategists argue, the most important factor in determining the target's response. When we examined the behavior of pairs of states engaged in three successive militarized disputes with each other, however, we found that there was a strong association between an unsatisfactory outcome in one dispute and the decision to move to a more aggressive strategy in the next confrontation.

The last result suggests the dark side of political realism emphasized by the conflict strategists. When the losing party in the previous dispute moved to a more aggressive bargaining strategy in the next, it was quickly matched by its adversary. If the statesmen in our studies often followed the dictates of political realism in their conflict behavior, their reactions to attempts at coercion by the other party were also consistent with the dark side of the realist prescription emphasized by the counterrealists. Highly credible threats, unaccompanied by any face-saving positive inducements, were positively correlated with defiant responses and with conflict escalation. This was particularly true of threats accompanied by physical demonstrations of force. In disputes between states of comparable military capabilities, the association between outright threats of force and defiant responses was greatest, while defiant responses to other types of inducements declined. Moreover, in disputes between evenly matched adversaries, we found a high degree of reciprocity in all types of actions.

A similar picture emerged when we examined the overall influence strategies employed in the disputes. Coercive "bullying" strategies were likely to lead to war outcomes. The most effective strategies were "reciprocating" strategies that combined firmness in the face of threats with a willingness to initiate and reciprocate cooperative moves, a finding that is consistent with the observed association between carrot-and-stick inducements and positive responses.

Conclusions

Taken together, the behavior of statesmen in the militarized disputes that we examined supports the argument that *realpolitik* considerations—power, prestige, a state's reputation for resolve— stand at the forefront of interstate conflict bargaining. But the same findings indicate that when national leaders follow the prescriptions of the realists and the conflict strategists to their logical extreme—to employ coercive bargaining tactics to the point of demonstrating willingness to accept a high risk of war to achieve credibility—without recognizing that the adversary may be strongly motivated by the same *realpolitik* considerations, it can lead to a strategy that invites disaster. That the findings from the five studies suggest that statesmen may be motivated more by that aspect of political realism that stresses the need to demonstrate resolve than by the realist prescription to act with prudence—to give the other state its due—is not encouraging.

There is cause both for encouragement and for concern in the past crisis behavior of the two superpowers. Both sides exhibited prudence and restraint in managing the two Berlin crises. The Cuban Missile crisis exhibited the dangers of a purely coercive U.S. bargaining strategy in dealing with the Soviets, but a carefully designed strategy of carrot-and-stick diplomacy mirroring the "firm-but-fair" influence strategy found effective across a wide variety of interstate crises brought the dispute to a successful conclusion. The Soviet response to the initial U.S. attempts at coercive bargaining over Cuba, coupled with the outcome—a serious blow to the Soviet reputation for resolve—however, warn against the dangers of "brinkmanship," of accepting a high risk of war to demonstrate credibility in any future crisis. This is especially true in future crises, where the Soviets are less likely to be at the same disadvantage in usable military power or motivation, not to mention our finding that the loser in one militarized dispute is likely to adopt a more aggressive bargaining strategy in the next.

Perhaps what all of this suggests, in its simplest terms, is that along with the cold, calculating analysis of power and strategy, there is a decidedly human element that influences the behavior of national leaders in even the most serious interstate disputes. This is not to say that the stresses of crises are likely to cause statesmen to act irrationally, but that human values, such as pride or a sense of one's status, can play an important role in interstate conflicts between states of comparable capabilities. That may be why statesmen—and their constituents—react so strongly to overt threats from states of comparable military strength. It may also be one reason why the states that are unsuccessful in one dispute are likely to turn to a more belligerent bargaining strategy in the next confrontation with their previous adversary.

Traditional realism posits that the management of crises requires self-restraint and a sense of proportion as well as a firm demonstration of resolve. That the states in the five studies so often appeared to place a stronger emphasis on the latter confirms the descriptive validity of the conflict strategist' view of crisis bargaining. That this so often resulted in the escalation of conflicts predicted by their critics raises serious questions about the prescriptions offered by the conflict strategists. For if the realists have generally been accurate in describing how statesmen are most likely to respond to crises, the counterrealists have been more correct in describing the high costs and risks of statesmen's actions. The warnings of the counterrealists are especially important in managing any future crises between the United States and the Soviet Union, where a high degree of symmetry in military capabilities and in motivation places severe constraints on the ability of either party to coerce the other without risking an unwanted war.

Ronald Reagan began his first term in office by denouncing detente and by announcing a more offensive strategy for dealing with the Soviet Union. Beyond the president's ideological rhetoric, this included an acceleration of the arms race and promises to demonstrate the U.S. willingness to use military power. Reagan's rhetoric embodied the essence of the approach presented by the conflict strategists. So far, with the exception of a couple of minor military adventures in the Third World, U.S. policies have been more restrained than the rhetoric; however, Reagan has not been tested by a serious confrontation with the Soviets. As the president's second term in office begins, the rhetoric has become restrained; there has been more emphasis on "confidence-building measures" between the superpowers and less on "giving the Russians something to worry about." One can only hope that the change reflects a greater awareness of the costs and risks of attempting a coercive approach to bargaining with the Soviets in a future confrontation, as well as in day-to-day relations.

REFERENCES

BOX, G. E. P., and G. M. JENKINS (1976). *Times Series Analysis: Forecasting and Control*. San Francisco, Calif.: Holden–Day.

BREHM, J. W. (1960). *A Theory of Psychological Reactance*. New York: Academic Press.

CARR, E. H. (1939). *The Twenty Years' Crisis*. London: Macmillan.

GOCHMAN, C. S. AND R. J. LENG (1983). "Realpolitik and the Road to War: An Analysis of Attributes and Behavior." *International Studies Quarterly*, 27:97–120.

JERVIS, R. (1976). *Perception and Misperception in International Politics*. Princeton, N.J.: Princeton University Press.

LENG, R. J. (1980). "Influence Strategies and Interstate Conflict." In J. D. Singer (ed.), *Correlates of War II*. New York: Free Press. Pp. 124–60.

LENG, R. J. (1983). "When Will They Ever Learn? Coercive Bargaining in Recurrent Crises." *Journal of Conflict Resolution,* 27:379–419.

LENG, R. J. (1984a). "Reagan and the Russians: Crisis Bargaining Beliefs and the Historical Record." *American Political Science Review,* 78:338–55.

LENG, R. J. (1984b). "Behavioral Correlates of War Project: Data and Findings." Paper Presented at the Annual Meetings of the International Studies Association, Atlanta, Ga., March 21–24.

LENG, R. J., and G. GOCHMAN (1982). "Dangerous Disputes: A Study of Conflict Behavior and War." *American Journal of Political Science,* 26:664–87.

LENG, R. J., and J. D. SINGER (1977). "Toward a Multitheoretical Typology of International Actions" In M. Bunge, J. Galtung, and M. Malitza (eds.), *Mathematical Approaches to International Politics.* Bucharest: Rumanian Academy of Social and Political Sciences. Pp. 71–93.

LENG, R. J., and H. WHEELER (1979). "Influence Strategies, Success, and War." *Journal of Conflict Resolution,* 23:655–84.

MORGENTHAU, H. J. (1978). *Politics Among Nations.* New York: Alfred A. Knopf.

RAPOPORT, A. (1960). *Fights, Games, and Debates.* Ann Arbor, Mich.: University of Michigan Press.

SCHELLING, T. C. (1960). *The Strategy of Conflict.* Cambridge, Mass.: Harvard University Press.

SCHELLING, T. C. (1966). *Arms and Influence.* New Haven, Conn.: Yale University Press.

4

Flirtations with the Apocalypse: American Nuclear Strategy in Reagan II

Louis René Beres

With the atomic secret torn from nature, humankind has brought all life to the brink of an obscene and abrupt conclusion. Although we have always feared extinction without significance, the perversion of species ingenuity through nuclear war would represent the final triumph of meaninglessness. Since the stockpiled nuclear weapons that now exist could make any further reproduction of living cells impossible, the consequences of a nuclear war might be nothing less than *omnicide*. Spawning death without rebirth, nuclear war would destroy not only all of nature, but even the natural relation of death to life.

Curiously, our leaders fail to understand. Anesthetized to reason, the Reagan administration begins its second term with its original assumptions intact. Tantalized by falsehoods, the president and his strategic mythmakers still substitute cliches and empty witticisms for correct inference. Having reached the point where life and death, reality and imagination, fact and fantasy are no longer seen as contradictory, their thought is bereft of object. Turned inward upon itself, this thought reflects not critical analysis but self-deception and political ritual.

While the beginning of Reagan II was marked by Soviet–American agreement in Geneva for further arms control talks, the basic plan of U.S. nuclear strategy has remained needlessly provocative. Exceeding the requirements of purposeful deterrence, this plan goes beyond the legitimate objective of survivable and penetration-capable strategic forces to accelerated preparations for fighting a nuclear war. The administration certainly does not seek such a war, but it believes that U.S. preparedness to fight a nuclear war is essential to successful deterrence.[1]

Such reasoning is sorely deficient. Endorsing a counterforce targeting program with mutually reinforcing fears of first-strike attack, the president's "rearmament" of the United States makes nuclear war much more likely. The dangers are heightened, as we shall see, by specific U.S. plans for the MX, Euromissile deployments,[2] and "strategic defense."

Buttressed by its hopes for "Star Wars" technologies, the administration has also stepped up plans for civil defense of the nation's population. Supported by $4.2 billion in budget authority over the next seven years, these plans call for the "temporary relocation" of approximately 150 million people from about 400 "high-risk" metropolitan and defense-related areas to about 2,000 allegedly safer "host areas" during periods when nuclear attack appears imminent.

There is, however, no reason to believe that such relocation would ever work (in New York City, for example, evacuation is to take place largely by subway), or even if it could work, that it would protect even a tiny fraction of our population from the effects of a "nuclear winter." As FEMA, the federal agency charged with statutory responsibility on these matters, itself admits, if the Soviet Union were to mount an all-out attack on the United States, "almost the whole population would be located within less than 100 miles of at least one nuclear detonation."[3] The significance of this expectation is that: (1) virtually the whole U.S. population would be within range of serious fallout radiation exposure; and (2) almost half the U.S. population would be involved in direct weapons effects.

The Reagan administration's nuclear strategy is hopelessly flawed. With its plans to "prevail" in a "protracted" nuclear war with the Soviet Union, this strategy now resembles an eschatological scheme, a plan for the Final Battle. Although the president's most recent policy statements have been free of his earlier references to an "Evil Empire," there has been no effective change in his fundamental orientation—that the struggle with our principal adversary is nothing less than a death-struggle between the Sons of Light and the Sons of Darkness.

This view contributes to a profoundly unrealistic and dangerous assessment of historical and political circumstances. Prodding the United States into irrational forms of adventurism, it creates a precarious "syndrome" from which there may be no escape. Borrowing from a recent book by Yehoshafat Harkabi, a former chief of Israel's military intelligence and now a professor at the Hebrew University in Jerusalem, the Reagan administration has become captive of the "Bar Kokhba Syndrome," a pattern of excessive risk-taking that places the very national existence in ultimate jeopardy. As in the case of the second-century-A.D. rebellion of Jews against imperial Rome in Judea, from which this "syndrome" draws its name, current U.S. nuclear strategy is destined to fail; indeed, since the stakes are much higher today than they were in A.D.132, it may not only be suicidal, but omnicidal, pushing an entire species to the margins of history.[4]

Nuclear strategy is a game that sane people may play, but not—as the Reagan administration suggests—with frivolity. Since all of the administration's planned force expansions and "improvements" would add nothing to our assured destruction capabilities, they can only undermine U.S. security. This is the case because such measures, especially as they are interwoven with apocalyptic visions of confrontation, are apt to be regarded as first-strike preparations.

This is the central flaw in President Reagan's nuclear strategy. Virtually every element of this strategy occasions doubts among Soviet leaders about this country's rejection of a nuclear first-strike option. By encouraging a climate of strategic interaction in which the Soviet Union must exist in a continual expectation of imminent attack, the United States compels its adversary to take steps to strike first itself. Naturally, these steps are perceived as aggressive in turn, and in "reaction" to apparent Soviet designs, an unstoppable cycle of move and countermove is initiated. The net effect, of course, is insecurity for all concerned.

It is wrong to assume that neither side will ever strike first if it believes that by doing so it will bring down overwhelming carnage upon itself. Even perfectly rational states can be expected to preempt, whatever the expected consequences, if they believe that the other side is about to strike first. This is the case because in the theater of the absurd logic of nuclear strategy, the country that strikes first in such a situation can expect to suffer less than if it waits to strike second. Sadly, everything now being done by the Reagan administration contributes to the Soviet fear of a U.S. first strike.

Ironically, the president's nuclear strategy—intertwined with an elaborate canon of nuclear theology—will cause evil by wanting heroically to triumph over it. But there is still time for a change in direction if those who preside over our safety learn to reverse still-advancing superstitions with a less "heroic" vision of world politics. In abandoning the ruins of apocalyptic thought, the administration could begin to confront the ashes of endless ruins-in-the-making not as a victim, but as a gifted survivor.

One fact is clear! A nuclear war between the superpowers must be considered like any other incurable disease; the only hope lies in prevention. Even if evacuation could be accomplished in time, there is no reason to believe that "host areas" would be free of lethal radioactivity. Moreover, within weeks after an exchange involving some 5,000 megatons between the superpowers, soot, smoke and dust from nuclear fires and groundbursts would reduce the amount of sunlight at ground level to a few percent of what is normal. According to comments by astronomer Carl Sagan at a conference on "The World after Nuclear War" held on October 31, 1983: "An unbroken gloom would persist for weeks over the Northern Hemisphere."[5]

But this would be only the beginning. For the succeeding months, the light filtering through this pall would be unable to sustain photosynthesis. As a result, there would take place a devastating impairment of the process whereby plants convert sunlight to food—an impairment that would cascade through all food chains, producing long-term famine.

The lack of sunlight could also produce a harsh nuclear winter, with temperatures dropping by as much as 25°C in inland areas. Many regions could be subject to continuous snowfall, even in the summer. In addition to killing all crops in the Northern Hemisphere, a nuclear war between the superpowers would freeze surface waters in the interior of continents, causing a great many animals to die of thirst.

These effects, of course, would accompany an exchange that could kill immediately 1.1 billion people and injure severely the same number. Moreover, because radioactive debris in huge amounts—an estimated 225 million tons in a few days, according to Sagan—would be carried throughout the atmosphere, exposure to radioactive fallout would be likely not only nationwide but worldwide. And urban fires set off by the nuclear blasts would generate large amounts of deadly toxins by vaporizing the huge stockpiles of stored synthetic chemicals.

The most devastating effects would be long-term. Contrary to conclusions supported by our leaders, nuclear war would have a major effect on climate lasting for several years. High-yield nuclear explosions would inject nitrogen oxides into the stratosphere, resulting in large reductions of the ozone layer. Since this layer screens the earth from excessive amounts of ultraviolet light, this could have a marked impact on microorganisms in the soil and on aquatic life.

Although such information is just now beginning to penetrate the consciousness of informed publics throughout the world, much of it has been known for some time. In a classic work of the early 1960s, biologist Tom Stonier (1964) identified correctly the serious outbreaks of famine and disease, the ensuing shock to individuals and environment that could persist for decades, the legacy of genetic damage and the disappearance of civilization. In a 1975 study titled *Long-Term Worldwide Effects of Multiple Nuclear Weapons Detonations,* a special committee of the National Research Council, National Academy of Sciences, introduced its findings with the disclaimer that, "No report can portray the enormity, the utter horror which must befall the targeted areas and adjoining territories"—a disclaimer that we now know must extend to every nook and cranny of the Soviet Union and the United States and beyond.

In considering such informed expectations, it is important to understand that they are very conservative estimates of what would happen after a superpower nuclear war. As the NAS committee indicated, its findings do not even consider the probable social, political, and economic consequences of the hypothesized nuclear exchange. Nor do they address the probable interactions between individual effects, interactions that might be utterly unexpected and lethal. To understand completely the effects of a nuclear war between the United States and the Soviet Union, we will ultimately have to go beyond the separate examinations of the consequences of blast, nuclear radiation, and thermal radiation, to a full consideration of possible synergy among these consequences.

What would be the medical consequences of a nuclear war? Happily, there is now available a great deal of information on this question, much of it (ironically) supplied by the U.S. Government (e.g., Office of Technology Assessment, *The Effects of a Nuclear War*) and most of it supplied through Physicians for Social Responsibility (PSR). Let us consider only the briefest overview of these consequences. It should be enough.

According to PSR: "Nuclear War, even a 'limited' one, would result in death, injury and disease on a scale that has no precedent in the history of human existence."[6] Should this assessment appear exaggerated, let us consider the dangers associated with only one of the myriad health threats in the postattack environment—the threat posed by dead human beings. According to Dr. Herbert L. Abrams (1981:201) of PSR:

> The health threat created by millions of post-attack corpses is a serious one. In many areas, radiation levels will be so high that corpses will remain untouched for weeks on end. With transportation destroyed, survivors weakened and a multiplicity of post-shelter reconstruction tasks to be performed, corpse disposal will be remarkably complicated. IN ORDER TO BURY THE DEAD, AN AREA 5.7 TIMES AS LARGE AS THE CITY OF SEATTLE WOULD BE REQUIRED FOR THE CEMETERY.

For anyone who has studied the effects of the atomic bombings of Japan, it is clear that a nuclear war would bring not only death, but incoherence. And such incoherence would be accentuated by the impairment of symbolic immortality, a process by which human beings ordinarily feel that they can "live on" through their posterity. Since the occasion of nuclear war would represent an assault on the very idea of posterity for millions (and perhaps billions) of people, the continuity of life would give way to authentic feelings of disintegration.

Even the most limited nuclear exchange would signal grievous catastrophe. The immediate effects of the explosions—thermal radiation, nuclear radiation, and blast damage—would cause wide swaths of death and devastation. Victims would suffer flash and flame burns. Retinal burns could occur in the eyes of persons at distances of several hundred miles from the explosion. People would be crushed by collapsing buildings or torn by flying glass. Others would fall victim to raging firestorms and conflagrations. Fallout injuries would include whole-body radiation injury, produced by penetrating, hard gamma radiation; superficial radiation burns produced by soft radiations; and injuries produced by deposits of radioactive substances within the body.

In the aftermath, medical facilities that might still exist would be stressed beyond endurance. Water supplies would become unusable as a result of fallout contamination. Housing and shelter would be unavailable for millions of survivors. Transportation and communication would break down to almost prehistoric levels. And overwhelming food shortages would become the rule for at least several years.

Since the countries involved would have entered into war as modern industrial economies, their networks of highly interlocking and interdependent exchange systems would now be shattered. Virtually everyone would be deprived of a means of livelihood. Emergency fire and police services would be decimated altogether. Systems dependent upon electrical power would cease to function. Severe trauma would occasion widespread disorientation and psychological disorders, for which there would be no therapeutic services.

In sum, normal society would disappear. The pestilence of unrestrained murder and banditry would augment the pestilence of plague and epidemics. With the passage of time, many of the survivors could expect an increased incidence of degenerative diseases and various kinds of cancer. They might also expect premature death, impairment of vision, and a high probability of sterility. Among the survivors of Hiroshima, for example, an increased incidence of leukemia and cancer of the lung, stomach, breast, ovary, and uterine cervix has been widely documented.

Left unchecked, this government's plans for fighting nuclear war will contribute to our increasingly likely rendezvous with extinction, a rendezvous that would bring us all face to face with the torments of Dante's *Inferno,* "Into the eternal darkness, into fire, into ice." We must, therefore, begin to take measures to halt this encroachment of death. More than anything else, this means a far-reaching rejection of current nuclear strategy.

The time has come to challenge the strategic mythmakers on their unfounded pretensions to expertise and on their delusions of immortality. There is very little time left. Now, without further hesitation, citizens of the United States must acknowledge the imperative to survive. Only then can we hope to escape the predatory embrace of annihilation.

But what exactly must be done to prevent a nuclear war? At one level, the answer is obvious. Instead of fine-tuning their over-worked scenarios of nuclear gamesmanship, the United States and the Soviet Union must accept a return to less volatile strategies of nuclear deterrence, a joint nuclear freeze, a comprehensive test ban, and steady expansion of nuclear-weapon-free zones. In addition, this country must take steps to parallel the Soviet policy of no first use of nuclear weapons—steps that would require prompt abandonment of Euromissile deployments.[7] We must also move to abandon the MX missile and illusory plans for space-based defense.

It is all so terribly obvious. Placing new warfighting missiles within existing Minuteman silos would not improve the survivability of this country's ICBM forces. Instead, the stationing of these missiles in existing silos would generate a U.S. shift to "launch-on-warning"—a shift in which U.S. nuclear forces might be launched before Soviet weapons had actually struck their targets.

How must this look from the Soviet vantage point? Threatened by the hard-target, countersilo qualities of the MX as well as by the prospect of U.S. first-strike weapons on "hair trigger," their incentive to preempt in the near term may be considerable. And even if we could make it past an initial deployment of MX, the Soviets would certainly respond with their own launch-on-warning tactics, a response that would enlarge the probability of both accidental nuclear war and a U.S. first strike.

We witness another curious development. President Reagan's plan for space-based ballistic missile defense has elicited virtually no support from the independent scientific community.[8] Moreover, at a time when deficit reduction is an overriding consideration of U.S. security, the plan will cost an initial $26 billion for research. Why then, does the plan proceed?

The answer, it would appear, lies in the plan's association with *defense*. Since the president calls only for a "Strategic *Defense* Initiative," what possible rationale can exist for opposition? Why should anyone resist plans for high-level protection of the United States?

Upon examination, however, it becomes clear that the only association between Star Wars and defense is linguistic. In a world where stable nuclear deterrence has always been based upon mutual vulnerability, an ambitious program by one side to preclude the other's "assured destruction" capability is manifestly *offensive*. Indeed, such an understanding led to the ABM Treaty of 1972, an agreement severely restricting the development of ballistic missile defense measures. Without this treaty, it is likely that a major expansion of the arms race would have begun much earlier.

The Soviets, of course, will never sit by and watch us develop a potentially destabilizing technology, one that would put them at a significant disadvantage. Rather, they will accelerate their work on an entire new generation of offensive missile systems—a configuration of nuclear weapons that could reliably penetrate U.S. laser and other directed energy beam defenses. The net effect of this cycle of move and countermove can only be a greatly heightened prospect of nuclear war.

Strangely enough, the president seems to recognize these lethal implications of Star Wars. In his original announcement of the plan on March 23, 1983, he commented that defensive systems "lead to certain problems and ambiguities," and that "they can be viewed as fostering an aggressive policy." Yet, he seems to feel that these deficiencies would prove unimportant if the shift toward defense were accompanied by graduated, mutual reductions of offensive systems.

The chief problem with the president's reasoning is that he chooses to ignore Soviet uncertainty. Notwithstanding his assurances of the United States' peaceful intentions toward the Soviets, there is little cause for optimism in the Kremlin. From Moscow's perspective, everything points to a major U.S. flirtation with the idea of a disarming first strike.

Where has the president gone wrong? Seeking to appear "tough," he has created the impression that we might prefer relative victory to nonwar. Even if this impression is erroneous, all that matters is that it is perceived as genuine in Soviet strategic calculations.

The president fails to understand that in the post-war balance of terror, safety is inextricably intertwined with mutual vulnerability. Clearly, this situation of deadly logic cannot go on forever. But the replacement of "mutual assured destruction" with a more enduring pattern of safety cannot be accomplished by illusory programs for defense.

The answer to the problem of nuclear war lies not in such esoteric technologies as lasers working in conjunction with orbiting optical elements (a scheme, incidentally, with a power requirement on the order of the output of 300 1,000-megawatt power plants, or more than 60% of the current electrical generating capacity of the entire United States). Instead, it lies in a well-reasoned, incremental disengagement from all forms of strategic competition.

But such disengagement can never take place amidst the current climate of suspicion, competition, and hostility. Before any real risk-reduction can occur, both countries will require prior assurances of cooperation and goodwill. In the final analysis, the two superpowers can control the nuclear threat to their existence only by first accommodating their rivalries across the whole spectrum of nonmilitary differences.

FIRST President Reagan must give substance to his retreat from the imagery of a holy crusade. There is no place for *jihad* in the process of reconciliation. Indeed, by approaching the Soviet Union not as a secular adversary but as the agent of Belial, the president makes any sort of reconciliation impossible. In this connection, Mr. Reagan would do well to heed the warning in

George Washington's Farewell Address that the "nation which indulges toward another an habitual hatred ... is in some degree a slave."

SECOND, the president must understand that we exist, as a nation, firmly within the arena of mortality. Before we can survive, he must accept that arms control treaties are not a gift to be bestowed upon the Soviets for good behavior, but a mutual requirement of avoiding extinction. Just as repression of the fear of death by individuals can impair the prospects for self-preservation, so can the administration impair prospects for national survival by denying the feasibility of collective disintegration. Although it is true that the fear of death must be tempered in both individual and national drives lest it create madness and paralysis, to insulate ourselves from such fear altogether is to make the threat of annihilation more imminent.

THIRD, President Reagan must begin to ensure that our own house is in order. At the moment, there is little evidence that U.S. foreign policy exhibits a singularly greater commitment to virtue. A kaleidoscope of shame and abjection, especially in Latin America and South Africa, this country's continuing disregard for human rights in anti-Soviet states suggests that *Realpolitik,* not goodness, animates our global affairs. There is, therefore, no meaningful difference between U.S. and Soviet foreign policies.

FOURTH, President Reagan must attempt to see the world from the Soviet point of view. In their plans for deploying Euromissiles, for example, it seems inconceivable that U.S. policy makers have been so insensitive to Soviet fears of first-strike weapons in West Germany. Have we completely forgotton what happened to the Soviet Union in June 1941? The Soviets have *not* forgotten!

But what of the Soviets' own modernization and expansion of nuclear forces? Are they not coresponsible for a deteriorating state of affairs? Indeed, they are. Yet, there is no reason to believe that mimicry is the correct strategy for the United States. Even if our worst-case assumptions about Soviet intentions were right, it is not true that our interests are best served by escalating the levels of tension and uncertainty.

In developing a sensible nuclear strategy, the United States should be guided only by a meticulous comparison of the costs and benefits of alternative courses of action. Instead of commitments to the vague need for "matching Soviet moves," "filling the void" created by the Soviet SS-20s, or "meeting the political litmus test for NATO" (the ritualistic arguments for cruise and Pershing II), our leaders must focus on the fact that there is *no* defensive use for any of the new weapons.[9] They must then consider whether such alleged expected gains are worth the expected losses. Unless the West is prepared to accept such gains as worth the very heightened risk of nuclear war, it must abandon the Euromissile deployments. For nations that are still moved by reason rather than by rhetoric, it should be an easy decision.

FIFTH, President Reagan must abandon his crusade to undermine the entire Soviet system. In this connection, he must resist the inclination to conduct diplomacy by ultimatum. And he must begin to promote an expanded array of cultural and scientific exchanges, a policy that could "spill over" into the security arena.

SIXTH, President Reagan must learn to understand that the rivalry between the Soviet Union and the United States, once spawned and sustained by genuine considerations of purpose and power, is now essentially a contrivance. Contrary to what we are led to believe, the underlying point of contention between the superpowers is not now ideological or economic, but a self-fulfilling and groundless rhetoric reinforced by self-serving elites. In what is perhaps the greatest single irony of world politics, these elites and their "defense community" handmaidens are true allies, supporting each other while they corrode the security of both countries.

While this country must continue to ensure the survivability and penetration capability of its strategic forces, it is altogether clear that this objective can be harmonized with a new framework of deescalation and collaboration. In moving toward such a framework, a new and infinitely more hopeful pattern of interaction could replace the lethal lure of primacy, a pattern that could serve U.S. interests and ideals simultaneously.

Violence is not power. Sometimes they are opposites; the less power, the greater the inclination to violence. From the standpoint of avoiding nuclear war, this suggests a U.S. imperative to recognize the demands of coexistence. Now that we have passed the 50th anniversary of the establishment of formal relations between the United States and the Soviet Union, it is fitting that we seek to strengthen such relations through energetic dialogue rather than through megaphone diplomacy.

There is nothing about current strategic postures that suggests malevolence or deliberate war-mongering. Indeed, in considering these postures, one is reminded of the statement by Albert Camus: "It seems to me that every one should think this over. For what strikes me, in the midst of polemics, threats and outbursts of violence, is the fundamental good will of every one."

But good will is not enough. If we are to transcend an unbearable fate there must also be *understanding*. To survive into the future, the Reagan administration must learn to recognize that nuclear *Realpolitik* can never work. Insubstantial from the start, it is an unrealistic policy whose corrosive effects are accentuated with each passing day.

NOTES

[1]The Reagan administration argues that since nuclear deterrence has worked since the dawn of the Atomic Age, it may work forever. But this argument is very much like that of the chain smoker who contends that he has been smoking cigarettes for 25 years without ill effects and that smoking must therefore be safe. The real question, of course, is whether smoking will *ultimately* kill him. If it does, the final assessment of costs and benefits will turn out to be dramatically less optimistic. Just as significantly, the notion of nuclear deterrence embraced by the Reagan administration is not the notion that has been with us from the start. Today, it is assumed that successful deterrence requires not only the capacity to assuredly destroy an aggressor after absorbing a nuclear first strike (MAD) but also the capacity to fight a nuclear war (NUT). With such an assumption, the United States plans to deploy a variety of weapons that are unsuitable for anything but an initial move of war.

[2]Amidst the din and controversy surrounding the cruise and Pershing II missiles, the most vital point is always overlooked. In the event of a Soviet/Warsaw Pact conventional attack against Western Europe—the scenario that gives rise to the NATO Euromissile deployment—a reprisal by any number of the projected 572 missiles directed at the Soviet homeland would almost certainly lead to all-out nuclear war. It follows that the threat to use these weapons to deter such an attack is wholly incredible. It could be argued in response that this threat might still be credible if the Soviets believed the U.S. president to be irrational, but if this were indeed the case, that country would have an irresistible incentive to strike first. What if the Soviets should launch their nuclear weapons as a first offensive move of war? In such a case, the cruise and Pershing II missiles would also prove useless, since they would add nothing to our existing strategic capabilities. Whatever feeble damage-limitation benefits might accrue to the United States from its arsenal of counterforce-targeted nuclear weapons, they would not be improved by the firing of up to 572 new intermediate-range missiles. This is the case because there would be very little left of this country to protect after the first round of Soviet attacks had been absorbed. Moreover, the United States does not even target Soviet submarine-launched ballistic missiles.

[3]See FEMA (1982), *Attack Environment Manual.*

[4]See Harkabi (1983). Harkabi himself does not apply the lessons of the Bar Kokhba thesis to U.S. nuclear strategy. This application is mine alone.

[5]For more on the concept of a "nuclear winter," see P. Ehrlich et al. (1983); Turco et al. (1983); Sagan (1983/84); Covey et al. (1984); Turco et al. (1984); A. Ehrlich (1984). For the layperson, an excellent nontechnical overview of the concept can be found in Sagan (1983).

[6]See Physicians for Social Responsibility (1980).

[7]The key to such abandonment lies, in turn, in the realization of approximate parity in conventional forces between the two alliances. This is because NATO's commitment to a nuclear "defense" stems from fears of the Warsaw Pact's numerically superior conventional forces. Should there be substantial success in producing equalization of conventional forces, the U.S./NATO side could be expected to diminish its long-standing reliance on theater nuclear forces and on the associated policy of "first use."

[8]See, for example, Arkin (1984); Bethe et al. (1984); Drell et al. (1984); Bundy et al. (1984/85); and Union of Concerned Scientists (1984).

[9]A dominant obstacle to stopping and reversing Euromissile deployments is the continuing and misconceived preoccupation with "balance" in medium-range nuclear forces. Although it is fashionable for supporters of the new European weapons to invoke requirements of equilibrium as if they were incontestable elements of our nuclear theology, these requirements are nonexistent. There is absolutely no relationship between balance and successful nuclear deterrence. Since credible deterrence requires the capacity to deliver "assured destruction" in a retaliatory blow, it is possible that a markedly inferior arsenal, so long as it were survivable and penetration-capable, could keep the peace. At the same time, a nation with a vastly superior nuclear arsenal might undermine deterrence and occasion a first strike by the other side if it were sufficiently provocative—that is, if it were the sort of nuclear warfighting arsenal now being developed by NATO and the United States. In this connection, the very worst sort of nuclear arsenal is one that occasions the other side to configure its own forces under "launch-on-warning" status. This is, of course, exactly what the Soviet response to the Euromissile deployment will ultimately be, a response increasing the chances both for U.S. preemption and for accidental nuclear war.

REFERENCES

ABRAMS, H. L. (1981). "Infection and Communicable Diseases." In R. Adams and S. Cullen (eds.), *The Final Epidemic.* Chicago, Ill.: Educational Foundation for Nuclear Science.

ARKIN, W. M. (1984). "SDI—Pie in the Sky?" *Bulletin of the Atomic Scientists,* 40/4:9–10.

BETHE, H. A., et al. (1984). "Space-Based Ballistic Missile Defense." *Scientific American,* 251/4:39–49.

BUNDY, M., G. KENNAN, R. McNAMARA, and G. SMITH (1984/85). "The President's Choice: Star Wars or Arms Control." *Foreign Affairs,* 63:264–78.

COVEY, C., S. SCHNEIDER, and S. THOMPSON (1984). "Global Atmospheric Effects of Massive Smoke Injections from a Nuclear War: Results from General Circulation Model Simulations." *Nature,* 308/5954:21–25.

DRELL, S. D., et al. (1984). *The Reagan Strategic Defense Initiative: A Technical, Political and Arms Control Assessment.* Stanford, Calif.: Center for International Security and Arms Control, Stanford University.

EHRLICH, A. (1984). "Nuclear Winter." *Bulletin of the Atomic Scientists,* Special Supplement, 40/4.

EHRLICH, P. R., et al. (1983). "Long-Term Biological Consequences of Nuclear War." *Science,* 222/4630:1293–1300.

FEMA (1982). *Attack Environment Manual,* May, CPG 2-1A1, Washington, D.C., Panel 14.

HARKABI, Y. (1983). *The Bar Kokhba Syndrome: Risk and Realism in International Politics.* Chappaqua, N.Y.: Rossel Books.

PHYSICIANS FOR SOCIAL RESPONSIBILITY (1980). "An Open Letter to President Carter and Chairman Brezhnev," *PSR Newsletter,* 1(2). P. 1.

SAGAN, C. (1983). *The Nuclear Winter.* Boston: Council for a Liveable World, Education Fund.

SAGAN, C. (1983/84). "Nuclear War and Climatic Catastrophe." *Foreign Affairs,* 62:257–92.

STONIER, T. (1964). *Nuclear Disaster.* New York: Meridian.

TURCO, R. P., et al. (1983). "Nuclear Winter: Global Consequences of Multiple Nuclear Explosions." *Science,* 222/4630: 1283–92.

TURCO, R. P., et al. (1984). "The Climatic Effects of Nuclear War." *Scientific American,* 251/2: 33–43.

UNION OF CONCERNED SCIENTISTS (1984). *Space-Based Missile Defense.* Cambridge, Mass.

5

Behavioral Theories and Global Strategies

Anatol Rapoport

In examining the relations between behavioral theories and global strategies, I will argue that the behavioral theories that may shed some light on the development of global strategies (i.e., geopolitics) are not those that purport to explain the behavior and the inferred psychological underpinnings of normal human beings, but, rather, of much larger entities—of systems called states and of particular subsystems of these, which could be called "defense communities." Admittedly, decisions that govern the behavior of these large systems and design the rules of that behavior (i.e., foreign policies) are made by predominantly normal individuals. It seems, however, that in that role the decision makers differ from normal human beings. Rather, they seem to be extensions of the larger systems, whose "needs" (if one may speak of such) are very different from human needs.

These conclusions suggest that in our time, when humanity as whole is faced with formidable problems bearing on its very survival, the concerns that shape the foreign policies of the superpowers are disconnected from the concerns that are central in the lives of the vast majority of human beings.

THE SYSTEM-THEORETIC VIEW

In constructing a behavioral theory in which aggregates rather than individuals appear as actors, there is no need to invoke mystical concepts like "group mind," "Zeitgeist," and the like. Or, better said, these concepts can be demystified and made usable in a responsible scientific theory. The "mind" of an organization needs to be no more obscure a concept than the "mind" of a person. To insist that no such "collective mind" exists, that only minds (i.e., perceptions, motives, affects, etc.) of individuals "really" exist, is no more justifiable than to insist that there is no such thing as "mind" altogether, even of an individual, because behavior is the only manifest evidence of "mind," and "in the last analysis" behavior consists of firing neurons and twitching muscles.

Here the holistic slogan, "The whole is greater than the sum of its parts," if properly interpreted, seems to say something significant. The proper interpretation is not a dogmatic negation of all forms of reductionism or a naive warning against assuming a universal additivity of effects, but rather a pragmatic principle of research. It is hopeless to *try* to derive patterns of gross behavior of an organism by concentrating only on the physiology of its nervous system (at least in our present stage of knowledge) and refusing to ascend from that particular level of abstraction. (Note that all levels of observation are particular levels of abstraction.) By the same token, let us resign ourselves to the circumstance that we cannot derive the gross behavior patterns of aggregates, organizations, and so forth by concentrating on what we know about individual behavior, even though in *principle,* the behavior of aggregates "consists" of behaviors of interacting individuals, just as the behavior of an individual consists (in principle) of interacting physiological units.

Once the relativity of abstraction is recognized as an epistemological principle, we can speak without embarassment about structure, behavior, and evolution not only of aggregates or organisms (e.g., social or ecological systems) but even of systems that have no material existence as such but can be regarded as emanations of organized aggregates. Examples are languages, systems of beliefs, ideologies, doctrines, and so forth.

That such ideational systems have identifiable structures is evident. They also evolve, and some aspects of their evolution show striking similarities to aspects of biological evolution—the evolution of languages from common ancestors being a prime example. The "behavior" of such conceptual systems is more difficult to define. One aspect of behavior, however, is discernible—namely, a sort of inertia, a tendency to preserve a structure. The same aspect is observable in the behavior of living systems, in the sense that they respond defensively to stimuli. Much of this behavior relates to homeostasis, the tendency of living systems to keep certain state variables within certain limits and in this way to preserve an identity. Homeostatic mechanisms of this sort can be supposed to operate in languages or in conceptual systems in the form of "filtering devices," keeping "foreign" elements out of the system. To take an example, consider foreign words being admitted into the vocabulary of a language. Upon being incorporated, the pronunciation of these words is changed to fit the phonetic structure of the language. Thereby, the phonetic structure is "protected" against the infusion of alien elements. Of course, in the long run the phonetic structure can change, but these changes reflect the evolutionary rather than the "behavioral" aspect of a language perceived as a system.

In developing a behavioral theory of a large organized aggregate, such as a state or of subsystems of states such as their military establishments, one must continually refer to a particular environment. It consists of a repertory of concepts that constitutes a remarkably stable framework, and this framework delineates the range of possible actions that can be taken by that system. The point I wish to make is that the semantic environment sharply constrains the options available to actors on the international scene. The system of concepts characteristic of organized aggregates need not resemble the system that guides the behavior and decisions of normal human beings. One suspects, therefore, that the actors in the game of global strategy—diplomats, military leaders, and so forth—only seem to be normal human beings. At the same time, they play the role of extensions or effector organs, if you will, of large interacting systems. In that role, they think, speak, and act in ways that one cannot expect a normal human being to think, speak, or act.

NORMAL HUMAN NEEDS

These remarks may seem provocative or to beg the question in the sense that they imply a definition of a "normal human being" so as to deliberately exclude the global strategist (acting in that role) from this category. So let us substitute "vast majority" for "normal." For this vast majority of human beings on this planet, everyday concerns revolve around, in the first instance, matters related to survival in the immediate future (which for a very considerable fraction of humanity constitutes a serious problem), then to matters related to reduction of misery or, in the case of the more fortunate, to increase of comfort, to relationships with other human beings, such as, mates, children, and others, with whom more or less close contacts are maintained. In cultures where people are expected to improve their position in life, they are concerned with matters pertaining to the advancement of careers. People with intellectual bent are concerned with ideas; those with artistic bent with creating beauty, with self-expression, with acquisition of public approval and acclaim, or with new ways of organizing perception. In the business world, people may be concerned with accumulating wealth. In practically all walks of life, people are concerned with the images they project, that is, with self-respect and with respect or affection of others. There are also feuds among people, and these induce feelings of hostility toward specific individuals or specific identified groups. Hostility is sometimes manifested in actions designed to harm others. On occasions, people may kill each other in passionate outbursts of hostility or even (but only rarely) in cold blood.

Now, I believe that I have covered a broad enough range of concerns of "normal human beings" (including also some that lead to destructive acts) to forestall an accusation of stacking the cards in favor of a very special definition of "normality." If so, then I can safely say that the concerns of modern global strategists are not among the concerns of normal human beings, even though, regarded as individuals, very few of the global strategists can be singled out as differing radically from individuals who must be regarded as "normal." This is the reason for my assertion that concerns related to global strategies are not concerns of normal human beings but of another type of "living system." These concerns are *imposed* on human beings through the medium of the semantic environment.

THE WAR OF EVERY ONE
AGAINST EVERY ONE

Over 300 years ago, Thomas Hobbes depicted what he thought was "man in the state of nature." His model of "man" was a bundle of appetites, to satisfy which, men had to act. Since all overt actions can be depicted as motion, Hobbes pictured humanity as a large aggregate of individuals all moving about and bumping against each other. These bumps were interpreted as frustrations of actions directed at satisfying appetites or drives. Consequently, every human encounter was depicted as a frustration. Every one got into every one's way. And so every one was every one's natural enemy.

Had this state of affairs continued, "man in the state of nature" would eventually have exterminated himself. He was saved from this fate, according to Hobbes, by inventing the state. The typical state of the time was a more or less absolute monarchy. It arose, according to Hobbes, in consequence of men giving up their liberty (freedom, autonomy) to a prince in return for being protected from each other. The exercise of violence became the monopoly of the state, embodied in the person of the prince. This is a thumbnail sketch of the theory of human society according to Hobbes.

Now, the sort of atomized humanity that supposedly represented "man in the state of nature" never existed. Man was probably social even before he became man, as Marx wisely observed. On another level, however, Hobbes' "war of every one against every one" became a much closer representation of reality, namely, on the level of the state. The European continent, a patchwork of sovereign states that arose after the Thirty Years' War, finally demonstrated the futility of trying to impose political unity on the basis of religious hegemony. The European "community of states" became a fairly accurate representation of Hobbes' "war of every one against every one." This political philosophy was forcefully and clearly formulated by Carl von Clausewitz, the outstanding philosopher of war.

Although a follower of Kant rather than of Hegel, Clausewitz enthusiastically embraced the Hegelian idea of the state as the embodiment of the collective will of a people. This will was imagined by Clausewitz to be directed by a drive to expand, to force others to submit. The realization of this will was for Clausewitz the meaning of politics, the "continuation of politics by other means." "War," wrote Clausewitz in the opening statement of his magnum opus, "is an act of violence to force our opponent to submit to our will." By "us" he meant the Kingdom of Prussia.

It is true, of course, that the Hobbsian war of every one against every one arose wherever militarily organized political units appeared, perhaps already in the Neolithic Age. But Clausewitz was probably the first to base an articulated political philosophy on the assumption that perpetual war is a normal state of the international system. It is instructive to view this philosophy against the background of the changing nature of war.

At its inception, war was probably "democratic" in the sense that the entire manhood of a tribe was engaged in fighting other tribes. But wars in the Europe of the eighteenth century did not have this character. Wars were fought by professional armies. The soldier was drilled to respond with standardized jerky movements to a limited repertoire of commands. The emotional concomitants of war—such as, patriotism, hatred of the enemy, glorification of a "cause," and so forth—were minimized. This situation changed radically in the wars following the French Revolution. Napoleon's soldiers were recruits strongly motivated by induced patriotic fervor or by Napoleon's charisma. They could be used much more flexibly than the dehumanized living tin soldiers of the Prussian and Austrian armies. They were also much more expendable than the highly trained soldiers of the monarchies. This enabled Napoleon to use more murderous tactics than eighteenth-century commanders were accustomed to.

Clausewitz understood the basis of Napoleon's military successes and, although he was anything but a democrat, he sponsored reforms of the Prussian military establishment that can be interpreted as steps toward "democratization." Clausewitz's treatise even contains a chapter on the "People's War." For the first time, morale was recognized explicitly as an important component of military potential. The army was now regarded not merely as an extension of a prince's personal power but as a political instrument, an embodiment of a national "will."

Since the "national will" was always supposed to be directed (in Clausewitz's implicit estimation) toward expansion of power, perpetual warfare appeared as a *normal* state of affairs. It was senseless to ask why nations went to war. One should rather ask why war alternated with periods of peace. To this question, Clausewitz gave answers: exhaustion, waiting for a better opportunity to start a war, failure to utilize existing opportunities, predilection for compromise—a fault, according to Clausewitz, who viewed the only purpose of war as the imposition of one national will on another, to be effected by destroying the adversary's army and hence his will to resist.

Thus, the Hobbsian vision of a perpetual war of all against all was reconstituted. This time, however, there was no way for the participants to "surrender their autonomy" to a higher authority in order to avoid eventual extermination.

CHANGING CONCEPTIONS OF WAR

The Clausewitzian system prevailed in Europe throughout the nineteenth century, culminating in the spasm of the First World War. The advances of killing technology based on the rapid development of the physical sciences, as well as on the temporary advantage of defensive strategies over offensive ones, turned the initial war euphoria into a trauma. The result was that the foundations of the Clausewitzian system—the total identification of a nation with the power appetites of its rulers—was shaken. The idea became widespread that war, far from being a normal phase of relations among states, was an anomaly akin to a disease. The search for the "causes" of wars, now called "peace research," began.

Understandably, attention was paid to psychological determinants of war because of the prevalent idea that wars were triggered by existing or induced hostile attitudes between people. Both the "hawks" and the "doves" entertained this idea. The difference was that the hawks believed that hostility toward aliens was natural and even approved of it as nature's way of maintaining vigor, survival of the fittest, and so forth, whereas the doves believed that such hostility was induced by propaganda in the interests of those who derived advantages from war itself or from the fruits of victory.

Aspects of human psychology, reflected, for example, in aggressive tendencies, susceptibility to propaganda, and so on, may still be important in outbursts of violence on the periphery of the highly industrialized, urbanized, secularized world. For example, the war between Iran and Iraq may be kept going by a state of mind resembling that pervading the Arab world in the days of Mohammed. The chronic war between Israel and the Arabs may also be reminiscent of a religious war, whether rationalized in terms of a covenant with God or as an Islamic "holy war." The communal strifes with occasional outbursts of genocide, as those between Hindus and Moslems or in the Nigerian civil war, were also rooted in human passions. Here, too, psychology or behavior theory could be expected to shed some light on the perennial problem of mass violence in human affairs. It is evident, however, that these outbursts on the "periphery" have little or nothing to do with global strategies, except possibly to the extent that the conflicting parties act as clients of the superpowers, who alone think in terms of global strategies. This may be the case in the Middle East.

As we regard geopolitics or the "global strategies" as they are designed and pursued today, we see that the institution of war has undergone "de-democratization," reversing the process that inspired Clausewitz's philosophy of war. This present process could also be described as a "de-psychologization" of war, if I may be forgiven for this bizarre term. It is meant to designate a growing independence of the events of war (both its incidence and its course) from psychological determinants. As a result, we see a diminishing relevance of behavioral theory (as it is usually understood, that is, focused on the individual) to a theory of war of global dimensions.

Actually, this "de-psychologization" began long ago as a concomitant of advances in the technology of killing. There was a time when a warrior had to be strong, brave, and fierce. He had to be strong, because survival in battle depended on the ability to wield heavy weapons. He had to be brave, because in order to be steadfast in battle, he had to suppress the instinct of self-preservation. He had to be fierce, because he also had to suppress inhibitions against killing his own kind.

As the development of killing technology made killing at ever greater distances possible, these military virtues progressively lost their importance, until today we see battles fought no longer by strong, brave, fierce men but by ordinary people operating immensely complex machines and hardly ever coming into contact with the enemy.

This trend, far from being deplored by professional military men (although it spells the demise of traditional martial values) is, on the whole, heartily welcomed. Strength, bravery, and fierceness as determinants of victory have been replaced first by industrial might, then by technical ingenuity conferred by sophisticated science.

The First World War was sometimes called the chemists' war, since in it the level of violence was propelled by advances in explosives, poison gas, and so forth. The Second World War has been called the physicists' war, because of the crucial role played in it by advances in aviation, telecommunications, radar, and so on. The apotheosis of Hiroshima and Nagasaki fixated that image.

I recall a mathematicians' meeting in Chicago in the late fall of 1945, when some of us were still in uniform. There was a distinct air of satisfaction with the vindication of "abstract mathematical theory," until then contemptuously dismissed by "practical" men of affairs. Now $E = Mc^2$ became something to conjure with. Cybernetics, information theory, game theory, mathematical disciplines, all sprouted immediately after the Second World War and were gladly received in the war community as useful tools in planning future wars. What we have witnessed, therefore, in the last decades, along with the de-democratization and de-psychologization, has been the intellectualization of war.

Progressively, the planning and conduct of war becomes ever further removed from the sort of events associated with corpses, mangled bodies, explosions, and screams. I recall a scene from the film *Dr. Strangelove*. The Soviet ambassador is invited to a meeting with Pentagon chiefs in the operational control center. He seizes the opportunity to photograph the huge map on the wall with its markings indicating global strategies. Someone sees this and grapples with him, whereupon another pulls the two men apart, admonishing them, "Hey, you can't fight in here; this is the War Room!"

Simulated global wars, from parlor games to realistic mock-ups of control centers, are as common as bridge. Lectures on "controlled" nuclear exchanges begin with the statement of rules and the assignment to each side of chips representing cities. It is not inconceivable that the next global war will be "fought" by young ladies seated at consoles resembling typewriters. The image of the strong, brave, fierce warrior has vanished without a trace.

It seems that this was the way the war community adjusted to changed public moods. What I will now say may seem fantastic, but I ask you nevertheless to give it some thought. It is one way (by no means absurd) of looking at the root of the predicament in which civilization presently finds itself.

THE "DEFENSE" COMMUNITY

Members of certain professions or employed in certain positions in the United States sometimes refer to themselves collectively as the "defense community." They do indeed form a community in many respects, being united by a spirit of collegiality, by communality of professional interests, and so on. The defense community comprises far wider circles than uniformed personnel, since many people working in the industrial and scientific infrastructure of the military establishment belong to it. Surely, a defense community exists also in the Soviet Union.

Encompassing both defense communities is the global war community. This war community cannot even pretend to defend anything. Its total destructive potential is directed against itself (and, with the advent of weapons of total destruction, at everything else). In this context, one cannot, of course, speak of collegiality, old friends, and so on, features that mark every professional community. But one can nevertheless regard the combined defense communities as a single system in one very important respect. Each component supports the other. Without the existence of one, the existence of the other would be extremely difficult to justify, given the climate of opinion and attitudes toward war that have developed since the demise of the Clausewitzian system on the European continent.

This is what I mean in referring to the adjustment of the war community (or war as an institution) to changed public moods. At least in Europe, glorification of war as the highest expression of national will is a burst balloon. Neither drum beating, nor bugle blaring, nor flag waving have the effect they once had. The conception of war as a pageant disappeared along with peacock-feathered uniforms. If *these* were what the war community had to depend on to insure the continued existence of the institution, we would have got rid of it long ago. However, all the old trappings have been discarded. The war community masquerades as an elaborate system of security against disaster based on the latest, constantly up-dated products of research and development. The strength of the military arm reflects not pomposity but know-how, not fanaticism but science. The image fits the prevailing religion of the superpowers—technolatry, worship of machines.

Now let us return to the question of whether it is permissible to speak of an "adjustment" of the war system to the public mood. Again I speak from the standpoint of the systemic view, which recognizes the existence of quasi-organisms on different levels of organization. In this view, "adjustment" is regarded as a consequence of certain selective pressures. The classical instance of adjustment is the adaptation of a species to its environment. All teleological conceptualizations of this process have been excluded from modern theories of evolution. No goal-directedness, no consciousness needs to be ascribed to the individuals comprising the adjusting species, let alone to the species as a whole, to justify the concept of adaptation. The individuals go about their business without a shadow of awareness of the large scheme. Their adjustment is effected over generations by ruthless culling of the unadapted. If we shift our attention from the individuals to the species as a whole and watch it in an immensely accelerated time, so that millenia are compressed into seconds, it will seem to us that the species, represented by a typical individual, "intelligently" adjusts to the changes of the environment and even changes the manner of adaptation as required by the pattern of environmental changes.

What is regarded as "learning," especially the learning of muscular skills, speech, and so forth, can be conceived of as a similar process. Certain patterns of neural impulses and muscle contractions are reinforced positively, some negatively—that is, inhibited. To the outside observer, however, the process may appear as "purposeful" adaptation—a sort of Lamarckian process instead of a Darwinian one.

Going further along these lines, we can easily imagine an organization adapting to its social environment not only in the sense of the members learning certain patterns of behavior by positive or negative reinforcement, but also in the sense that its *membership* is modified by a selection process.

There is, therefore, no difficulty in conceiving an organization as a generalized organism. The analogy need not be pushed beyond its realm of validity, but the realm of validity is probably quite broad. If so, the "defense community" of a nation can be regarded as a generalized organism within the nation, itself a generalized organism; and the global "defense community" can be regarded as a generalized organism living within humanity. It behooves us as social scientists to study these "defense communities": their structure, their behavior, their evolution, especially their relation to the "host" organisms within which they live.

Stated in the language of system theory, the generally accepted view is that a defense community is a functional subsystem of a society regarded as a supersystem—functional in the sense of performing a constructive function, such as defense against encroachment by external enemies. The idea that the *global* war machine is a single system is not widespread. If, however, it were accepted as a reasonable conception, it is unlikely that the war machine would be regarded as functional. A functional role can be ascribed, perhaps, to one "hemisphere" of the global war machine, for presumably this military establishment defends the society in which it is imbedded from attack by the other "hemisphere." But if we ask against what the *entire* machine defends the system in which it is imbedded—that is, humanity—the only reasonable answer is "against itself." And this is manifestly absurd.

THE WAR MACHINE AS AN ORGANISM

Thinking in categories of global strategies is a manifestation of the thought processes of the war machine. Objections to the effect that the war machine does not think, that only people think, carries no more force than the insistence that artificial intelligence devices do not "really" think. This is a truism if thinking is deliberately defined so as to exclude the processes that go on in artificial intelligence devices, which is, of course, anyone's right. It may even be ethically justifiable to do so as a rationalization of a sharp distinction between sentient beings, to whom we want to extend empathy, compassion, and so forth, and insentient objects, which we want to exclude as objects of affection, reverence, and so on. But if any *operational* definition of thinking is offered, then it will follow almost certainly that some aspects of "thought" will have to be attributed to artificial intelligence devices.

The situation with the war machine is analogous. Of course, human beings are among the components of the machine, and they may have retained some habits characteristic of human thinking. But these habits are, for the most part, vestiges rather than functional aspects of the thought processes governing the behavior of the war machine, in particular the design of global strategies. Indeed, the actual behavior of the war machine—that is, its responses to stimuli—are being steadily automated.

The larger outlines of this thinking process, what are called global strategies, are still charted by human beings, but not as normal human beings in the sense I have indicated earlier. At the risk of tedious repetition, I must nevertheless point out once again (to forestall misunderstanding or resentment) that the "normality" of these human beings in their everyday life—for example, in relation to other human beings—is certainly not put in question. Nor is their moral character questioned. Most of these people are probably in no way differentiated from others, who think predominantly about ordinary human life situations in human terms or of political life in political terms. The point I am making is that people whose job is to think in terms of global strategies do not think or act as normal human beings in this setting but rather as components that have not yet been replaced by artificial intelligence devices of the war machine.

If any distinction is to be made between these people and others, it is simply that they find themselves in their present positions in consequence of a selection process. But they are replaceable. If they ceased to think as components of the war machine, they would surely be replaced by others who can continue to fulfill that function. It is for this reason that behavioral theories, worked out in the context of human behavior, motivation, affect, and so on, are of little relevance to the analysis of the sort of thinking that guides the design of global strategies.

I hope the picture that I have tried to project of the war machine as an organism sui generis, "living" within mankind, is sufficiently clear to reveal the parasitic nature of this organism. The term "parasite" may appear as an affect-laden metaphor, but it is not meant as such. I see the word in its technical sense. A parasite is defined in biology as an organism that derives its nourishment at the expense of another organism—the host—without contributing to the functional processes of the latter. If an organism nourished by another does contribute to the maintenance of the latter, the relation is called symbiotic rather than parasitic. It is my contention that the global war machine is parasitic on its host—humanity—in the above sense. Many more will agree with this contention than with a stronger one I am about to make—namely, that even the presumably (but not actually) autonomous parts of the war machine, that is, the military establishments of sovereign states, are, for the most part, parasitic on their respective societies.

THE EROSION OF WAR AIMS

The contention that national military establishments are parasitic on the societies in which they are imbedded may not have been as defensible in former times as it is today. At any rate, within particular value systems, military establishments could at one time be seen as functional. If the people of a tribe regard only themselves as fully human (a conception reflected in some languages) and deny the right of existence to others, then their military potential serves a purpose—say to drive other tribes from land to be appropriated. When the overriding social value in ancient Sparta was to keep the helots in slavery, the complete militarization of that society as a means to that end was functional. Specific war aims were formulated and sometimes achieved in the era of so-called cabinet wars in Europe. The Second World War was thought by many, perhaps by most people on the Allied side, to have been the only means to avoid enslavement by rampant dictatorships. The wisdom or the morality of the various aims, which the military establishments served, is not the issue. The point is that there *were* such aims, so that military action could still be rationalized as a means to an end, that end being something outside the range of needs of the war machine itself.

At present, at least with reference to the superpowers, this is no longer the case. If the Clausewitzian principle of matching the magnitude of the war effort with the utility of expected gains is applied, there is no war aim *outside* the needs of the war machine itself that can be seriously regarded as commensurate with the cost of achieving it by a war, given the destructive potential available to the superpowers. The conclusion is inescapable that the only war aim for which the next global war is now planned and for which global strategies are designed in the think tanks are those that are governed by the war machine itself.

Clausewitz must be turning over in his grave. For him, an inalienable principle of military philosophy has always been a clear subordination of military aims to political ones. As the war machine broke away from its moorings, this principle fell by the wayside.

The existence of each hemisphere of the global war machine is justified publicly in one and only one way—namely, by the existence of the other hemisphere. It is assumed, as a matter of course, that if one of the hemispheres were dismantled, the disarmed state would be at the mercy of the armed one. Just how and, above all, to what purpose this power to subjugate would be used is not ordinarily explained, except quite vaguely. Whatever explanations are offered must remain highly hypothetical, since there has been no historical situation that could reasonably be regarded as analogous. At any rate, it is usually unnecessary to invoke any detailed scenarios of a "take-over," because the image of "being at the mercy of the enemy" is sufficiently terrifying to make unilateral disarmament appear as the epitome of folly.

However, unilateral disarmament is rarely an issue in discussions of this sort. Sometimes the issue of general complete disarmament is raised, but this is usually dismissed as "utopian." There remain proposals for very slight bilateral reductions of destructive potential or even more modest proposals of freezing existing levels. It appears that all such attempts to reverse, stop, or even control the arms race are most likely to fail. The reason is that *political* issues never seriously enter the discussions. That is, the question is hardly ever raised *why* it should be in the interest of one side to destroy or, for that matter, subjugate the other. On the rare occasions when this question is raised (always by people outside the decision-making cohorts, not within them), it is answered by pointing to "obvious" expansionist, imperialist, or subversive ambitions of the other. Each side denies these allegations about itself as a matter of course and, in turn, makes exactly the same allegations about the other.

THE ONE REMAINING WAR AIM

In only one context does the assumption about the unalterable aggressive intent of the other make sense: in the military context. There, the assumption *is* axomatic, since it coincides with the fundamental military maxm that not the inclinations nor the actual intentions of the adversary but his *capabilities* should be decisive in planning strategy. To put it another way, capabilities are identified with intent: what the adversary *can* do to harm you (and therefore obviously to benefit himself), he will.

In playing chess, this assumption is the only rational one. An experienced chess player does not expect the opponent to make poor moves, at least not if there is reason to believe that the opponent is also experienced and rational. On the contrary, we must expect the opponent to make good moves—that is, moves good for them and therefore bad for us. We must, therefore, always expect the worst and make our plans accordingly. Since the situation is symmetrical, both sides must strive to inflict as much damage on the other as possible. In the context of chess this makes perfect sense, because there are no "aims" in chess other than beating the opponent or avoiding being beaten. When military thinking loses its anchorage in political (or any other) considerations, this sort of thinking is the only mode that makes sense. For the object of military action is victory. What the victory is supposed to accomplish, or its social costs, is not the soldier's concern. In this respect, the soldier can be disarmingly modest: he leaves the answer to the question to others better qualified to utilize the fruits of victory. His job is to deliver it.

How victory is *defined,* however, is for the soldier to decide, for the soldier is the expert in these matters. Or, rather, the criteria of victory are given by established implicit rules of the game of war. At one time, victory was regarded as won when the opposing army left the field of battle. But battles are not fought on "fields" any longer; so the criterion is no longer relevant. Clausewitz defined victory in larger terms, namely, as the destruction of the opponent's army, an end toward which all military strategy should, according to Clausewitz, be directed. As the nature of war changes, so does the concept of victory, but this concept never encompasses more than a purely military condition.

In modern total war, there are no fields of battle, where armies meet and victories are decided. Moreover, a state's armed might is no longer concentrated in its army but diffused throughout the industrial and scientific infrastructure of the country. Total war is the logical extension of the Clausewitzian principle: the army's job is to destroy the enemy's ability to resist.

The extreme unpopularity of total war in the nuclear age has stimulated other doctrines. For example, since the destructive potential of a nuclear power is concentrated in its nuclear arsenal, it seems sufficient to limit the blow to that system. This strategy is not only in accord with the venerable Clausewitzian doctrine but appears to be more humane since the destruction of civilian population is reduced to an unavoidable minimum.

But now a serious problem arises. A strike against the enemy's nuclear arsenal makes sense only if it is a preemptive strike. Moreover, such a strike becomes suicidal if the enemy still has sufficient capacity to retaliate, whereby the retaliatory strike must be aimed not at the initiator's military installations (which have already done their job), but at the population centers. Therefore not only must the first-strike capacity be overwhelming, but it must also be a complete surprise. Obviously, both sides are concerned with the same "problem." The result is an arms race producing not only an exponential growth of destructive potential but also reducing the time between the initiation and consummation of the strike to minutes.

The first-strike situation can be represented by the parable of two scorpions in a bottle. Assume that neither scorpion derives any benefit from stinging the other, *except* that by killing the other, it insures itself against being killed by the other. From this point of view, it *is* advantageous to each scorpion to sting the other. And since both scorpions, if they are "rational," must come to the same conclusion, both are compelled to sting each other, and both die. If they had not been "rational," they would both have lived.

By "rationality" in this case I mean military strategic rationality: not what the other wants or can benefit from, but what he can do to you should guide the design of strategy. Pursuing the logic further, we see that if scorpion A thinks that scorpion B intends to sting him, then scorpion A should sting scorpion B, and vice versa. Even if scorpion A does not believe that scorpion B intends to sting him but has somehow received the (mistaken) impression that he, A, intends to sting him, then A must conclude that B must conclude that he, B, should sting A, and therefore A must sting B first. In this way, rationality of "higher order" (one that takes into account the rational thought processes of the other) reinforces the conclusion fatal to both.

Realization of the "destabilizing" effect of the first-strike capability has led to the rejection of this strategy in some circles of the military establishment. These "moderates" espouse a second-strike capacity, which requires a strongly protected nuclear capacity, not strong enough to destroy the opponent's strike capability but able to withstand a first strike in order to inflict a second strike. Note that the second strike must be aimed at the population centers of the opponent.

The second-strike strategy, being essentially a deterrent strategy, requires credibility. Our opponent must believe that we can and will retaliate if attacked. He must also be convinced that we have no intention of striking first (otherwise he may convince himself that a preemptive strike is mandatory.) One way of convincing the opponent that we do not intend to strike first is to leave our population centers vulnerable to his attack, since this shows that we do not expect a retaliatory strike and therefore do not intend a preemptive strike. Thus, if both sides adopt a second-strike strategy, both must aim at each other's population centers, and both must keep their cities defenseless—a situation that must seem bizarre to any human being not entrapped in the "logic" of global strategy.

THE HEGEMONY OF MILITARY VALUES

The normal human being with normal human concerns may feel entitled to ask why humanity must continue to live under the Sword of Damocles. The answer given in terms of the logic of global strategy is that there is not one sword but two hovering over us, and that each is a protection from the other. Moreover, the answer usually contains an implication that the heavier these swords are, the safer we are.

Values underlying discussions of global strategy are purely military values. Whatever logic underlies them is purely military logic, constructed on an axiomatic base of military thinking: the format of the two-person zerosum game, in which whatever one wins, the other must lose. That virtually no real-life situations (except two-person parlor games of strategy) can be cast into this model makes practically no impression on the design of global strategies, dominated completely by thought cast into military categories. No more than lip service is paid to politics undominated by the needs of the war machine. Ideological underpinnings of politics have been reduced to a farce. Among the grave dangers to world peace is the chronic threat of war between the two communist giants. U.S. "defense of freedom" is often a defense of murderous gangster regimes. The Soviet Union, the self-proclaimed most exalted people's democracy, rules an empire of subjugated sullen populations with regimes beholden only to the Kremlin bosses. All of these regimes are labeled "people's democracies."

Of the various explanations offered of these deplorable policies, the one that makes the most sense and the one for which most concrete evidence exists is the hegemony of the military in the formulation of global policies. The hegemony may not be apparent in the proportion of generals in the highest decision-making bodies. It is apparent in the design of the global strategies themselves, which very clearly reveal the primary needs not only of the components of the global war machine (strategic advantages on the global arena) but also the needs of the global war machine as a whole: unlimited growth insured by the positive feedback between the two hemispheres. Here "need" is, of course, meant metaphorically. A malignant growth has no "needs" in the sense that we as human beings experience them. But the physiology of a cancer is such that its growth cannot be inhibited. Hence we can say that its "need" to grow indefinitely is satisfied at least until it kills the host.

The perpetual threat of total destruction is not generated by clashes of political interests, except to the extent that these interests are subservient to the needs of the war machine. It is not generated by clashes of incompatible ideologies, except to the extent that diatribes of ideology are used as demagogic rationalizations of the war machine. It is not generated by greed, because no gains of territory or treasure can compensate for the losses incurred in a total war by victor and vanquished alike. It is not generated by hatred or xenophobia, because these human emotions are no longer necessary for precipitating and conducting war.

I believe military thinking enjoys its primacy precisely because it has been admirably adjusted to technocratic thinking, requiring a new kind of expertise. Both technology and expertise are self-propelling. Technology begets technology, and expertise begets expertise. Technological expertise is the most credible, being concrete and directly related to the exercise of power. For this reason, the needs of the war machine can be most clearly formulated, much more clearly than political aims or human needs. Consequently, policies guided by these needs appear "realistic."

For this reason, attempts to break out of the vicious cycle propelling humanity to destruction mostly fail. These attempts are manifested in plans to reach some sort of arms control agreements, and rightly so, because effective arms control agreements might be a prelude to arms reduction, perhaps eventual disarmament, which certainly ought to have priority in coming to grips with global problems.

But arms control negotiations are dominated by military experts and by their conceptual repertoire. Most prominent in the latter is the concept of "equilibrium." The term sounds reassuring, evoking images of stability and safety. It is rationalized by an assumption that the stronger party must be motivated to attack and by the conclusion that therefore to inhibit attack, one must prevent either party from becoming stronger than the other. (One is reminded of the "wonderful One-Horse Shay" of Oliver Wendell Holmes, all of the parts being equally strong, which led to the instantaneous collapse of the whole contraption when all the parts wore out at once.) Note the hegemony of military thinking in this faith in "equilibrium." The question why the stronger party must be motivated to attack is not raised. "Pressing an advantage" is an obvious value in the military sphere.

Note also that "equilibrium" or "balance of power" is only a metaphor here. It is not the sort of equilibrium that can be established on a beam balance. It can be said to exist only if it is *believed* to exist by both sides. But the war machine must grow. Therefore there is a strong tendency to deny the existence of an equilibrium, where each side claims to be behind. These claims can always be substantiated because of the complexity of the war machine. Unlike the parts of the "wonderful One-Horse Shay," all equally strong, the paired parts of the two hemispheres of the war machine cannot be made perfectly equal. There will always be some components of destructive potential in which one or the other is behind.

Now, in principle, balance could be restored in either of two ways: either the side that is ahead cuts back, or the side that is behind catches up. I have never seen a preference for the first option. The needs of the global war machine force recourse to the second option. Again I must reiterate what I mean by "needs": the pressure generated by the internal dynamics of a system.

The hegemony of military thinking is evident also in the global strategies of both superpowers. In the decades following World War II, the global strategy of the United States was an encirclement of the communist land mass, Russia/China. The chain of states allied with the United States stretched from Norway over Denmark, West Germany, Italy, Greece, Turkey, and the countries of the so-called Baghdad Pact (now defunct). It was to include the Indo-Chinese peninsula, to continue over the Philippines, South Korea, and

Japan to Alaska. The U.S. invasion of Vietnam and Cambodia and the attendant devastating 20 years of war must be ascribed to this global strategy, since U.S. economic interests were essentially insignificant in that region and, at any rate, cost-benefit analysis could never justify that war. As for ideological considerations, I have already pointed out that they are no longer to be taken seriously.

As has been said, the brutal domination of Eastern Europe by the Soviet Union, the aggression in Afghanistan, the intrigues in the Middle East, the hostility toward China, the attempt to establish missile bases in Cuba—all these components of Soviet global strategy can be satisfactorily explained only by the needs of the war machine.

CONCLUDING REMARKS

In sum, behavioral theory can shed light on the global strategies designed by the superpowers and on the horrendous dangers that this behavior entails only if behavioral theory is extended to include the structure, the functioning, and the evolution of a system that has arisen as an emanation of civilization and now threatens to destroy its source—namely, the global war machine that has broken away from its political moorings, has acquired its insatiable appetite, and has dehumanized armies of experts, technocrats, and strategists who nurse it.

One final remark. Military thinking is not the only mode that cuts people off from what I have called "normal human concerns." The tendency toward ever-increasing abstraction of conceptualizations mediated by symbolic language is a distinctly human trait, inherent in all types of creative activity. Mathematics is a prime example. Initially spawned by practical activities such as counting and measurement, mathematical thought became more and more independent of "normal human needs." The same can be said of many forms of artistic activity, abstruse philosophy, and the like.

Some thinkers, notably Tolstoy, for example, rejected these typical emanations of high civilization as perversions. Anti-intellectual overtones of many populist movements point to further examples of such rejection. I would exonerate flights of fancy, whether in increasingly more abstract science or in esoteric art or even in metaphysical speculation, from charges of subversion of human values. In excluding these concerns from the range of "normal human needs" enumerated earlier, I only wished to emphasize that they are concerns of a small minority. By no means did I wish to imply that because a mode of thought has cut itself off from its anchorage in "normal human needs," it is to be regarded as pathological or wicked. On the contrary, the faculty of pursuing open-ended, in principle unbounded, abstraction is what, to my way of thinking, makes it worth while to be born human. I condemn geopolitics not because it is totally unrelated to "normal human needs," but because it is the one system of thought that is sure to precipitate irreversible catastrophes (from the point of view of normal human needs) if translated into action. It ought to be confined to parlor games and declared a crime in real-life applications, just as dueling is a crime that has been rendered harmless in its surrogates, such as fencing, chess, or other forms of two-person zerosum games.

In this way, I draw a sharp line between geopolitics and other forms of "dehumanized" concerns. However, what I have said about the inapplicability of most presently available behavioral theories to the dynamics of global strategies applies equally to the analysis of other forms of abstruse thinking—mathematical, esthetically esoteric, and so on. Analysis of these forms of thought requires an examination of systems that have "taken off" on their own, so to say. Again mathematics is a prime example. It cannot possibly be understood with reference to familiar human experience. This is why I reject all "anthropological" interpretations of mathematics as just another emanation of Western culture. I agree with Martin Gardner that this is a view characteristic of people who cannot imagine anything that has a validity of its own, transcending human experience.

In the case of geopolitics, however, it is not a matter of autonomous "validity" but, rather, as I have already suggested, of an autonomous malignant growth, especially difficult to combat, because unlike invading parasites, biochemically foreign to the host, malignant growths are generated by the host's own biochemistry and consequently are mistaken for a functionally integrated subsystem of the host organism.

In the light of the events of the last two or three years, it is difficult to evade the conclusion that the foreign policies of the superpowers are now completely geared to sustaining the malignant growth parasitic on humanity—the global war machine. For this reason, discussions aimed at evaluating these policies with respect to some standards of rationality, practicality, or ideological commitment (let alone ethical principles) miss the mark. The

predominant determinant is an obsession stemming from traditional military conceptions of "security" as something that is
directly related to one's own destructive potential and inversely
related to that of the adversary. The obvious implication of this
view—namely, that striving for security by both produces a
mounting threat to both—is shut off from the consciousness.

III

EVALUATING
SPECIFIC POLICIES

6

Reagan's Soviet Policy: Economic Linkage Unchained

Neil R. Richardson

Most observers believe that tensions between the United States and the Soviet Union receded appreciably in the early 1970s. There is also widespread agreement that this detente was itself short-lived; in the early months of the Carter presidency—if not before—detente was clearly on the wane.

This analysis does not aim to determine the causes of detente. Neither are the reasons for its subsequent demise of immediate interest. Instead, discussion is focused on the "linkage" strategy for detente and on the potential for misunderstanding the opportunities "linkage" may afford. "Linkage" is the term adopted by Henry Kissinger to describe U.S. efforts to engineer detente with Moscow beginning in the late 1960s. A decade later, the word had fallen out of favor in the Carter White House, only to be embraced again by president-elect Reagan's transition team in 1980 (*New York Times,* November 7, 1980, p. 1). As discussed in these pages, there is reason to believe that the Reagan administration fails to appreciate how "linkage" might be used to reestablish a detente in U.S.–Soviet relations.

THEORETICAL CONSIDERATIONS

An evaluation of East–West linkage necessarily begins with some explication of definitions and premises. Linkage itself refers to interaction in one issue area that the initiator intends to use to affect interaction in a different issue area. Notice that this conception has two principal ingredients, (1) the notion of linkage between issue areas and (2) the requirement that the parties to the interaction understand that the linkage exists.

Linkage, then, is an arrangement between parties, even if the understanding is tacit. In turn, this means that at least two conditions must be satisfied. One, referred to just above, is that clear communication must be established in order that each party understands what it is promising and, in exchange, what the other is offering in the bargain. Another requisite is that each side must supply something that the other values.

From the initiator's perspective, the first order of business is to establish interactions in one issue area that can subsequently be used to induce the target to agree on linkage between relations of the first sort and relations on an otherwise separate issue dimension. An appealing avenue is thus for the initiator to provide the target country with benefits from the interaction, benefits substantially greater than those that accrue to the initiator itself. This "asymmetrical interdependence" (Keohane and Nye, 1977) may then provide the initiator with bargaining advantage by virtue of its control over the continued provision of those benefits. In the words of a prominent social exchange theorist,

> A person [nation] who has services or resources at his disposal and who is independent of any with which others could reciprocate can gain power over them.... The supply of recurrent unilateral (or asymmetrical) services is a source of power, since it obliges those who cannot reciprocate in kind to discharge their obligation to the supplier by complying with his wishes. (Blau, 1964, pp. 314, 322.)

As Secretary of State Kissinger said more diplomatically in a 1974 Senate testimony, his hope was that,

> by acquiring a stake in this network of relationships with the West, the Soviet Union may become more conscious of what it would lose by a return to confrontation. Indeed, it is our hope that it will develop a self-interest in fostering the entire process of relaxation of tensions. (U.S. Congress, 1974, p. 240.)

The second order of business is to communicate to the target the desired linkage to the latter's behavior in a previously separate issue area. Clarity is very important. Relatedly, it is important to establish over time an understanding between the parties regarding fair expectations of just what constitutes reciprocity in the exchange (Blau, 1971).

PRIOR EVIDENCE

As is true of many foreign policy premises, the linkage between access to U.S. commerce and conciliatory Soviet behavior was not based on a solid empirical foundation. Data-based studies have produced no more than mixed results in this connection. The multivariate studies of Rummel (1966, 1972) and Russett (1967), for example, have found that economic cooperation fails to reduce the likelihood of war when large numbers of countries are studied. In a similar vein, Goldmann (1980) has concluded that perceived tension levels in eight of today's "great power" dyads are not significantly related to trade and diplomatic cooperation.

On the other had, for 30 countries pooled over a decade, Polachek (1980, p. 67) discovered that "trade tends to increase cooperation ... and decrease conflict" between states. This, of course, is of some comfort to advocates of detente linkage. However, Weede argues that because Polachek did not include war among the conflict variables, one can conclude only "that *verbal* conflict is reduced by trade" (Weede, 1981, p. 148, emphasis added).

In short, there is scattered and unclear evidence about the likely success of an economic linkage strategy for engineering detente. For, not only are different countries incorporated into these inquiries, but different time periods are used, as well. Perhaps more troubling is that none of them isolates the United States and the Soviet Union for analysis. Because there are grounds to suspect that the superpower relationship has unusual dynamics (for example, see Waltz, 1979), the direct relevance of these studies to the linkage strategy is uncertain. Even Rummel's (1976) work, aimed directly at U.S.–Soviet relations, is based mainly on pooled data for scores of countries. Nevertheless, these studies raise in broader terms the pertinent question: Can closer economic ties between the two countries produce more conciliatory Soviet foreign policy behavior?

In an earlier study (Richardson, 1982), I examined U.S.–Soviet relations over the period 1963 through 1978. Operationally, the linkage period was confined to 1971 and thereafter, for, as Kissinger himself believed, efforts at even attempting linkage were frustrated in the first two years of the Nixon presidency (Kissinger, 1979, pp. 159–62).

The data source was the Conflict and Peace Data Bank (see Azar and Sloan, 1975), an events data collection that permits each country's actions toward the other to be subdivided by issue area. This feature of the data allowed for "cooperative" U.S. economic acts to be plotted against Soviet "conflictual" acts on all noneconomic issues (where all verbal behavior of both parties had been removed). The juxtaposition of these two variables in Figure 6.1 suggests that economic linkage may have occurred. Soviet conflict toward the United States was never above a modest level between 1971 and 1976. Furthermore, as U.S. economic cooperation began to mushroom in 1972 and 1973, Soviet conflict fell to zero in nine of the ten quarterly periods after the start of 1972. It was only with the Senate's December 1974 passage of two controversial amend-

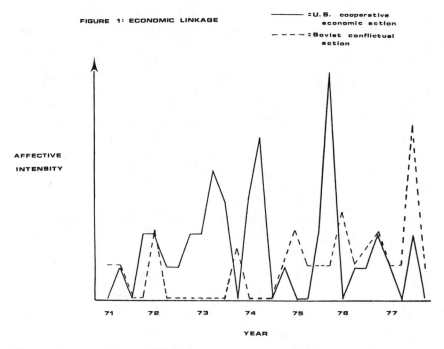

FIGURE 1: ECONOMIC LINKAGE

———— =U.S. cooperative economic action

— — — =Soviet conflictual action

AFFECTIVE INTENSITY

71   72   73   74   75   76   77

YEAR

Figure 6.1.   Economic linkage.

The scale for the "Affective Intensity" axis is, in principle, infinite because each act is weighted according to Azar's intensity scale and all acts are then aggregated quarterly. (For elaboration on the scaling procedure, see Azar and Sloan, 1975.)

ments to the U.S.–Soviet Trade Agreement—amendments that infuriated Moscow and led it to reject the two-year-old Trade Agreement—that low-level Soviet conflict reappeared.

This evidence suggests that Kissinger's strategy had merit. The United States asymmetrically provided economic benefits to the Soviet Union in the form of grain, computers, trucks, tools and equipment, and the like and also loaned hundreds of millions of dollars to Moscow for purposes of buying these goods. It appears that Soviet behavior toward the United States became markedly less belligerent as a result, at least until the Senate intervened in a way that led the Kremlin to doubt that the United States was a reliable trade partner.

THE REAGAN RECORD

The deterioration of detente was rapid. By the time President Reagan was sworn into office, only the memory remained. But because all could agree that relations with Moscow were crucially important, and because the new president was seemingly pledged to the prospect of linkage in superpower relations, the prospective use of economic ties for political purposes was never far from mind.

Of course, the Carter legacy and the Reagan campaign both helped to define the broad outlines of President Reagan's policies regarding the Soviet Union. The president was pledged to restore U.S. military forces, which his campaign had said were falling dangerously behind those of the adversary. He was also committed to steering a more consistent and sterner course in East–West relations. An important part of this consistency and firmness was to depend on closer policy coordination with Japan and the European allies.

In addition to the planned arms buildup, there were three East–West items high on the foreign policy agenda at the beginning of Reagan's first term. One was the Soviet military presence in Afghanistan. Another was the planned construction of a natural gas pipeline from Siberia to Western Europe. Third, and most recent, were concerns brought about by labor unrest in Poland. At least partly because linkage was to be a policy guide, these three East–West confrontations were soon intertwined.

The problems in Afghanistan had begun with a bloody coup that installed a "revolutionary" president in April 1978. By the end of that year, a 20-year treaty of friendship and cooperation was signed with Brezhnev. In the next eight months, rebels and government forces were fighting heavily, deaths were reported to be in the thousands, and Carter issued his first warning against Soviet intervention.

Red Army troops were first airlifted into Afghanistan on December 26, 1979. Ten days later, President Carter, appearing on national television, characterized the act as "a callous violation of international law and the United Nations Charter." It was, he said, "a deliberate effort of a powerful, atheistic government to subjugate an independent Islamic people." "The world simply cannot stand by and permit the Soviet Union to commit this act with impunity." "Neither the United States nor any other nation which is committed to world peace and stability can continue to do business as usual with the Soviet Union"(New York Times, January 5, 1980, p. 1). He then announced that several steps would be taken in response. The United States would resume provision of military equipment to neighboring Pakistan; a series of bilateral meetings on agriculture, business, health, and civil aviation were to be canceled; Ambassador Watson was to be recalled from Moscow—and the list continued. While Carter's response was thus a broad one, the centerpiece was economic punishment.

Soviet fishing privileges in U.S. waters were being severely curtailed, although denial of some 350,000 tons of fish annually was of very little consequence. On the other hand, the trade embargoes were meant to hurt. One category of embargoed goods was high-technology exports (such as advanced computers, oil-drilling equipment, and machine tools). Combined, they comprised about 25% of the $700 million in nonagricultural sales from the United States to the Soviets. Nevertheless, high-technology goods accounted for only 5% of all exports, because grains alone constituted some 80%.

Grains, then, were the other category of Carter's embargo. To be denied were 17 million metric tons of U.S. grain already on order. This amount explicitly did not include eight million additional tons guaranteed annually on long-term contract since 1976 (of which five million tons had already been shipped). Nevertheless, the 17 million tons equaled about 13% of Soviet livestock fodder. Furthermore, administration officials reported that Canada, New Zealand, and Australia had given assurances that they would not take up the slack by increasing their own grain exports to the Soviet Union. Argentina, the remaining major world grain supplier, went on record as "sympathetic" to Carter's decision. Indeed, it was plausible to believe that none of these countries would have been able to increase its shipments of Soviet-bound grains for 1980 anyway, having already committed most of its crop (see Chapman, 1980).

If so, Moscow would have faced a considerable international grain embargo; it would have had little recourse but to do without those imports. Because the grain was all in animal feed, the effects of the shortage would have reached the market by summer. In all probability, pigs and poultry would have been slaughtered early, and the cattle would have eaten less. Milk production would soon have fallen, while meat supplies would have, later on, been smaller than ever.

However, all did not go according to plan. The Argentinians defected from the embargo almost immediately, selling well more than they had previously planned to the Soviet Union. The others later followed suit, leaving the United States alone to continue to withhold grains. Carter's grain embargo would remain in effect for 15 months before being rescinded by newly elected President Reagan.

If January 1980 marked the undertaking of the grain embargo, it also witnessed exploratory talks between Soviet planners and West German energy and banking representatives. The subject of their discussions was a multibillion-dollar pipeline that would bring natural gas to West Europe by the mid-1980s. Subsequent estimates indicate that West Germany's gas consumption, then 15% reliant on the Sovient Union, would become 30% dependent on that source. French consumption, also at 15%, would jump at least to 35% from the Eastern bloc leader. It was to become the largest single East–West trade agreement on record.

After Ronald Reagan's election in November of that year, and as pipeline negotiations intensified, West Germany's Chancellor Schmidt was apparently concerned that the president-elect would oppose the deal on the grounds that the European allies would become overly energy-dependent on the East. On this, however, Reagan was silent, and one week before his inauguration both Caterpillar Tractor and International Harvester were negotiating for participation in the mammoth project.

It was not until mid-1981 that Reagan's position on the pipeline became clear. In July, there were reports that Caterpillar's license to supply pipe-laying equipment might be revoked. At the same time, and while attending an economic summit meeting of Western leaders, Reagan warned the Europeans of the dangers of energy dependence on Moscow. Despite these signs of discontent in the administration, Caterpillar's license was approved, and several

French, Japanese, and Italian firms entered the project. These European firms were bolstered by their governments' reply to Reagan; the rebuttal was that the new pipeline would diversify their countries' energy sources. Exxon, Mobil, Texaco, British Petroleum, and Royal Dutch/Shell soon announced their participation. In short, by November 1981, President Reagan's doubts seemed to be overwhelmed by the momentum of business deals. In fact, November 21 marked the signing of the capstone agreement—between the Soviet Union and West Germany's Ruhrgas—for annual deliveries covering 25 years. The matter seemed to be settled.

Indeed, had it not been for events unfolding simultaneously in Poland, the pipeline might well have disappeared from public sight within Reagan's first 12 months in office. But even in the final months of the 1980 election campaign, the labor unrest in Poland was vying for newspaper headlines. By the time martial law was declared in December 1981, Poland's difficulties were if anything greater than they had been when, in January, Solidarity had wrung initial concessions from the government. In the interim, both authorized and unauthorized strikes were commonplace. Genera Jaruzelski replaced Kania (who himself had lasted only 13 months). The country's international debt service obligations were quickly outrunning the government's capacity to make payments or even reschedule them. The West repeatedly cautioned the Soviet Union against interference or, more pointedly, military invasion.

One noteworthy development during this period was the announcement, on April 25, that President Reagan had decided to lift the 16-month-old grain embargo of the Soviet Union imposed by his predecessor at the time of the Afghanistan invasion. Strikingly, just one day after the embargo was lifted, Secretary of State Haig threatened to ban *all* trade with Moscow, including all grain, should Soviet troops invade Poland.

So, when martial law was declared, the United States immediately suspended economic assistance—$100 million in grain—to Poland. In the two weeks following, other sanctions were spelled out. Again, economic penalties were the primary ingredients. Furthermore, the sanctions were expanded to apply not only to Poland but also to the Soviets for their presumed complicity in the martial law decision. The renewed U.S. trade embargo against Moscow this time did not include grain, then contributing about 75% to the mix of goods exported; high-technology products were prohibited instead.

Perhaps in response to Haig's plea, the Common Market quickly met to consider potential West European sanctions. After several weeks, its Executive Commission proposed that West European sanctions not include any export embargoes. Rather, they recommended a $350 million reduction in planned 1982 imports. This figure represented about 3.5% of Common Market purchases from the Soviets and was reportedly comprised of automobiles, fur, caviar, and diamonds. By mid-March, however, the Council of Ministers had diluted the list; all but the caviar seems to have been exempted from the boycott.

All of these developments surrounding Poland's difficulties—culminating by the end of 1981 in Warsaw's crackdown and the West's economic sanctions—invited the White House to reconsider the massive pipeline project. The pipeline became to the administration a symbol of the West's outright gift of high technology to a belligerent adversary. For, not only was the Soviet Union still fighting in Afghanistan, it had also just bullied Polish leaders into declaring martial law.

In brief, Jaruzelski's harsh response to Soviet pressure led the United States to do more than simply impose the direct trade sanctions mentioned above; the White House also reversed its six-month "drift" of tacit permissiveness with respect to the pipeline. Such permissiveness was no longer so easily reconciled with Soviet behavior. Accordingly, Reagan at first decided to bar new licenses to U.S. firms applying to export pipeline-related goods, meanwhile allowing existing licenses to be honored. He asked allies to do the same, but they refused to comply.

Allied resistance led the administration on another tack. By April 1982, the White House was expressing hope that further conflict over the pipeline could be avoided within the Atlantic community. It proposed instead that the impending economic summit be the occasion to establish agreement on trade credit restrictions placed on future dealings with Moscow.

However, no such alternative was forthcoming at the June summit. Accordingly, President Reagan returned to the pipeline sanctions with a vengeance. Not only were pertinent U.S. sales barred, but the embargo was to extend to foreign companies producing pipeline equipment under licensed patent from U.S. firms. This declaration created an uproar across the ocean. Several European governments challenged the legality of extraterritoriality in this application (as did most U.S. experts in trade law). The French government ordered its firms to produce under U.S. license with or without Washington's approval. Even Margaret Thatcher's government enacted laws that would allow Parliament to insist that British firms defy the U.S. embargo.

The controversy continued into the early winter, fueled by the administration's prosecution of several U.S. firms for having overseas subsidiaries that were producing goods for the pipeline. But, by late October of 1982, all governments were conferring on ways to compensate for an end to the current embargo. Finally, in mid-November, Reagan lifted the pipeline sanctions, announcing that the allies had reached agreement on a broader trade strategy toward the Soviet bloc. Just what this new strategy entailed was left unclear, but the impression was allowed that curtailment of trade credits such as had been proposed before the June summit had now been adopted. Despite this announcement, allied leaders said off the record that they had made no major concessions to the United States.

Thus, the end of 1982 marked only the end of the attempted pipeline sanctions. It did not mark the end of martial law in Poland. Neither were Soviet troops withdrawn from Afghanistan. Finally, the United States also resumed full-scale grain shipments to its superpower rival. In short, there is prima facie evidence that the Reagan administration was unable to manipulate economic rewards and punishments in a fashion that induced the desired Soviet behavior. Why was this so?

DISCUSSION

The failure to modify Soviet behavior through the use of economic instruments can be explained in a variety of ways. For example, a linkage strategy requires that one's willingness to use economic incentives is believed. It can therefore weaken the appearance of resolve when a government's internal differences are publicized, as happened when Alexander Haig prevailed over Secretary of Defense Weinberger with respect to allowing General Electric's licensed turbines to go to a pipeline compressor manufacturer in France (Safire, 1982). It was not their disagreement that weakened linkage, but rather the fact that their differences were made public.

A government's vacillation can likewise contribute to unsuccessful attempts at linkage. The appearance of a policy change can often be explained, but rapid shifts suggest uncertainty and hence a lack of resolve. This sort of difficulty haunted the Reagan administration's treatment of U.S. firms and, in this instance, was compounded by a clear miscalculation of allied response to the imposition of martial law in Poland.

The pipeline sanctions also illustrate a commandment of any bargaining effort: "Thou shalt not be vague" about either part of the bargain. There is some room to argue that the United States wavered over just how tightly it would try to enforce the embargo on pipeline equipment firms. However, the dramatic vagueness here was with respect to what the United States demanded over a period of months. At one time or another, the sanctions seem to have been motivated by (1) concern that European allies would become inordinately dependent on Soviet gas, (2) hopes that a portion of Moscow's military expenditures would be thereby diverted, and (3) hopes that General Jaruzelski would be made to lift martial law and come to terms with Solidarity and the Church, even granting that the third motive was clearly dominant.

Notice that explanations such as these imply that circumstances allowed for linkage, but that policymakers were guilty of human error resulting in failed strategy. However, all explanations such as these presuppose two larger and interrelated assumptions. One of them is the belief that U.S. policymakers understood *how* economic linkage is to work. The other assumption is that the United States had an opportunity to make a linkage strategy work. Neither of these important assumptions was satisfied.

Economic linkage is predicated on enmeshing the Soviet Union in an unequally beneficial economic relationship that it perceives to be durable. For it is only the expectation of a *continued* supply of valued goods that would permit Moscow to begin to think in terms of developing an appropriate and acceptable reciprocal "currency" of behavioral conciliation in other foreign policy issue areas— behavior that is thereby linked to its receipt of asymmetrical economic benefits provided by the United States. As we have seen, there is evidence from the early 1970s that such a link may be feasible when Kremlin leaders can reasonably expect that U.S. economic provisions will not be quickly suspended, an expectation that was embodied in the Trade Agreement signed in 1972 and awaiting Senate ratification for the next two years.

The Reagan record clearly shows that this administration used economic incentives quite differently (and quite unsuccessfully). In the first instance, Carter's grain embargo was lifted shortly after Reagan's first term began. Alone, that act might have paved the way toward the emergence of a long-term expectation of grain sales on which the adversary could depend. Unfortunately, Haig threatened to suspend those sales (if Soviet troops should enter Poland) the very next day. There could be no mistaking the message: Grain supplies to the Soviet Union would be subject to *immediate* suspension upon the commission of any specific act that met with White House disapproval. A similar impermanence characterized Reagan's position on the pipeline. The long-term expectations necessary to linkage could hardly be engendered under such circumstances.

Thus, the Reagan administration's use of grain and pipeline equipment sales to the Soviet Union amply demonstrates that it may have misunderstood the meaning of economic linkage. For this reason, the second major assumption would necessarily be unsatisfied as well. That is, a linkage strategy will never find opportunity if policymakers fail to understand that it requires a long-term investment in one's partnership.

Thus—and whether by intent or inadvertence—the record shows that these economic instruments of foreign policy were used simply as means by which to impose sanctions instead. Sanctions are tangible signs of disapproval. Common market officials remarked that the ultimate decision to boycott Russian caviar after the crackdown in Poland was "intended to be a gesture of displeasure" and was "never intended to cause Moscow serious inconvenience" (*New York Times*, March 12, 1982, p. 1). And, of course, they also signal to constituents that one is "doing something."

However, economic sanctions as political instruments have not fared well historically (see, for example, Doxey, 1971; Losman, 1979). This is because the success of such moves depends upon the (rare) convergence of a variety of factors that render a target "vulnerable" (see Caporaso, 1978). Among them are (1) the initiator's ability to withhold benefits, (2) its capacity to convince all other potential suppliers to do likewise, (3) the target's real need for the benefits, (4) the target's inability to supply itself, and (5) whether those groups or classes within the target society that are most hurt by the sanctions are also politically important to the government.

In the case of the grain embargo, we have seen that at least three of these conditions were not met. The United States could not convince other grain exporters to cease shipments, the Soviets mainly supply themselves, and the average Soviet citizen—not politically potent—bore the brunt of whatever dietary costs may have ensued. In the pipeline case, the most glaring deficiency was

Washington's inability to forestall alternative supplies of the needed equipment.

Still, these sanctions may have served some symbolic purposes valued by the Reagan administration; but two further points might be added. One of them is that sanctions usually involve costs for the initiator, whatever their political value may be. For a time, midwestern farmers paid most of the price of the grain embargo as the market value of their product declined. Likewise, a number of U.S. firms were denied equal opportunity to bid for pipeline construction contracts.

Second, it might be noted that these two sanctions were applied in instances where Kremlin leaders were highly unlikely to succumb to economic pressure unless they were quite vulnerable. Surely the political future of neighboring Poland and Afghanistan would be regarded in Moscow as matters of very great importance. Assuming, then, that Reagan's policymakers sensed this, it would seem that these two embargoes were largely meant to serve as symbols of displeasure, despite their costs to specific sectors of the U.S. economy.

There is a larger lesson to be drawn from these episodes. What seems clear is that the Reagan administration either misunderstood or intentionally eschewed the possibilities for engineering detente by means of economic linkage. The objective opportunity to supply the Soviet Union with asymmetrical economic benefits over the long term was available, and there is evidence from the Kissinger years that such a strategy can succeed. In this light, one can bemoan the missed opportunity to modify Soviet behavior in desired ways. But one can also hope that the 1984 signing of a long-term grain agreement between the superpowers represents a change of strategy in favor of economic linkage as President Reagan carries out his second term of office. Of course, whether economic linkage is on the president's agenda remains to be seen. In view of the inadequacy of Reagan's sanctions, however, a linkage strategy in pursuit of renewed detente seems to be much the wiser course of action.

ACKNOWLEDGMENT

The author gratefully acknowledges comments on this chapter offered by Charles Hermann and John Vasquez.

REFERENCES

AZAR, E., and T. SLOAN (1975). *Dimensions of Interaction: A Sourcebook for the Study of the Behavior of 31 Nations from 1948 through 1973.* Pittsburgh, Pa.: University of Pittsburgh, International Studies Occasional Paper No. 8.

BLAU, P. M. (1964). *Exchange and Power in Social Life.* New York: John Wiley & Sons.

BLAU, P. M. (1971). "Justice in Social Exchange." In H. Turk and R. L. Simpson (eds.), *Institutions and Social Exchange.* Indianapolis, Ind.: Bobbs-Merrill. Pp. 56–68.

CAPORASO, J. (1978). "Dependence, Dependency and Power in the Global System: A Structural and Behavioral Analysis." *International Organization,* 32:14–43.

CHAPMAN, S. (1980). "Grain of Truth." *The New Republic,* January 19, pp. 12–15.

DOXEY, M. (1971). *Economic Sanctions and International Enforcement.* New York: Oxford University Press.

GOLDMANN, K. (1980). "Cooperation and Tension among Great Powers: A Research Note." *Cooperation and Conflict,* 15:31–45.

KEOHANE, R., and J. NYE, Jr. (1977). *Power and Interdependence: World Politics in Transition.* Boston, Mass.: Little, Brown.

KISSINGER, H. A. (1979). *White House Years.* Boston, Mass.: Little, Brown.

LOSMAN, D. (1979). *International Economic Sanctions: The Cases of Cuba, Israel, and Rhodesia.* Albuquerque, N.M.: University of New Mexico Press.

POLACHEK, S. W. (1980). "Conflict and Trade." *Journal of Conflict Resolution,* 24:55–78.

RICHARDSON, N. R. (1982). "Economic Linkage as a Detente Strategy." Paper presented at the Annual Meetings of the International Studies Association, Cincinnati, March.

RUMMEL, R. J. (1966). "Some Dimensions in the Foreign Behavior of Nations." *Journal of Peace Research,* 3:201–24.

RUMMEL, R. J. (1972). *The Dimensions of Nations*. Beverly Hills, Calif.: Sage Publications.

RUMMEL, R. J. (1976). *Peace Endangered*. Beverly Hills, Calif.: Sage Publications.

RUSSETT, B. M. (1967). *International Regions and the International System: A Study in Political Ecology*. Chicago, Ill.: Rand McNally.

SAFIRE, W. (1982). "The Kremlin Pipeline." The *New York Times*, January 3, Sec. IV, p. 19.

U.S. CONGRESS, SENATE COMMITTEE ON FOREIGN RELATIONS (1974). *Hearings, Detente*. 93rd Cong., 2nd Sess.

WALTZ, K. (1979). *Theory of International Politics*. Reading, Mass.: Addison-Wesley.

WEEDE, E. (1981). "Detente-Related Policies: An Evaluation." In D. Frei (ed.), *Definitions and Measurements of Detente*. Cambridge: Oelges-chlager, Gunn & Hain. Pp. 141–54.

7

Human Rights: Assessing the Impact on Nongovernmental Organizations

E. Thomas Rowe

The role of human rights issues in United States foreign policy has a long history.[1] In recent years the experiences of the 1960s, combined with the blatant violations of widely-held values by several U.S. administrations, led to an increasing assertion in Congress of the necessity for human rights issues to be explicitly incorporated into U.S. foreign policy. The result was a number of laws and regulations designed to press the U.S. executive toward more attention to human rights and the use of human rights criteria in aid decisions and other aspects of policy (see Weissbrodt, 1977).

Initially, under presidents Nixon and Ford, there was resistance to this pressure. While there were some changes in policy, the actual impact was certainly quite limited. However, circumstances changed substantially with the election of Jimmy Carter to the White House. He decided to make human rights one of the hallmarks of his administration.

THE CARTER AND REAGAN HUMAN RIGHTS POLICIES

In his inaugural address, President Carter spoke of the increasing demands worldwide for "basic human rights" and of the role the

United States would assume in helping to shape a more humane world. In remarks directed to an international audience, the new president indicated the United States would cooperate with others to ensure "the basic right of every human being to be free of poverty and hunger and disease and political repression." (Carter, 1981a, pp. 1–4). A few weeks later, in an address at the United Nations, President Carter emphasized that all U.N. members had committed themselves "to respect basic human rights." In light of that, he said, U.N. members could not claim that mistreatment of their own citizens was simply a domestic matter. All members had a responsibility to speak out against violations of rights. The United States, he declared, would "be steadfast in [its] dedication to the dignity and well-being of people throughout the world" (Carter, 1977).

The actual implementation of those promises proved to be far more difficult than the declaration (see, e.g., Bloomfield, 1982). The last two years of the Carter administration involved a much more moderate policy than the first two years (American Association for the International Commission of Jurists, 1984). Nevertheless, in his last "State of the Union" speech of January 23, 1980, President Carter pledged that the United States would continue to seek "protection of human rights." This served U.S. national interests, he argued, because "the basis for stability and peace" would be stronger and more enduring where human rights were observed (Carter, 1981b, pp. 194–200).

Despite the difficulties in implementation, there can be little doubt now that the Carter administration's emphasis on human rights did have some impact on a variety of specific circumstances and contributed to improvements in particular human rights conditions in a number of countries. A number of works have detailed some of this evidence (see, e.g., Cohen, 1982; Quigley, 1978; Hammarberg, 1978; Schoultz, 1981). Certainly there were also effects on the media, on intergovernmental organizations, on the organization of the Department of State, and on various non-human-rights policies of the United States (see Bloomfield, 1982; American Association for the International Commission of Jurists, 1984; Forsythe, 1983).

At the same time, the Carter administration's policies had come under considerable attack. There were some who argued that the human rights commitment was purely rhetorical from the outset, designed to conceal other interests and considerations actually shaping policy (see, e.g., Pastusiak, 1978). Still others felt that there was not a clear enough conception of the relationship between the goals being sought and the possible ways in which those goals might be implemented. Instead, the Carter administration was engaging in a "global evangelism" that advanced neither the cause of human rights nor the interests of the United States ←— (Haas, 1978). The policy produced an arrogance and interventionism that was ineffective and sometimes counterproductive.

In more conservative circles, the policy was even more severely criticized and seen as having a long-term, pernicious impact (see, e.g., Kirkpatrick, 1979; Lefever, 1978). For these critics, the most serious threat in the world—both to human rights and to other values—was to be found in the Soviet Union and in "communist" governments and movements tied to the Soviet Union. These "totalitarians" were viewed as more thoroughly suppressing human rights than more conventional "authoritarian" governments, seeking to extend their repressive systems worldwide, and unwilling and unable to undergo the internal liberalization that would gradually lead to a regime observant of human rights. At the same time, they were hostile to the United States and other "democratic" states. Because of these characteristics, the most important aim of any human rights campaign had to deal with the Soviet threat. Anything that undermined that effort, however laudable it might seem in the short run, was undesirable.

These critics argued that the Carter human rights efforts were having precisely that effect. The governments most amenable to U.S. influence and most easily undermined by U.S. actions were those friendly to and allied with the United States. Some of these were "authoritarian" governments that engaged in human rights practices the United States would deplore. However, they were not seeking to extend their rule to other areas, they were not as thoroughly or severely repressive, and they might gradually evolve into democratic systems. Moreover, as U.S. allies against the Soviet Union, they were part of the resistance against the spread of "communism." To denounce their violations of rights, especially in public forums, or to take punitive actions against them in the form of aid or trade sanctions would have the effect of undermining the regimes and making them more vulnerable to "communist" subversion.

In the view of these critics, then, the human rights policies of the Carter administration would not help those suffering from Soviet oppression but could damage friendly regimes and hence serve Soviet interests. The results might be some short-term relief for a few individual victims of abuse; however, the long-term results would be greater oppression.

These views were common among supporters of the administration of President Ronald Reagan when he assumed office in 1981. At least initially, there was a de-emphasis of the issue area generally in public pronouncements. Indeed, this downplaying of human rights was even explicitly acknowledged (see American Association for the International Commission of Jurists, 1984, p. 33). Moreover, the first nominee for the position of Assistant Secretary of State for Human Rights and Humanitarian Affairs was Ernest Lefever. He had in 1979 indicated to Congress his view that there was little the United States could or should do to advance human rights, other than serving as a good example and maintaining a strong military posture against the Soviet Union (see U.S. Congress, 1979; also see U.S. Congress, 1981; Lefever, 1978). Opposition to Lefever was fierce, and he was not approved. The administration then let the office remain vacant for several months. This fact alone was a clear indication of the lower priority the new administration had decided to give to human rights. In contrast, Patricia Derian, the Assistant Secretary under the Carter administration, had been a strong advocate of human rights both in relationships with other governments and within the Carter administration itself.

Eventually the Reagan administation did propose and get approval for Elliot Abrams to serve as Assistant Secretary. The nomination was generally well received among human rights activists. Moreover, by the fall of 1981, the administration was again arguing that the promotion of human rights was central to U.S. foreign policy (see, e.g., Kirkpatrick's essay in Barrett et al., 1981).

Still, the human rights policy had been and continued to be quite different from that of the Carter administration in both theory and practice. "Totalitarian" regimes—in the contemporary world, the Soviet Union and its allies—were the most serious threat and the most necessary to resist. Hence, U.S. military policy and adequate defense were important parts of the human rights equation. "Authoritarian" regimes were to be viewed as lesser evils than "communist" and hence preferred if a choice had to be made. Still, there was to be a realistic commitment to democracy and rule of law. Attempts were therefore to be made to move those authoritarian systems in that direction, realizing that the power of the United States was limited and that such an evolution was necessarily a slow process. Moreover, the preferred method became "quiet diplomacy" rather than public denunciations or punitive use of military and economic assistance. Public pressures would sometimes be used; but, especially for friendly governments, traditional or quiet diplomacy was more likely to be effective (see Schultz speech in U.S. Department of State, 1984, pp. 87–90; and Abrams, 1984).

At least in terms of public diplomacy, the Reagan administration followed through on this in practice. In the United Nations and before the Inter-American Commission on Human Rights, the United States was more hesitant than had been true under Carter about criticism of human rights abuses by governments friendly to the United States. At the same time, strong positions were taken on abuses by the Soviet Union and its allies. Similarly, the Reagan administration was much more supportive than under Carter of bilateral and multilateral loans, military aid, and the sale of police equipment to friendly governments even when they had questionable records on human rights.[2]

These changes from the presidency of Jimmy Carter to that of Ronald Reagan provide a good opportunity for an examination of the impact of different policies in the same issue area. A full assessment would be a major project beyond the scope of this present study.[3] Instead, I want to focus on one important aspect: the impact of the policies on other organizations and actors involved in pursuing similar goals.

The international promotion and protection of human rights is an activity pursued by a complex of actors—governmental, inter-governmental, and nongovernmental. This is true of a large portion of the goals pursued through foreign policies, of course, but it is especially true of the human rights area. Hence, one way of assessing policy is to determine its impact on others seeking the same goals—both directly on the actors themselves and indirectly on the context within which they must operate. My aim here is to look at the impact of U.S. policy on nongovernmental organizations (NGOs) active on human rights issues.

Data and Methodology

To examine this, a mail survey was conducted in the spring and summer of 1984. The list of organizations surveyed was taken from the *North American Human Rights Directory,* published by the Human Rights Internet. It included all listed NGOs with offices in the United States that were still active and had current addresses, and that had the protection and promotion of human rights as a central purpose. Except where specific, separate, action-oriented units were identified, educational and research institutions, trade union organizations, professional associations, and churches were excluded.

In total, 195 organizations were identified in this way and sent questionnaires. Of these, 40%, or 78 organizations, replied. The types surveyed and responding, using the same categories as those in the *Directory,* are shown in Table 7.1. The range of organizations

Table 7.1

Nongovernmental Organizations Surveyed

	Questionnaires sent (N)	Responses (N)
Type of Organization		
Secular NGOs with broad concerns	6	3
Coordinating networks	3	1
Religious-based NGOs	18	9
Legally Oriented NGOs	24	9
Academic NGOs	2	1
Medically Oriented NGOs	3	1
Types of Rights		
Prisoners' rights	7	2
Freedom of expression	3	1
Freedom of religion	5	3
Rights of indigenous people	3	1
Refugees	14	6
Scientific freedom & scientists' rights	6	4
Regional Focus		
Africa	26	8
Asia	22	6
Soviet Union & Eastern Europe	29	15
Western Europe & North America	8	6
Latin America	33	13
Totals*	195*	78*

*Groups may be classified in more than one category, so that the totals are not the sum of the columns.

Table 7.2

**Were there Significant Differences between
the Carter and Reagan Administrations in Human Rights Policies?***

	Yes	Mainly rhetoric	No	No answer
Focus of NGO				
Worldwide or several regions (*N* = 30)	80.0	3.3	6.7	10.0
Soviet Union & E. Europe (*N* = 15)	80.0	0.0	13.3	6.7
Latin America (*N* = 13)	92.3	7.7	0.0	0.0
Africa (*N* = 8)	75.0	25.0	0.0	0.0
Asia (*N* = 6)	83.3	0.0	16.7	0.0
W. Europe, N. America (*N* = 6)	100.0	0.0	0.0	0.0
All NGOs (*N* = 78)	83.3	5.1	6.4	5.1

*In percentages.

responding is wide and seems to represent adequately the diversified character of the U.S.-based groups seeking to promote human rights.

The survey was made up of a series of open-ended questions asking the respondents to identify the purposes and activities of their organizations, to explain whether or not they considered that there were significant differences between the human rights policies of the Carter and Reagan administrations, to identify the nature of any differences, and to assess the extent and nature of the impact of the change in administrations on the activities of their organizations. Because of the open-ended nature of the questions, some of the responses were difficult to quantify. However, as will be seen below, there was a large degree of uniformity in the responses.

Results

The first question to be addressed is whether or not the differences between the Carter and Reagan administrations were judged to be substantial. While there were some obvious differences, as noted above, these might have been viewed as relatively unimportant. If so, then the comparisons would not have been very interesting. However, there was widespread agreement among those active in

Table 7.3

**Comparing the Human Rights Policies
of the Carter and Reagan Administrations***

	Yes	No	No answer
Compared to the Carter period, has Reagan:			
De-emphasized particular geographic political regions?	74.4	14.1	11.5
Given greater emphasis to any regions?	39.7	44.9	15.4
De-emphasized any type of human rights?	65.4	14.1	20.5
Given greater emphasis to any rights?	25.6	52.6	21.8
De-emphasized any types of activities?	61.5	11.5	26.9
Given greater emphasis to any activities?	26.9	53.8	19.2

*In percentages ($N = 78$).

human rights organizations that there were significant differences. A few respondents saw no differences, and a few saw them as primarily matters of rhetoric. As shown in Table 7.2, however, 83% saw the differences as substantial.

Partly because of the open-ended nature of the questionnaire, identification of what those differences were showed somewhat greater variation. Even here, however, there was still a considerable degree of agreement. Table 7.3 shows a summary of the results. The most commonly expressed view was that the Reagan administration had generally de-emphasized human rights as a factor in foreign policy. Where human rights were considered, they tended to be subordinated to East–West considerations and to be part of a global confrontation between the United States and the Soviet Union.

When asked whether particular regions had been de-emphasized, a few (about 14%) said no. The more typical responses, however, were either that all regions had been de-emphasized, or that human rights violations by authoritarian governments friendly to the United States were ignored. Where these governments were specified, Latin American regimes and South Africa were most frequently mentioned. Concerning whether the Reagan administration had given any region greater attention, the most common response (about 45%) was simply no. Still, a substantial portion (about 40%) argued that human rights violations by communist, socialist, or left-wing regimes had been given more emphasis under Reagan. A few respondents contended that this impression was an illusion. Human rights, they argued, had been de-emphasized generally. On the few occasions when they were raised as issues, they tended mainly to relate to communist regimes, and hence this gave an appearance of greater emphasis simply because of the relative amount of attention. The actual frequency and intensity of attention to human rights in communist countries, they argued, was greater under the Carter administration.

With regard to the types of human rights given emphasis, the most frequent response was that all types had been de-emphasized and that none received greater emphasis under the Reagan administration. Where particular rights were specified, the respondents usually felt that the Reagan administration had de-emphasized economic, social, and collective rights. The right to have basic needs met, particularly for the poor and oppressed, the rights of refugees, and the right to self-determination were frequently mentioned as having been de-emphasized. Several respondents also identified civil and political rights and freedom from gross violations of personal integrity (torture and death squads). While relatively few (about 26%) saw any specific rights as receiving greater emphasis under the Reagan administration, those who did saw those as the rights of transnational business enterprises, the right to private property, and certain political rights associated with democratic systems (regular and free elections, freedom of religion, freedom of the press, and freedom of assembly).

Finally, with regard to types of activities emphasized or de-emphasized, the typical view was that all efforts to promote human rights had been de-emphasized by the Reagan administration; the specific de-emphasized activities mentioned were public denunciations of violations of rights, the use of human rights criteria in determining trade relationships and in allocating economic and military assistance, an activist role by the Assistant Secretary for Human Rights and Humanitarian Affairs, and the use of international intergovernmental agencies. While few said any activities had been given increased emphasis, those who did saw "quiet" diplomacy, the use of positive incentives with South Africa, the use of military action, and anticommunist activities generally as all having been given particular stress by the Reagan administration.

In short, the view among these NGO activists was that the Reagan administration had given less emphasis to human rights issues than did the Carter administration, it had especially downplayed violations of rights by right-wing authoritarian regimes allied with the United States, and it had been primarily concerned with violations by socialist or communist countries tied or believed to be tied to the Soviet Union. Moreover, economic rights, group rights, the right to have basic necessities met, and freedom from violation of the person were viewed as having received relatively little attention. At the same time, some of the freedoms associated with parliamentary systems—elections, assembly, and religion, for instance—were given emphasis along with the right to private property. Finally, the respondents saw an increase in support for anticommunist activities and a continuation of public denunciations of human rights practices in the Soviet Union and countries tied to the Soviet Union. However, there was a decrease in the use of public pressures on other countries, trade and aid were less likely to be used as a lever to attempt to press for human rights, a visibly activist role for the human rights division of the State Department was avoided, and less support was given for continued growth in the human rights tasks of international intergovernmental organizations.

The fact that activists in human rights NGOs saw such differences between the Carter and Reagan administrations does not necessarily mean that they would see the activities of their own organizations as being affected, either positively or negatively. In fact, a larger portion did see differences in the administration than believed those differences had an impact on them. However, the majority of respondents reported that the changes significantly affected their activities. As Table 7.4 shows, about 56% saw a substantial impact from the change in administration, with those NGOs focusing on Latin America and Africa particularly affected.

The more interesting responses, however, deal with the nature of the impact. Table 7.5 indicates that the majority of respondents found pursuit of some of their activities more difficult as a result of the change from Carter to Reagan, and a clear plurality also thought this meant less impact than in the past.

Further exploration of the responses indicates a sharp difference between those from individuals active on human rights issues in the Soviet Union and Eastern Europe and those concerned with other regions or with human rights worldwide. Respondents from NGOs concerned with the "communist" countries tended to give a

Table 7.4
Were Your Activities Significantly Affected?*

	Yes	No	No answer
Focus of NGO			
Worldwide (*N* = 30)	46.7	36.7	16.7
Soviet Union & E. Europe (*N* = 15)	40.0	46.7	13.3
Latin America (*N* = 13)	92.3	7.7	0.0
Africa (*N* = 8)	75.0	25.0	0.0
Asia (*N* = 6)	33.3	33.3	33.3
W. Europe, N. America (*N* = 6)	50.0	16.7	33.3
All NGOs (*N* = 78)	56.4	29.5	14.1

*In percentages.

much more favorable evaluation of the impact of the change. Tables 7.6 and 7.7 show the two groups separately and indicate the striking differences in both perceptions of the problems encountered because of the Reagan administration and whether or not the NGO impact had been affected.

In general, as Table 7.6 shows, the majority of respondents from organizations active on a worldwide basis and in areas other than Eastern Europe reported that their organizations had greater difficulty pursuing many of their activities and much of what they did had less impact as a result of the human rights policies of the Reagan administration. About 19% also reported that some activities were easier to pursue and had more impact. However, most of these tended to be the result of hostile reactions to the Reagan administration rather than a directly intended result. Basically, what this points out is that almost none of these respondents evaluated the intended effects of the Reagan administration's policies positively. Instead, where any of the effects were seen as positive, it was essentially because the concerned public and other organizations had such a strong negative reaction to the Reagan administration that it was sometimes easier than in the past to organize that public and cooperate with other NGOs. In addition, the more adverse conditions for human rights under the

Table 7.5

Assessing the Impact on NGOs*

	Yes	No	No answer
As a result of policy changes, are any of your activities:			
Easier to pursue?	23.1	64.1	12.8
More difficult to pursue?	59.0	26.9	14.1
Having greater impact?	35.9	46.2	17.9
Having less impact?	46.2	34.6	19.2

*In percentages ($N = 78$).

Reagan administration forced groups to be more active and more effectively organized. Finally, the stark contrast between the administration's policies and the reality of human rights violations sometimes made it easier to justify the necessity for action among potential supporters. These then were positive outcomes of what were seen as undesirable policies. While there were a couple of reports of directly positive impact—in one case because of a change

Table 7.6

**Assessing the Impact:
All NGOs Except Those Concerned with the Soviet Union
and Eastern Europe***

	Yes	Yes, as a hostile reaction to Reagan	No	No answer
As a result of policy changes, are any of your activities:				
Easier to pursue?	4.8	14.3	68.3	12.7
More difficult to pursue?	66.7	—	19.0	14.3
Having greater impact?	6.3	28.6	47.6	17.5
Having less impact?	55.6	—	25.4	19.0

*In percentages ($N = 63$).

Table 7.7

Assessing the Impact:
NGOs Concerned with the Soviet Union and Eastern Europe

	Yes	Yes, but not due to Reagan's policies	No	No answer
As a result of policy changes, are any of your activities:				
Easier to pursue?	40.0	—	46.7	13.3
More difficult to pursue?	20.0	6.7	60.0	13.3
Having greater impact?	40.0	—	40.0	20.0
Having less impact?	6.7	—	73.3	20.0

*In percentages (*N* = 15).

in an ambassador and staff and in another because of support for an adult literacy program—these were rare for groups operating outside the Eastern European bloc.

Instead, the most most frequent responses involved ten types of problems.

1. There were reports of reduced access to administration and State Department officials. Whether because of lack of interest or the low priority assigned human rights issues, or actual hostility on the part of officials, many respondents reported much greater difficulty in gaining access than during the Carter administration. According to some respondents, this was also true of getting support from the State Department for individual cases. Neither officials in Washington nor the countries where abuses were occurring were as responsive to requests for assistance in casework.

2. Similarly, many respondents reported reduced access to Congress, particularly the Senate. Congress tended to follow the administration lead in the low importance assigned to human rights issues and to rely on the information that the administration provided. The Carter administration, on the other hand, had helped to create an atmosphere in which members of Congress would welcome NGO information and advice on human rights.

3. According to some respondents, the low priority that the administration gave to human rights tended to make it more difficult than it had been to get media attention, both for general human rights issues and for specific cases of abuses.

4. Many said they were facing greater difficulty in raising funds. While none of the groups reported receiving government funds, the Reagan administration's reduction in government funding for various other programs and agencies increased the competition for private donations and hence reduced the amounts readily available for any particular NGO. Moreover, the groups' members now saw more serious dangers of nuclear war and more desperate situations for the poor as a result of the Reagan administration and hence sought some reallocation of funds to these purposes at the expense of human rights.

5. Related to this, some reported they were having greater difficulty in keeping their supporters' attention focused on human rights. Their members were so concerned with other policies of the Reagan administration that human rights issues were assigned less importance.

6. It was also contended that there were greater problems in gaining access to officials of foreign governments involved in violations of human rights. The low priority the United States currently assigned to human rights and the reduced attention to human rights criteria in trade and aid decisions made officials of other governments less concerned and less responsive to criticism. According to others, the fact that human rights issues had become an instrument in the U.S.–Soviet confrontation and were otherwise given little attention reduced the legitimacy of raising such issues generally. The area was seen as part of a political, ideological, and power conflict. It had become more difficult for U.S. groups to contend that there were basic universal stantards that all countries could be expected to observe since the U.S. government seemed to be so selectively concerned with violations.

7. Some respondents said they were having increased problems in getting a hearing among less committed groups in the population because of the chilling effects of the administration's emphasis on the threat of communism. While their regular supporters had become more mobilized, other portions of the population were more nervous about being seen as associated with "left-wing" causes. Moreover, there was even some fear of U.S. government surveillance and harassment of

human rights activists. Several respondents expressed concern about what they labeled as a "new McCarthyism" in the country.

8. Similarly, the rhetoric of the Reagan administration, according to some of the respondents, had unintentionally encouraged extremist groups on the right to promote more publicly racist and other views antithetical to the cause of human rights.

9. There were also common reports of greater difficulty in getting full and accurate information from the Reagan administration on human rights issues. Some respondents reported increased problems in carrying out some activities because they were unable to obtain accurate and timely information.

10. Finally, some respondents contended that because of the low priority assigned to human rights issues, the Reagan administration was less effectively organized to receive and consider information or requests from NGOs. Even if the ultimate response would be sympathetic, the NGO had to work harder than under the Carter administration to get attention and some action or response.

These responses were, as I have already stated, in sharp contrast to the responses from individuals in those groups active on human rights issues in the Soviet Union and Eastern Europe. Overall, the latter saw more positive effects on their activities because of the change from Carter to Reagan. Among this group of organizations, however, there were substantial differences between those concerned with basic changes in the nature of the government—those concerned with what they regard as Soviet communist subjugation of the peoples of the Soviet Union and Eastern Europe—and those concerned with changes in the policies of existing governments to ensure the rights of religious and ethnic groups, the right to emigrate, or the rights of dissenters. About half of the 15 groups in the Eastern-bloc category fell into each of these, and the differences in their responses are reported in Table 7.8. There are interesting differences on the questions of whether any activities had been easier or more difficult to pursue and whether any activities had greater impact as a result of the change in administrations.

The respondents from organizations seeking basic governmental changes generally reported a more favorable situation under the Reagan administration. They said they found administration officials more receptive to their approaches and more responsive to

Table 7.8

Assessing the Impact:
NGOs Concerned with the Soviet Union and Eastern Europe,
Regime Change Versus Policy Change*

	Yes	No	No answer
As a result of policy changes, are any of your activities:			
Easier to pursue?			
NGOs seeking regime change (*N* = 8)	50.0	25.0	25.0
NGOs seeking policy change (*N* = 7)	42.9	57.1	0.0
More difficult to pursue?			
NGOs seeking regime change (*N* = 8)	0.0	75.0	25.0
NGOs seeking policy change (*N* = 7)	57.1	42.9	9.0
Having greater impact?			
NGOs seeking regime change (*N* = 8)	62.3	12.5	25.0
NGOs seeking policy change (*N* = 7)	14.3	71.4	14.3
Having less impact?			
NGOs seeking regime change (*N* = 8)	0.0	75.0	25.0
NGOs seeking policy change (*N* = 7)	71.4	14.3	14.3

*In percentages.

their needs. High-level officials in the State Department, the National Security Council, and the White House under the Reagan administration had shown greater understanding, cooperation, and attention. As a result, the NGOs' activities had been enhanced, and the impact was more substantial because of the change from Carter to Reagan.

A less favorable picture emerges from those NGOs concerned more with changes in policies in Eastern-bloc countries. Here there were reports that high-level contacts and negotiations with Soviet officials had become more difficult under the Reagan administration, that contacts with dissidents were also more problematic, and that the intensification of the cold war had made it hard to publicize issues in a nonideological way. Human rights issues became too entangled with left–right or war–peace arguments.

These negative effects, however, were not uniformly reported. Two respondents indicated strong cooperation from Reagan administration officials in specific casework. Moreover, one reported that at least one specific case had been handled more effectively by officials in the Reagan administration than had been the case under Carter. Also, there were some who reported that while the situation had deteriorated during the Reagan administration, they thought this was caused by developments in the Soviet Union and Soviet intransigence rather than any U.S. policies. Hence the change in U.S. administrations was not seen as a central factor.

The final question in the survey asked for an overall comparative assessment of the general situation under the Reagan and Carter administrations for the pursuit of human-rights goals. In light of the results already reported, the figures shown in Table 7.9 are not suprising. Approximately 62% of the respondents reported

Table 7.9

**Overall Assessment of Conditions
for Achieving NGO Human Rights Goals***

	More favorable	Largely unaffected	Less favorable	No answer
Focus of NGO				
Worldwide (*N* = 30)	3.3	10.0	66.7	20.0
Soviet Union & Eastern Europe (*N* = 15)	46.7	20.0	20.0	13.3
NGOs seeking regime change (*N* = 8)	75.0	12.5	0.0	12.5
NGOs seeking policy change (*N* = 7)	14.3	28.6	42.9	14.3
Latin America (*N* = 13)	7.7	7.7	84.6	0.0
Africa (*N* = 8)	0.0	0.0	100.0	0.0
Asia (*N* = 6)	33.3	16.7	50.0	0.0
W. Europe, N. America (*N* = 6)	0.0	16.7	66.7	16.7
All NGOs (*N* = 78)	14.1	11.5	62.8	11.5

*In percentages.

that conditions were less favorable under the Reagan administration, while less than 15% (only 11 respondents) reported they were more favorable. Moreover, the majority of those reporting better conditions in recent years were activists in NGOs concerned with ending communist rule in Eastern Europe. Two others of the 11 total reported that conditions had improved, but they thought this was despite policies followed by the Reagan administration rather than because of those policies. They contended that the situation could have improved further with more supportive policies from the U.S. government.

Not all of those who saw a deterioration of conditions thought policies of the Reagan administration had helped produce the deterioration. Three respondents contended that the less favorable situation might have had little to do with U.S. policies and resulted instead from policies of the Soviet Union. In general, however, most respondents thought that the Reagan administration was a major factor in creating conditions less favorable to the advancement of human rights than had been the case under the Carter administration.

CONCLUSIONS

President Carter was sometimes criticized by human rights advocates for failing to carry through on his promises in the area of human rights. His human rights commitments were said to fade quickly in the light of U.S. economic and security interests. President Reagan was more frequently criticized, especially in the first half of his administration, for failing even to pay lip service to the area except as part of the renewed cold war. As someone once remarked, "Where there's hypocrisy, there's hope." Even a largely rhetorical commitment provides some leverage. The absence of even that often means there is almost nothing to work with.

The Reagan administration did change its posture somewhat by the fall of 1981 and began to argue that human rights were at the core of U.S. foreign policy. At the same time, to the extent that this implied creating conditions conducive to the operation of human rights NGOs, the policy would seem to have failed. Certainly this was the perception of the majority of the activists surveyed in this study.

Any administration that seeks to promote human rights as one of its foreign policy goals might well wish to create conditions to facilitate the operations of human rights NGOs. These groups can take actions and pursue goals in ways inappropriate for governments but quite compatible with governmental aims. Moreover, they provide important sources of alternative information and interpretations of events and policies. Hence, they can serve a vital role both for government and for the public domestically, in addition to the impact they may have on the behavior of other governments or the conditions of their people.

In the area of human rights, the activities of NGOs would be helped by several measures:

1. a self-conscious effort to ensure access to government officials;
2. a reassertion by governmental officials of public attention to human rights as a legitimate and important issue area;
3. a willingness to provide assistance through diplomatic staff or others in specific cases of alleged violations of rights;
4. a readiness to make judicious use of public as well as "quiet" diplomacy to attempt to change policies of governments violating rights, as long as this is combined with some humility and sensitivity to national autonomy;
5. a clear commitment to the application of universal standards to both "friends" and "enemies";
6. support for the establishment and strengthening of international legal and institutional mechanisms that would promote human rights while removing some of the opportunities for manipulation of such issues for national purposes, including our own.

These types of measures could be compatible with the policies of any U.S. administration interested in the promotion of human rights. In fact, they might serve as a set of general guidelines that would minimize the likelihood of either global evangelism or cynical manipulation of human rights for political purposes.

NOTES

[1]A good overview of the issues, including reviews of the Carter and Reagan administrations, is contained in Forsythe (1983). Also see Kommers and Loescher (1979), Nanda, Scarritt, and Shepherd (1982), Farer (1980), the American Association for the International Commission of Jurists (1984), Schlesinger (1979), and Vogelgesang (1980).

[2]These policies have produced scathing criticisms by some human rights advocates. One review of the Reagan record suggested the administration had come "close to endorsement of offenses condemned at the Nuremberg War Crimes Tribunals. ..." (Maechling, 1983, p. 118). Another contended that the administration had "cheapened the currency of human rights" by its political use of human rights standards and it had disregarded and violated the law in several specific cases (Americas Watch, Helsinki Watch, Lawyers Committee for International Human Rights, 1983). For further evaluations, see Derian (1981), Dodd (1984), Leach (1984), Posner (1984), Forsythe (1983), and the American Association for the International Commission of Jurists (1984). While these vary somewhat, none provide favorable conclusions about the administration's record.

[3]Such an assessment would have to include evaluation of the internal consistency of the goals sought and the policies designed to achieve those goals, the reliability of the historical and contemporary evidence upon which the policies are defended, the impact of the policies in terms of the immediate aims they are trying to achieve, and the impact of the policies over the longer run and in areas not necessarily intended.

REFERENCES

ABRAMS, E. (1984). "A View from the Department of State." *Federal Bar News and Journal,* 31:202–4.

AMERICAN ASSOCIATION FOR THE INTERNATIONAL COMMISSION OF JURISTS (1984). *Human Rights and U.S. Foreign Policy, the First Decade, 1973–1983.* New York: American Association for the ICJ.

AMERICAS WATCH, HELSINKI WATCH, LAWYERS' COMMITTEE FOR INTERNATIONAL HUMAN RIGHTS (1983). "The Reagan Administration's Human Rights Policy: A Mid-Term Review." *Human Rights Internet Reporter,* 8:616–19.

BARRETT, W., et al. (1981). "Human Rights and American Foreign Policy: A Symposium." *Commentary,* 72:25–63.

BLOOMFIELD, L. (1982). "From Ideology to Program to Policy: Tracking the Carter Human Rights Policy." *Journal of Policy Analysis and Management,* 2:1–12.

BUHL, C. (1981). "Human Rights and the Reagan Administration." *CALC Report,* 7:1–3.

CARTER, J. (1977). "Transcript of the President's Address at the U.N. on Peace, Economy and Human Rights." *New York Times,* March 18, p. 4.

CARTER, J. (1981a). *Public Papers of the Presidents of the United States, Jimmy Carter, 1977: Book 1, January 20 to May 24, 1977.* Washington, D.C.: U.S. Government Printing Office.

CARTER, J. (1981b). *Public Papers of the Presidents of the United States, Jimmy Carter, 1980–81: Book 1, January 1 to May 23, 1980.* Washington, D.C.: U.S. Government Printing Office.

COHEN, R. (1982). "Human Rights Diplomacy: The Carter Administration and the Southern Cone." *Human Rights Quarterly,* 4:212–42.

DERIAN, P. (1981). "Human Rights: Some of Our Best Friends are Authoritarians." *The Nation,* November 7:467–70.

DODD, C. (1984). "Two Views from Congress: A View from the Senate." *Federal Bar News and Journal,* 31:204–6.

FARER, T. (ed.) (1980). *Toward a Humanitarian Diplomacy: A Primer for Policy.* New York: New York University Press.

FORSYTHE, D. (1983). *Human Rights and World Politics.* Lincoln Nebr., and London: University of Nebraska Press.

HAAS, E. (1978). *Global Evangelism Rides Again: How to Protect Human Rights Without Really Trying.* Policy Papers in International Affairs No. 5. Berkeley, Calif.: University of California, Institute of International Studies.

HAMMARBERG, T. (1978). "Carter and Human Rights: What Results? A European View." *Human Rights Internet Newsletter,* 4:39–43.

HUMAN RIGHTS INTERNET (1980). *North American Human Rights Directory.* Washington, D.C.: Human Rights Internet.

KIRKPATRICK, J. (1979). "Dictatorships and Double Standards." *Commentary,* November, 36–45.

KIRKPATRICK, J. (1981). "Establishing a Viable Human Rights Policy." *World Affairs,* 143:323–34.

KOMMERS, D. and G. LOESCHER (eds.) (1979). *Human Rights and American Foreign Policy.* Notre Dame, Ind.: University of Notre Dame Press.

LEACH, J. (1984). "Two Views from Congress: A View from the House." *Federal Bar News and Journal,* 31:207–9.

LEFEVER, E. (1978). "The Trivialization of Human Rights." Reprinted in F. Sondermann, D. McLellan, and W. Olson (eds.), *The Theory and Practice of International Relations,* 5th ed. Englewood Cliffs, N.J.: Prentice-Hall. Pp. 353–71.

MAECHLING, C., Jr. (1983). "Human Rights Dehumanized." *Foreign Policy,* 52:118–35.

NANDA, V., J. SCARRITT, and G. SHEPHERD (eds.) (1982). *Global Human Rights.* Boulder, Colo.: Westview Press.

PASTUSIAK, L. (1978). "Human Rights, Carter's Motives." *Human Rights Internet Newsletter,* 4:38–43.

POSNER, M. (1984). "A view from a Non-Governmental Organization." *Federal Bar News and Journal,* 31:209–11.

QUIGLEY, T., et al. (1978) *U.S. Policy on Human Rights in Latin America (Southern Cone): A Congressional Conference on Capitol Hill.* New York: Fund for New Priorities in America.

SCHLESINGER, A., Jr. (1979). "Human Rights and the American Tradition." *Foreign Affairs,* 57:503–26.

SCHOULTZ, L. (1981). *Human Rights and United States Policy toward Latin America.* Princeton, N.J.: Princeton University Press.

U.S. CONGRESS, HOUSE OF REPRESENTATIVES (1979). *Human Rights and U.S. Foreign Policy.* Hearings before the Subcommittee on International Organizations of the Committee on Foreign Affairs, 96th Congress, 1st Session, pp. 222–37.

U.S. CONGRESS, SENATE (1981). *Nomination of Ernest W. Lefever.* Hearings before the Committee on Foreign Relations, 97th Congress, lst Session.

U.S. DEPARTMENT OF STATE (1984). *Realism, Strength, Negotiation: Key Foreign Policy Statements of the Reagan Administration.* Washington, D.C.: U.S. Department of State, Bureau of Public Affairs.

VOGELGESANG, S. (1980). *American Dream, Global Nightmare: The Dilemma of U.S. Human Rights Policy.* New York: Norton.

WEISSBRODT, D. (1977). "Human Rights Legislation and United States Foreign Policy." *Georgia Journal of International and Comparative Law,* Vol. 7, Supplement: 231–88.

8

Morality
and National Interest:
Vietnam and Central America

Howard Zinn

Reporting to President Reagan in the fall of 1984, after a six-day visit to Central America and presumably much research, the Kissinger Commission explained U.S. interests in Central America by listing seven points, the first of which was: "To preserve the moral authority of the United States. To be perceived by others as a nation that does what is right *because* it is right is one of this country's principal assets" (Kissinger Commission, 1984:44–45).

A British writer, Timothy Garton Ash, has pointed out that this was not a declaration of concern that right be done, but rather the expression of a desire to "be perceived" as doing right. Ash comments:

> But if you are doing (or claiming to do) what is right because you think it is in your own interest so to be seen, then you are not doing it because it is right. You are being self-interested, not disinterested; selfish, not selfless; political, not moral. If you pretend otherwise, you are being hypocritical (*New York Review of Books,* November 22, 1984).

It should be noted that the passage in the Kissinger Report, while it is all about being "perceived" as moral, does not preclude the possibility that the perception is accurate, that the policy is, indeed, moral. In fact, the report says, ". . . our strategic and moral interests coincide." Still, the emphasis on perception makes us suspicious. Whether U.S. policy is truly moral or merely moralistic (that is, hypocritical) needs to be tested by examining it.

As the need for mass armies has required the inspiration of a moral cause, nations have more and more defended their foreign policies in moral terms. Perhaps the last large-scale instance of aggression being defended in racist and jingoistic terms was given us by the Fascist powers. Their defeat in the Second World War, accompanied by the glowing language of the Atlantic Charter and the Charter of the United Nations, has put a burden or moral justification on all international behavior, especially for the victors of that war. Thus, Soviet aggression—as in Hungary or Afghanistan—is explained on moral grounds: the defense of socialism. U.S. aggression—as against Vietnam or Nicaragua—is defended similarly, to preserve the "free world" or to defend "national security."

The speciousness of the Soviet claim need not be argued strenuously in the English-speaking world, where no more than a handful of ideologues defend Soviet foreign policy and where large-scale defections from the communist party have been due mostly to abhorrence of Soviet actions. The size and power of the Soviet Union make implausible the claim that smaller, weaker powers in Eastern Europe had to be occupied and controlled for Soviet "security." And the internal departures from the historic ideals of socialism leave empty the claim that the protection of Soviet "socialism" requires certain ruthless measures.

It seems, therefore, more urgent—at least in our part of the world—that the claims of the United States to moral behavior abroad be confronted, analyzed, and examined to determine whether the Orwellian corruptions of language we find so easily on the Soviet side are absent here. It might be well to attempt that by a close look at the recent policy of the United States in Central America, with an occasional backward look at the Vietnam war. And, if we are going to test that policy against its moral claims, there may be no better place to start than with the most frequently used phrase for the justification of foreign policies: "the national interest."

It is a phrase with several variants—"national security," "national defense"—and many meanings, which may explain why it has proved so effective as a mobilizer of populations. Some of these meanings suggest moral considerations, others do not; the ambiguity has proved useful. (Nixon, in one of his famous secretly taped White House conversations with a worried aide regarding the need to cover up the "dirty tricks" that were coming to light, suggested that the whole thing might be simply explained by "national security.") There are raw jingoists, who mean by national interest nothing more than the growth of U.S. power in the world and bluntly say this is what they want. This is not the claim of political scientists such as Hans Morgenthau, who claim not to take sides in international conflicts, but who insist that international relations can only be studied in terms of power relations, that moral principles are not worthy of discussion; they are simply irrelevant.

Morgenthau urged "realism" in taking "the national interest" as "the one guiding star, one standard of thought, one rule of action" in international relations.[1] It is not clear whether Morgenthau believed morality *should not* guide international behavior, or whether, Machiavelli-like, he claimed simply to describe this behavior. To describe, however, is also, by implication, to prescribe, and thus sophisticated political scientists may find themselves, whether they like it or not, in the company of ordinary superpatriots, as both give the same tests to foreign policy.

The phrase "national interest" has far more appeal, however, and is much more useful to political leaders, when it carries implications of moral rectitude. Thus, it is often used in conjunction with "defense of liberty," "supporting freedom," "helping democracy," defending nations against attack, defending our own nation, abiding by agreements and treaties, supporting human rights. There is now in the Department of State a special "Undersecretary for Human Rights" to emphasize this concern (although there must be some suspicion accompanying this division of labor; does it mean that human rights are *not* the primary concern of the others in government?).

The connection of national interest with moral issues was expressed by Jeane Kirkpatrick, shortly after her appointment by Reagan as Ambassador to the United Nations, in an interview with *U.S. News & World Report.* Responding to a question about the policy of the United States in maintaining good relations with repressive governments, she replied: "Speaking generally, we must make it perfectly clear that we are revolted by torture and can never feel spiritual kinship with a government that engages in torture. But the central goal of our foreign policy should be not the moral elevation of other nations, but the preservation of a civilized conception of our own self-interest." (Reprinted in Gettleman et al., 1981:342–45.)

This is a tortured passage, from a moral point of view. I believe a fair paraphrase would be as follows, relating it to El Salvador, which was the initiating subject of that interview: "We are revolted by the torture that goes on under government protection in El

Salvador. We cannot feel spiritual kinship with such a government. But we must keep on giving it military aid, so that it can defeat the left-wing guerrillas, because our central goal is not to achieve some better moral condition in El Salvador, but (and here I must confess inability to paraphrase) "the preservation of a civilized conception of our own self-interest." We can only probe the meaning of that expression by looking very closely at the actual policy of the United States in El Salvador, which we must assume follows Kirkpatrick's "civilized conception" of national interest.

The first thing that is evident, both from her statement and from the facts about El Salvador, is that a civilized conception of national interest does not include the right of people in other countries to be free from torture. Her initial "But" is critical. We may not like torture, but we will accept it as a necessary condition for preserving our self-interest. Let us broaden the point: to "civilize" our conception of national interest does not mean, to Kirkpatrick and the policymakers of the United States, that the rights of people in other countries are equal to our own.

I would argue that morality in the field of foreign relations, if it is to have any reasonable meaning, must start from the proposition that the moral precepts of the Declaration of Independence are global—that all people in the world have an equal right to life, liberty, and the pursuit of happiness. That means that the torture of citizens in El Salvador is equivalent to the torture of "Americans." (If we stopped using the term "American" to describe only people in the United States, the truth of the statement would be self-evident.) Jeane Kirkpatrick clearly does not hold such a view, because if she did, her statement would become an absurdity: ". . . we are revolted by the torture of our people. . . . But the central goal of our foreign policy should be . . . the preservation of a civilized conception of our own self-interest."

What would make such a passage reasonable would be an admission that no political leader dares make: that "self-interest" really refers to the interest of certain elites and does not include the well-being of ordinary people in any country, including citizens of the United States.

A moralistic approach—that is, one pretending to morality—would insist that our policy helps people abroad, even while it neglects their most basic needs, contributes to their oppression, kills them in large numbers. Thus, in the Vietnam war, the government's claim, made repeatedly, was that the United States was fighting to help the South Vietnamese against invasion from the North. The claim was contravened by certain important evidence: that the insurrection against the Diem regime in Saigon was carried on mainly by people in South Vietnam; that North Vietnamese troops came in later and on a smaller scale after U.S. troops began to arrive in large numbers; that the Saigon regime itself was more a U.S. creation than a representative of the South Vietnamese people; that most of the U.S. bombing in Vietnam was directed at the South and, therefore, given the inevitably indiscriminate nature of aerial bombing, it was the South Vietnamese people who suffered most from this bombing.

If a basic moral principle in foreign relations is global equality in fundamental rights, then surely one of these rights is that of self-determination. Any claim to help people abroad must be connected to helping them determine their own fate. But helping is a kind of intervention, and a possible encroachment on self-determination, unless it is help to fend off threats to the self-determination of the aided people and unless it makes them more capable of determining their own destiny, while keeping that outside aid marginal. None of these were characteristics of U.S. intervention in Vietnam, which was so massive, so overwhelming, as to constitute in itself the chief threat to the self-determination of the Vietnamese.

The claim of the United States to be supporting Vietnamese self-determination was made suspect by one important historic fact: that when the French were fighting to conquer Vietnam, the United States gave massive aid to the French, directly against the attempts of the Vietnamese to gain independence. This was prefigured by the reneging on Roosevelt's promise in the Atlantic Charter to support self-determination in the postwar world. In the top-secret Defense Department history of the Vietnam war, known as the Pentagon Papers, there are a number of similar statements (of which I am selecting ˉone): In February, 1947, the U.S. Ambassador in Paris was instructed to assure Premier Ramadier that "we have fully recognized France's sovereign position in that area [Indo-China] (*Pentagon Papers,* Vol. I:31).

Later, when the United States took over the war, the secret internal documents contradicted the public statements about wanting South Vietnam, as Adlai Stevenson told the United Nations, to be free from "outside force." The Defense Department historians wrote, not knowing this would be made public: "South Viet Nam was essentially the creation of the United States" (*Pentagon Papers,* Vol. II:22). The *Pentagon Papers* give us a name, that of Brigadier General Edward Lansdale, Assistant to Secretary of Defense for Special Operations, and tells us of one of these special operations: "In 1955 and 1956 he was a key figure in installing and establishing Diem as president of South Vietnam" (Pentagon Papers, Vol. II:26).

Whatever the pretense to the U.S. public, U.S. officials made it quite clear that the desires of the Vietnamese were not predominant in determining U.S. policy. When Henry Cabot Lodge, U.S. Ambassador to Saigon, was shown the results of a Gallup poll in 1966 indicating a strong public desire to withdraw from Vietnam, he replied: "Some day we may have to decide how much it is worth to us to deny Vietnam to Hanoi and Peking—regardless of what the Vietnamese may think" (Pentagon Papers, Vol. IV:99–100).

If the motive for the long, ugly war in Vietnam was not self-determination for the Vietnamese, what was it? Official statements, some secret, some overt, make this fairly clear. In the midst of the massive effort to aid the French war, a National Security Staff study spoke of Southeast Asia as "critical to U.S. security interests" and in spelling this out spoke of many things, including the "critical psychological and political consequences." It also noted that Southeast Asia was "the principal world source of natural rubber and tin" and stressed the importance of this "in event of global war." (Pentagon Papers, Vol. I, Document 10, February 13, 1952.) Another National Security Council Statement of Jan 16, 1954, again spoke of security interests and emphasized the domino effect, that the loss of any single country would lead to other losses, in Southeast Asia, in the Middle East, in Europe. Nowhere was it explained how one domino would lead to any of the others.

The same paper talked of serious economic consequences: rubber, tin, oil from Malaya and Indonesia being threatened, as well as rice exports from Southeast Asia to other parts of Asia. It went on to say that the Southeast Asia area "has an important potential as a market for the industrialized countries of the free world." How these economic consequences affected "national security" was not made clear. That this conception of national security has any moral dimension is made dubious by John F. Kennedy's statement of July 17, 1963: "We can think of Vietnam as a piece of strategic real estate" (Pentagon Papers, Vol. II:162).

Let us now test U.S. policy in Central America, by Jeane Kirkpatrick's "civilized conception of our own self-interest," but with the assumption that a civilized conception would treat all people in the world as equal in their rights, including the right to self-determination. And let us apply the test not to an ephemeral policy of any one administration, but to a long-term policy, so that history can instruct us. And let us look first at El Salvador, which was the subject matter of Kirkpatrick's statement about self-interest.

Perhaps the central fact about El Salvador's modern history is the displacement, since the early 19th century, of food-growing land by coffee plantations, operating for the profit of plantation owners. This process left a population of landless harvest workers, unemployed nine months of the year, and deprived the mass of the peasants of land, food, and freedom, leading to periodic rebellions. By the late 1970s, according to Oxfam America, six families owned more farmland than 133,000 small farmers (Simon and Stephens, 1981).

In the midst of the current insurrection (March, 1980), a representative of the coffee plantation owners (Frente Unido Cafetalero) said: "Coffee growers should not anguish over the situation in El Salvador today; there was a similar one in 1932, and if it was solved then it can be now" (Gettleman et al., 1981:xi).

We must assume that he was referring to the fact that in 1932 a major uprising by peasants in El Salvador was crushed by the military dictator, one General Martinez. In a matter of days, Martinez killed at least 30,000 of the country's peasants, including Farabundi Marti, a socialist leader. This event became known as *la matanza* [the massacre]. Historian Walter LaFeber tells us: "Martinez suddenly became the oligarchy's hero. The bloodbath also changed the mind of Washington officials about the general. Before the slaughter, the State Department had been adamant about nonrecognition. Two weeks later it admitted that "the situation ... is a difficult one. Martinez appears to have strengthened his position ... as a result of having put down the recent disorders." That year, the United States granted the Martinez regime informal diplomatic status, and in 1934 Roosevelt gave formal recognition. LaFeber concludes: "Washington officials preferred military dictatorship to indigenous radicalism" (LaFeber, 1983:73–74).

That preference has continued down to the present day. Since 1979, when a military coup took place and the United States (under the Carter administration) began increasing its military aid, El Salvador has been ruled by a series of military juntas. The elections of 1982 and 1984 were touted by the United States as evidence that reformers had been elected and democracy was on its way, but control by the military was left intact. Between October 1979 and

January 1984, according to the legal office of the Catholic Church in San Salvador, 40,000 people were killed in that nation of 5 million people, and 500,000 became refugees.

The elections have not made any important change in the pattern of mass murders, tortures, disappearances. The 1984 report of Amnesty International (1984:55ff) makes this clear:

> Amnesty International has received regular, often daily, reports identifying El Salvador's regular security and military units as responsible for the torture, "disappearance," and killing of non-combatant civilians from all sectors of Salvadorian society. Such reports have been received with respect to the period following the October 1979 coup, when El Salvador was ruled by a series of governing juntas, as well as for the period since the elections for a Constituent Assembly in March, 1982.

For instance, in the fall of 1984, a Reuters dispatch from the town of Santa Lucia reported the accounts of witnesses that "Salvadoran troops encircled and opened fire on hundreds of unarmed peasants and a small number of armed leftist rebels here during a recent anti-guerilla drive. ..." (*New York Times,* September 15, 1984).

United States support for the El Salvador government did not waver through all this. Indeed, on exactly the same page of the *New York Times* that reported that army attack on civilians (the Roman Catholic Church's legal aid office counted at least 34 dead), there was an Associated Press dispatch: "Secretary of State George P. Shultz certified today that the Salvadoran Government was eligible for continued U.S. military aid because it had made progress in curbing human rights abuses and in other areas."

Does the United States bear any moral responsibility for those activities? In 1982, a former soldier in the El Salvador army testified that U.S. advisers were present at torture sessions conducted by the Treasury Police (*New York Times,* January 11, 1982). In the spring of 1984, it was disclosed that the head of the Treasury Police, Colonel Nicolas Carranza, had been paid $90,000 a year by the CIA for at least five years. The Treasury Police were notorious for their involvement in El Salvador's "death squads." A former official of the country said Carranza was involved in various terrorist acts (*International Herald Tribune,* March 23, 1984). Although the 1980 Arms Export Control Act forbade U.S. advisers from engaging in a combat role, Americans were flying reconnaissance flights from Honduras over El Salvador, U.S. Ambassador Pickering admitted (*Boston Globe,* April 22, 1984).

If "a civilized conception of our own self-interest" is not civilized enough to include the rights to life, liberty, and happiness of the majority of the people in El Salvador, then perhaps there is another rationale for U.S. policy—that the people there are being sacrificed for the benefit of other people in Central America. The premise there would be that the destruction of the revolutionary movement in El Salvador will protect neighboring governments from revolution. That begs the question of whether the neighboring governments are decent and not in need of revolution. Decent governments are hard to find in Central America; indeed, Costa Rica, the only liberal democracy in the region, is not a neighbor of El Salvador, while the countries that are—Guatemala and Honduras—can hardly be considered in good hands.

Guatemala, in particular, for most of the period since the CIA-engineered right-wing coup there in 1954 (see Schlesinger and Kinzer, 1983), has had one of the most brutal dictatorships in the world, and one supported for almost all of this period by the United States. In the fall of 1984, seven years after the Carter administration had suspended military aid due to human rights violations that had become too flagrant to be ignored, the Reagan administration and the Congress "quietly" lifted a seven-year ban on military assistance to Guatemala," according to a Knight–Ridder Service report.

There is another possible argument: that maintaining the present government of El Salvador in power, whatever its faults, is preferable to a rebel victory because, as Jeane Kirkpatrick put it (*Commentary*, November, 1974), "authoritarian" governments like El Salvador are more desirable than "totalitarian" governments, such as Cuba's, because there is a greater likelihood of change toward liberalism in such authoritarian regimes. At the time she presented this notion, Kirkpatrick was criticizing the withdrawal of support by the Carter administration from the Somoza government in Nicaragua and from the Shah in Iran. She compared those two situations to China and Cuba. In all these instances, she wrote, "the American effort to impose liberalization and democratization on a government confronted with violent internal opposition not only failed, but actually assisted the coming to power of new regimes in which ordinary people enjoy fewer freedoms and less personal security than under the previous autocracy—regimes, moreover, hostile to American interests and policies."

So, revolutionary governments of the left are worse than the preceding autocracies. And if we helped keep these autocracies in power, she argues, there would be a better chance for their self-transformation into liberal democracies than if "radical totalitarian regimes" came into being.

Are traditional autocracies preferable, as Kirkpatrick claims, to revolutionary governments, from the standpoint of the lives and liberties of the people living in those countries? I submit that if one were to range throughout the world for examples, only a careful selectivity would lead to a firm conclusion, one way or the other. The evidence is too complex, the contradictions abound: great numbers of people were killed by the Chinese Communists after taking power; how would you measure this against the millions who died of hunger and disease in the old regime? How would you factor in the undeniable evidence that the Communists in China had introduced universal health care, education, and minimal nutrition standards for everyone—all of which did not exist before?

Or take Cuba. Both Castro and Batista put people in jail for dissenting views; yet Castro has unquestionably given a new life to the ordinary Cuban worker or farmer, in terms of available work and social security. And if a very large number of Cubans were dissatisfied enough to emigrate, is that not also true of Puerto Ricans and Haitians, within the U.S. sphere of influence? What of Russia? How compare the horrors of Stalinism with those of Tsarism? For Yugoslavia, the case is easier: no Stalinist bloodbaths, and a better regime for working people than existed under the semi-Fascist regime before the Second World War.

Do Kirkpatrick's favored "authoritarian" governments have a shorter longevity, as she claims, than her despised "totalitarian" governments? The evidence there is not at all clear. The Kissinger Commission (1984:113) itself denies her point: It acknowledges the "systematic use of mass reprisals" by "certain reactionary forces in Central America" and notes that "such reprisals ... have often proved capable of preserving colonial rule and unpopular governments for a very long time, even centuries." The right-wing dictatorship in Portugal lasted at least 40 years, in Spain almost the same length of time. The Somoza dictatorship in Nicaragua lasted 45 years.

True, the Soviet dictatorship has been in existence almost 70 years. But is it true that Communist governments cannot change in a more liberal direction? Post-Stalin Russia under Khrushchev showed the possibilities for change: the elimination of the gulags, mass release of prisoners, elimination of censorship for the foreign press, greater freedom in the arts. Still a repressive regime, but different enough to suggest possibilities for even more change.

Hungary has a much more liberal atmosphere today than it did in its earlier Communist years. The point here is that predictions about change in this century are not easy.

The significance of this uncertainty is huge: it means that one cannot support a present policy of governmental terror on the ground that it is certainly better than what its opponents will install, or that it will evolve into a better situation. It is the very unpredictability of future events, the volatility of societies in the modern world, that should support the powerful moral precept that it is wrong to kill people in the present for some presumed future good.

One wonders whether the concern for change to liberalism is genuine, considering the history of U.S. interventions in which moderate left governments were overthrown and something akin to Fascism installed. The overthrow of the moderately left Arbenz government in Guatemala, of the moderately Marxist Allende government in Chile, to establish terror regimes in both countries (in one case with U.S.–CIA–United Fruit complicity, in the other with U.S.–CIA–ITT complicity) hardly supports the claim of moral concern. What Kirkpatrick inserts in her argument as a minor rationale—keeping out of power those elements "hostile to American interests and policies"—turns out to be her only criterion; the regime preferred by the United States is the one that is "friendly" to this government, whatever it does to its own people.

The pretense to morality in U.S. foreign policy can be tested by the most vivid current cases: those of El Salvador and Nicaragua. There is no doubt that for the U.S. government El Salvador represents the friendly authoritarian government that deserves our help, and Nicaragua the unfriendly totalitarian government that deserves our enmity. But the contrast between these two is sharp, by any measure of concern for human rights. Nicaragua is under the tight control of the left-wing Sandinista government, and there are political prisoners, but there are no death squads killing and torturing large numbers of people. The arming of the general population in Nicaragua suggests large-scale popular support for the government. There is censorship of the press in Nicaragua, but in El Salvador no opposition press is allowed. The editor of *La Prensa* in Managua complains, rightly, of censorship, while the editor of a comparable opposition newspaper in San Salvador, *La Cronica,* was simply taken out of his office, hacked to death with machetes, and left on the street. The Nicaraguan government cruelly displaced the Mesquito Indians from their homeland, presumably for purposes of military defense. But the El Salvador government has not just displaced comparable groups of poor peasants, but slaughtered them. Social reform in El Salvador has failed; social reform in Nicaragua has been extensive.

What of the issue of self-determination, surely a critical moral issue, since the freedom of individuals must include their right to make choices for themselves, and the freedom of associated individuals in a community or a nation–state must include that collective right. Self-determination is much more complex a concept for nations than for individuals. There may be a dispute over what constitutes the *self,* in a country engaged in civil war. There are easy cases and hard ones.

It seems reasonable that a critical factor in this determination is: which side in a civil conflict has popular support? And one good test of this would be: which side, lacking popular support, finds outside aid indispensable? Conversely, which side, enjoying the support of the population at large, finds outside aid useful, but not critical? In the case of Vietnam, the *self* of Vietnam could hardly be represented by the Saigon government, which, by the admission of the U.S. officials, was a U.S. creation, and which had so little popular support that it required a huge U.S. army to fight the war. The same could be said of the Soviet intervention in Afghanistan.

In the case of Central America, the history of that region is so full of military intervention by the United States that no estimate of self-determination today can ignore those episodes. Between 1900 and 1933, the U.S. intervened militarily in Guatemala once, in Nicaragua twice (sending 5,000 marines in 1926 and keeping them there for seven years), in Panama six times (starting with the creation of the state of Panama to get control of the canal), in Honduras seven times. After the Second World War, the interventions continued, there, and in other places in Latin America: Guatemala, Cuba, the Dominican Republic, Chile. That history, while not conclusive for an evaluation of U.S. policy today, must certainly throw some doubt on U.S. claims to be concerned for self-determination in that region.

That doubt becomes very strong when one looks at the actual situations in Central America. Honduras has become a U.S. military staging area, with at least nine military sites and up to 5,000 U.S. troops in continuing maneuvers, creating "a substantial, semi-permanent military capability" in Honduras, according to a congressional staff report of early 1984 (*International Herald Tribune,* January 13, 1984). In the fall of 1984, a long-time observer of Central American affairs, Lucy Komisar, returned from Honduras and told of the Honduran government's embarrassment at

U.S. interference. Local newspapers had reported that the U.S. ambassador met with the Honduran Foreign Ministry to discuss the position Honduras would adopt at the next meeting of the foreign ministers of Central America with the Contadora countries (Mexico, Panama, Venezuela, Colombia). Komisar wrote: "The government issued a lame communique proclaiming that it made its own foreign policy based on patriotic considerations. Yet not a few columnists wondered acidly what the ambassador was doing in a working policy meeting of their Government" (*New York Times,* October 11, 1984).

As for El Salvador, it is hard to claim support for self-determination when the government finds it necessary to resort to mass killing to terrorize an obviously hostile peasant population, whose support for the guerrillas has kept the insurrection alive for years. In Nicaragua, the revolution was enormously popular, and even with the defections of some of the revolutionary leaders, it remains so. The anti-Sandinista rebels have been unable to find a popular base inside the country, where an armed citizenry clearly supports the government, despite great economic hardships. These rebels, to survive, have required considerable U.S. aid, in the form of covert military assistance and CIA activity, and they have become desperate enough, in the face of popular opposition, to attack farmers in the tobacco fields and commit atrocities against civilians (*New York Times,* December 20, 1984). A sign of their desperation, in late 1984, was their use of a CIA-drafted pamphlet urging tactics of deception, blackmail, and assassination (*New York Times,* October 17, 1984).

I have tried to show that the concept of "national interest" has not become "civilized" enough to include the interests of other peoples. We are left, therefore, with the question of whether it refers to the interests of the people of the United States. Does *national* interest mean the life, liberty, and pursuit of happiness of the American people as a whole, or does it really mean the interests of the rich and powerful? Does "survival" mean the physical survival of the people in this country, or the survival of the profits of the hundred giant corporations that dominate our economy? The *self* of the United States is not unitary; as with other nations, it is a divided self, with many interests.

Even if "national interest" were truly national, and "national survival" meant just that, the argument can be made, as Terry Nardin does in his study, *Law, Morality, and the Relations of States,* that our own situation, precious as it is to us, does not warrant doing terrible things to other people. He challenges the common notion that national survival justifies *any* action: ". . . the prospect of being conquered cannot by itself justify measures of defense that make others the victims of injustice" (Nardin, 1983:303).

The technology of modern warfare makes Nardin's word "injustice" a mild one. One would have to substitute "mass slaughter" to be accurate about the means. To be accurate about the end, one would have to replace the misleading word "survival" (because if it were literally true, it would be a matter of trading one mass killing for another) and talk about "being conquered," to use Nardin's language. It is conquest that is the ultimate fear, since neither the Soviet Union nor any other nation would have any motive to destroy the United States (the Soviets would be destroying their own wheat supply, and the ensuing radioactive clouds would threaten the Soviet Union itself).

A morality concerned about human life cannot, Nardin seems to be saying, justify even a "small" war like Vietnam or Korea, in which millions die, just to avoid conquest. A conquered people can build resistance movements; a literature is developing about the concept of "defense without war."[2] There were movements of resistance even in Hitler-occupied Europe, strikes even in Soviet labor camps. Inside the Soviet bloc, there have been enough rebellions, defections, changes, to suggest that conquest still leaves hope; death does not.

There is another consideration. National decisions for war are made by governmental elites, which decide for the entire population that there is an issue worth dying for. The criers of the slogan "Give me liberty or give me death" are usually speaking of their own liberty and someone else's death. In short, the means of warfare are now so horrendous (even in non-nuclear war) as to make dubious any claim for a just or moral war, even for the end of avoiding conquest—that is, for national survival, for the strongest meaning of "national interest."

We can leave Nardin's point to gnat at us. The actual situations confronting us today don't reach the issue of war or conquest, I would argue. Despite the continued use of phrases such as "national defense," "national survival," and so forth, we have not been facing a situation where physical survival as a nation, or conquest by another nation, is a real issue.

Take Vietnam: Did Communist victory in Vietnam threaten conquest for the United States, even by some fantasy of dominoes swimming the Pacific to California? Did even the rubber, tin, oil of Southeast Asia mean, to the richest country in the world, a problem of survival? John F. Kennedy called Vietnam "a strategic piece of real estate," but that made it another piece in the international game of "Monopoly" rather than something vital for the existence of the United States.

Clearly, "national interest," and "national defense" have become phrases that distort all intelligence. They enabled the Soviet Union to invade Czechoslovakia, Hungary, Afghanistan, on the unsupported premise that if these countries were in "unfriendly" hands they would pose a threat to the Soviet Union. They enabled the United States to wage long wars in Korea and Vietnam, having persuaded at least a portion of the population that the national interest was at stake. In none of these cases was there proof of this sufficient to warrant the sacrifice of a single life, let alone hundreds of thousands.

Central America is closer, but can one say that "national interest" is in danger, in the sense of survival, even if Nicaragua or El Salvador become Communist states? What renders common sense inert is the emotionally charged word "Communism," and the accompanying words "Soviet Russia," "Cuba." Those words seem to make unnecessary any rational examination of what this threat consists of. No one can connect the dominoes in any credible sequences to show how one or more Communist victories in Central America can truly threaten the United States.

There is a certain set of facts that throw a powerful doubt on the claim that U.S. policy in Central America is based on stopping a Communist threat linked to the Soviet Union. I am speaking of the history of U.S. intervention in Central America, and in the Caribbean generally, *before 1917,* before there was a Soviet Union. It appears that long before the Bolshevik Revolution, the United States was doing in the Caribbean basically what it is doing today, trying to keep in power authoritarian governments that are "friendly" and using military power against revolutions that threaten those governments.

That history suggests the existence of reasons other than Communism, other than national security, for U.S. intervention. The economic exploitation of Latin America by U.S. corporations surely is one reason. That it is not a relic of the past is shown by the importance of United Fruit in the Guatemala coup of 1954 (McCann, 1976), and the role of ITT in the Chile coup of 1973 (see U.S. Senate, 1975).

One test of the sincerity of concern about a Communist conquest of the United States would be to look at situations in Latin America farther removed than Central America. For instance, Santiago, Chile, is 6,000 miles from Washington, D.C. (but, we

00 miles from Miami). How the Marxist–Social
rnment of Allende in Chile could pose a threat to
es cannot be understood except in some fevered
United States determinedly went about, secretly,
y the charter of the Organization of American
_____ and the charter of the CIA) to support a coup against
Allende, ushering in a reign of terror in Chile that has lasted over a
decade.

The Chilean affair does not prove conclusively that the same
fanaticism is operating in Central American policy, but it hardly
gives us confidence that concern for national security is really at
the heart of U.S. foreign policy. In fact, a supposed Communist
conquest of the United States is never spelled out, never given a
scenario, because if it were attempted it would soon look ridiculous.
The portentous section of the Kissinger Commission report headed
"Strategic Implications for the United States" is not persuasive.
That section speaks of "large stakes in the present conflict in
Central America" and "the direct national security interests of the
United States" and lists these "large stakes":

> A series of developments which might require us to devote large
> resources to defend the southern approaches to the United
> States, thus reducing our capacity to defend our interests
> elsewhere.
> A potentially serious threat to our shipping lanes through the
> Caribbean.
> A proliferation of Marxist–Leninist states that would increase
> violence, dislocation, and political repression in the region.
> The erosion of our power to influence events worldwide that
> would flow from the perception that we were unable to
> influence vital events close to home. (Kissinger Commission,
> 1984:109–11).

Would the United States need "to devote large resources to
defend the southern approaches to the United States" even if all the
countries in Central America were run by Communists? Would all
of them, combined, be able to invade the sourthern United States,
or take over Mexico or the Caribbean Sea, which are the only
"southern approaches"? No invasion of the United States is
conceivable, except as part of a general war with the Soviet Union,
which can only mean nuclear war, which would make invasion
irrelevant and Central America irrelevant.

We are dealing here with frenzy, not fact, hysteria, not
analysis. Indeed, the fears about "southern approaches" and

"shipping lanes" are clearly predicated on war with the Soviet Union, because in this section of the Kissinger report it says that "some 50 percent of the shipping tonnage that would be needed to reinforce the European front and about 40 percent of that required by a major East Asian conflict" would need to go through the Caribbean. To talk about "fronts" in any major war with the Soviet Union or China is surely nonsense. The members of the Kissinger Commission are still fighting the Second World War. We are to support right-wing dictatorships in Central America on the premise that we may be fighting a 1940s war, replete with fronts and shipping lanes, in an era when the major warring powers have 50,000 nuclear weapons in their arsenals.

As for the other worries, about the "proliferation of Marxist–Leninist states that would increase violence, dislocation, and political repression in the region," there is no proof offered. Indeed, it would be hard to show that the existence of Cuba and Nicaragua have added any violence, dislocation, or repression to a part of the world—Latin America—that has suffered from an abundance of all those evils during the century-long predominance of the United States there, and in the absence of Communist states.

The last point about "erosion of our power to influence events worldwide" is also unsupported by any evidence. It begs the factual question: do "perceptions" about U.S. power in Latin America affect U.S. power in other parts of the world? Unquestioned U.S. power in Latin America for that long period of the cherished Monroe Doctrine did not prevent the United States from "losing" China, being stalemated in Korea, being defeated in Vietnam, standing by helplessly while the Soviet Union established and then re-established its control over Eastern Europe. Do such "perceptions" about power in any one part of the globe really have an effect on powerful aspirations of oppressed people who see a need for revolution in another part of the globe?

There is a prior moral question: why should anyone concerned with human rights care about the erosion of U.S. power to influence events, given the record of the use of such power so far. That record shows too many uses of U.S. power for the purpose of establishing or retaining tyrannical and murderous regimes: the Greek intervention of 1947–48, the Korean war of 1950–53, the Iran coup of 1953, the Guatemala invasion of 1954, the long war in Vietnam, the Chilean coup of 1973, the long record of aid to governments all over the world with serious violations of human rights.

The Kissinger Commission fears "proliferation of Marxist–Leninist states," in Central America. Given the record of intra-

Communist rivalry in the world—Sino–Soviet, Yugoslav–Soviet, Sino–Vietnamese, Vietnamese–Cambodian—how can such proliferation suggest a fearsome monolith? All the Central American states together do not match, by the test of proximity, military power, or cohesion, the "threat" of West Germany to the Soviet Union, a threat that is still more a figment of Soviet paranoia than real. Similarly, talk of a proliferation of Communist states in Central America has become an irrational fear held by the most powerful, most geographically unapproachable world power.

The effect of such paranoia on the people of Central America is already evident. But what about the effects on the people of the United States? We might note, in passing, that the general population seems more rational than the political leadership. Public opinion surveys indicate widespread opposition to military intervention in Central America. In January, 1984, a *Washington Post–ABC News* poll showed only 23% in favor of covert aid to the anti-Sandinistas in Nicaragua (*International Herald Tribune*, January 21, 1984).

One effect is the devouring of national resources by the military budget (a $272 billion outlay for fiscal 1985, the rate now being more than a trillion dollars during any four-year presidency and going up). As the resulting huge deficits in the budget threaten economic growth, the first step has been to cut (as Reagan proposed shortly after his 1984 reelection) tens of billions from health, education, and welfare. There are direct effects of such cuts, already appearing in the statistics, on infant mortality, the health and living standards of the elderly, the housing of the poor in the cities, the education of children, the money available to the arts.[3] If morality in foreign policy means that governments must be concerned with "life, liberty, and the pursuit of happiness"—if "national interest" is to be defined in such human terms—then the starving of social programs and the obesity of military programs shows profound immorality.

Another domestic effect of a policy of military intervention in Central America—whether short of war, as by military aid, or actual war—is to endanger freedom of expression, as war atmospheres always do. We have had plenty of solid historical experience with that: the mass jailings of Civil War dissenters without benefit of habeas corpus, the two thousand prosecutions of dissenters in the First World War, the incarceration of Japanese in the Second World War, the blacklists, jailings, loyalty oaths of the cold war, the political trials of the Vietnam era.

The philosophical argument for such repression was supplied

early in the cold-war period by Dean Acheson, in the famous National Security Council report No. 68 of early 1950 (not declassified until 1975). Diplomatic historian Gaddis Smith has pointed out that most studies of this report have emphasized its discussion of the Soviet threat. "They have ignored the philosophical sections, which, although composed with Achesonian elegance, point as did McCarthy toward thought control and intolerance of dissent." In NSC No. 68, Acheson talked of the need to "distinguish between the necessity for tolerance and the necessity for just suppression." Acheson worried about "an excess of tolerance degenerating into indulgence of conspiracy." (Review of David McLellan, *Dean Acheson, the State Department Years.* In The *New York Times Book Review,* September 12, 1976.)

War atmospheres lead to obsessive secrecy, such as the classification, between 1946 and 1954, of 20 million government documents—about 300 million pages—as "top secret," "secret," or "confidential." William G. Florence, retired Pentagon security expert, who helped write the original classification order under Eisenhower, testified in 1971 before the Committee on Government Operations: "Only one-half of 1% of all the information currently classified top secret, secret, and confidential, deserves such protection. ..." (U.S. House of Representatives, 1971).

With increased military aid to Central America and the generally more bellicose attitude of the Reagan administration came more restrictions on foreign travel. Cuba was made off limits, except for certain specialized travelers; visas were denied to certain left-wing foreigners (as to Beatrice Allende, widow of Chile's murdered leader). A National Security Decision Directive of March, 1983, swears any federal employee with access to classified data to life-time secrecy. Such employees must pledge to submit all future writings, even after leaving government service, to prepublication review.[4] Explaining the Reagan administration's decisions to cut back on the collection of statistics, to eliminate hundreds of government publications, to reduce the staff of the National Archives, and to weaken the Freedom of Information Act, Assistant Attorney General Jonathan Rose explained: "Freedom of information is not cost-free, it is not an absolute good" (*New York Times,* November 15, 1982).

I have tried in this chapter to examine the most frequently used shorthand term to justify U.S. foreign policy morally: "national interest." My tests have been Vietnam and Central America. I argue that an enlightened definition of national interest must include two elements. First, it must go beyond national boundaries to grant equal consideration for the rights of people everywhere. Second, it must include the interests of that vast population beyond the political strategists and the corporate elite. That is, it must include the young summoned to fight in war, the general public deprived of national resources in the feeding of the military budget, and the rights of the unborn—yes, the "right to life" of future generations.

NOTES

[1]Hans J. Morgenthau, *In Defense of the National Interest.* N.Y.: Knopf (1951), p. 242; quoted in Cohen (1984).

[2]Boserup and Mack, 1975; see also Michael Walzer's (1977) brief final chapter, and Sharp (1970).

[3]A *Boston Globe* dispatch, May 24, 1984: "Infant mortality, which had been declining steadily in Boston and other cities in the 1970s, shot up suddenly after the Reagan administration reduced grants for health care for mothers and children and cut back sharply on Medicaid eligibility among poor women and children in 1981, according to new research."

[4]See David Burnham's article, *New York Times,* June 14, 1984, on censorship of employees' writings. Also Floyd Abrams article, *New York Times Magazine,* September 25, 1983, "The New Effort to Control Information."

REFERENCES

AMNESTY INTERNATIONAL (1984). *Torture in the Eighties.*

BOSERUP, A., and A. MACK (1975). *War without Weapons.* New York: Schocken.

COHEN, M. (1984). "Moral Skepticism and International Relations." *Philosophy and Public Affairs,* 13:299–346.

GETTLEMAN, M., et al. (1981). *El Salvador: Central America in the New Cold War.* New York: Grove Press.

KISSINGER COMMISSION (1984). *The Report of the President's National Bi-Partisan Commission on Central America.* New York: Macmillan.

LA FEBER, W. (1983). *Inevitable Revolutions.* New York: Norton.

McCANN, T. (1976). *An American Company.* New York: Crown.

NARDIN, T. (1983). *Law, Morality and the Relations of States*. Princeton, N.J.: Princeton University Press.

PENTAGON PAPERS (1971) [Gravel Edition]. Boston: Beacon Press.

SCHLESINGER, S., and S. KINZER (1983). *Bitter Fruit*. Garden City, N.Y.: Doubleday.

SHARP, G. (1970). *Exploring Non-Violent Alternatives*. Boston, Mass.: Porter Sargent.

SIMON, L., and J. STEPHENS, JR. (1981). *El Salvador Land Reform: Impact Audit, 1980–81*. Oxfam–America.

U.S. HOUSE OF REPRESENTATIVES (1971). *Hearings before the Sub-Committee on Government Operations*, 92nd Congress, 1st Session, June–July.

U.S. SENATE (1975). "Covert Action in Chile 1963–1973," *Staff Report of the Select Committee to Study Governmental Operations with Respect to Intelligence Activities*. December 18, 1975 Washington, D.C.: U.S. Government Printing Office, 1976.

WALZER, M. (1977). *Just and Unjust Wars*. New York: Basic Books.

IV

THE FUTURE
OF FOREIGN POLICY
EVALUATION

9

At the Impasse:
Epistemology
and the Scientific Evaluation
of Foreign Policy

Richard K. Ashley

INTRODUCTION

The evaluation of foreign policy, like the evaluation of any sphere or mode of action, is a practical endeavor—an endeavor both historical and social. It must proceed within the horizon of a community, its practical understandings, its symbols, its remembrances, its expectations and dispositions. It must proceed, in other words, within a *discourse* whose historically made structures make possible the differentiation of collective experience, the coordination of interpretive dispositions, the collective application of shared standards, and the production of mutually recognized, generally dependable understandings of the socially experienced world. This is not a matter of choice. There can be no evaluation outside a historical field of discourse or independent of a discourse's normative and normalizing structures. Deprived of its practical involvement in a social discourse, the act of "evaluation" is deprived of social value. It becomes, quite simply, a meaningless exercise.

To speak specifically of the *scientific* evaluation of foreign policy is not to introduce an exception to this general rule. As much as any other way of seeing and saying, approaches to evaluation meriting the label "scientific" must be grounded in the practical understandings and interpretive dispositions of a community and its discourse. To speak of the scientific evaluation of foreign policy is, however, to pose a challenge at once considerable and unique. The challenge inheres in the very special demands upon discourses claiming to be scientific. In order to be worthy of its name, scientific discourse must, as a minimum, satisfy two conditions—two related conditions that so-called "traditional" discourse typically need not satisfy. These may be called the conditions of *detachment* and *openness to criticism and correction.*

First, in contrast to the tradition-bound discourses of everyday participants in global life, scientific discourse effects a radical *detachment* from the primary experience of the social world. Traditional discourse—be it the discourse of, say, traditions of statesmanship, entrepreneurship, military service, journalism, international civil service, or liberal democratic citizenship—involves an unquestioning relationship of familiarity with the familiar world. It is bound up in sets of tacit presuppositions that give the world its self-evident, natural character. It takes for granted the adequacy of the divisions and categories by which social life is organized. It does not question the practical language by which action within those divisions is more or less normally coordinated, narrated, and understood. It does not ask whether these divisions and categories are contingent or necessary, specific or universal, historical or timeless. It merely accepts the social value-commitments implicit in the given practical order. In sharp contrast, scientific discourse presupposes an interpretive standpoint independent of the interpretive norms of the traditional community. It seeks a detached standpoint that breaks from the self-contented, tradition-bound subjectivity of the familiar world—a standpoint outside the hermeneutic circle of traditional belief. From this standpoint, scientific discourse aspires to apprehend the objective relations of society, not as participants do, but in their true paradigmatic coherence. It aspires to distinguish between those historical conditions and patterns that are products of the subjectivity of the given order—and, hence, define the deep value commitments of that order—and those truly objective relations that exist independent of knowledge or will. And it aspires to comprehend the practices by which, and the conditions under which, the familiar experience of the traditional order is made possible or could be transformed.

Second, scientific discourse is distinguished from traditionalist discourse by its *openness,* its commitment to criticism and self-correction, even with respect to its most elementary foundations. In general, competent participation within traditional discourse minimally requires the innocent acceptance of collectively recognized interpretive structures; the active questioning of a community's symbols, norms, values, and practical understandings bears a tinge of heresy, and it invites sanctions, perhaps even banishment from the community. In the case of *scientific* communities, on the other hand, such criticism and questioning is not just acceptable. It is an institutionalized expectation of competent performance. Scientific interpretations, it is generally conceded, cannot rest on a closed circle of consensual beliefs within a scientific community; indeed, they cannot finally come to rest at all. They must instead be continuously open to criticism and revision in the light of experience external to and independent of the discourse of the scientific community itself. It is this unceasing openness to externally grounded criticism, and this alone, that secures scientific interpretations in their claims to objectivity.

Quite evidently, the two characteristics go together. Just as evidently, the characteristics pose a special challenge for the scientific evaluation of foreign policy. The challenge can be phrased in terms of a potential strain between two requisites of a scientific approach to foreign policy evaluation. On the one hand, if it is to claim any significance at all, the evaluation of foreign policy must secure recognition and establish meaning in the context of the normative structures of one or another social discourse. It must preserve its practical relevance, its significance for action within the historical discourse and problematics of participants whose practices are subject to evaluation. On the other hand, if it is to claim the special significance of being a *scientific* evaluation, then the discourse within which it finds its grounding must minimally fulfill the normative conditions just named: it must effect a sharp break from the historically evolved normative structures of the social order whose practices it would examine and evaluate, and it must maintain a posture of openness to criticism and correction in light of external experience.

The potential tension between these two requisites is plain. How can both be satisfied? How can the conditions of scientific discourse be met without producing an approach to evaluation so thoroughly detached, so open to self-reflective criticism and correction, that it refuses direct engagement with the practical commitments and familiar, tradition-bound struggles of women and men, statesmen and entrepeneurs? How, conversely, can immediate practical relevance be achieved without compromising the self-critical openness and detachment that scientific discourse demands? To answer these questions in actual scientific practice—

this is the challenge for the scientific evaluation of foreign policy.

These are not idle questions prompted only by an abstract methodological concern. The challenge they pose is not merely of scholastic interest. Rather, the questions take form in the same context that occasions this volume as a whole: an awareness that the practice of foreign policy, perhaps especially U.S. foreign policy, bears critically on the most significant issues to which social science could possibly speak and, at the same time, a concern that the discourse of social science has yet to fulfill its responsibilities in this regard. The voice of social scientific analysis seems somehow halting, equivocal, unsure of itself. When it is not these things, it too often appears unable to connect with the historical subtleties and nuances of actual foreign policy practice. Worse, when it strikes a relevant chord, it is too often because scientific practice has sacrificed all claim to critical distance, has suspended its involvement in open scientific discourse, and has been reduced to the status of a technology of the state.

The task of this chapter is to offer a diagnosis of this impasse in the scientific evaluation of foreign policy—a diagnosis responsive to the methodological challenge posed just above. My approach to this task is in the form of a narrative. I want to tell a story whose central themes are subversion and redemption, so to speak. I want to tell a story of the subversion and possible redemption of the potentialities of science for the evaluation of foreign policy practice.

The theoretical inclinations of foreign policy analysts, this story suggests, are rich with potential insight into modern dilemmas of international political practice. Recurring arguments and avenues of investigation among scientific analysts exhibit promise of penetrating the self-satisfied practical understandings of international political participants while also speaking directly and forcefully to the value-linked problematics these participants experience. Yet, according to my story, this promise is unfulfilled. The scientific evaluation of foreign policy is at an impasse and can offer no satisfactory resolution to the challenge posed above, because its scientific practices have been subdued within a particular methodological discourse. Its scientific practices have been subordinated to a discourse anchored in liberal positivist understandings of the scientific enterprise—understandings that lay claim to objectivity and neutrality but that in fact bear specific normative commitments that are products of historical struggle. Naturalistic in its understanding of social science, liberal positivist discourse predisposes analysts to a particuar model of international political practice. Far from empty of empirical content, it rules out of order certain avenues of inquiry and criticism. Far from empty of normative content, it reduces the practical significance of scientific argument and criticism to an essentially technical enterprise, namely, the enhancement of the efficiency of means in the service of pregiven ends. In these ways and more, the privileging of liberal positivist interpretations of scientific practice guarantees that the promise of scientific foreign policy evaluation will continue to be unrealized. The challenge alluded to a moment ago will be unanswered.

The theme of promise subverted is complemented by the theme of promise redeemed, however. Liberal positivism, while still predominant, is not the only discourse of scientific practice. Taking heed of recent developments in German "critical theory" and French "poststructuralism," one can speak of a "critical scientific" discourse that is only recently beginning to find applications to international studies.[1] Critical scientific discourse does not conceive of social order on the model of natural order, and it does not comprehend the practical significance of science exclusively, or even primarily, in technical terms. Rather, critical scientific discourse starts from an appreciation of the power of normatively laden epistemic structures—structures of thought, language, and social practice—in the historical constitution of social reality, including the constitution of the subjects of social action, their self-understandings and their effective interests. It acknowledges the role of practice in the historical production and transformation of these epistemic structures. Within such a discourse, scientific evaluation is self-consciously emancipatory in its practical orientation. Knowing itself to be inescapably dependent upon the epistemic structures of society and bound to the normative dispositions embedded in those structures, the critical approach invokes a determination to explore and make plain the historical limits and transformational potential of the epistemic structures upon which historically effective political practice depends. Thanks to this determination, I shall be suggesting, critical scientific discourse makes possible the fulfillment of the promise of scientific foreign policy evaluation. It makes possible the answering of the challenge.

This, then, is the story I want to tell. My telling will proceed through four episodes. First, lest there be any misunderstanding, I want to begin with a rather careful description of liberal positivist discourse and its orienting structures. Second, I shall turn to the scientific study of foreign policy and consider its development within the framework of liberal positivist understandings. Third, I shall offer a brief diagnosis of the consequences. I shall suggest that the liberal positivist subversion of important avenues of argument and criticism accounts for the current impasse in the scientific evaluation of foreign policy. It undermines scientists' abilities to answer the challenge posed a moment ago. Fourth, I shall very briefly highlight the promise of a critical social science of foreign policy, an alternative discourse engaged in rethinking the relation of theory, research, and practice.

LIBERAL POSITIVISM

A reference to "liberal positivist" discourse is more than a little troubling. In part, this is because the word "liberal" and the word "positivism" have taken on a variety of rather definite, sometimes very restrictive meanings in philosophical literatures—often quite opposed meanings. In perhaps larger part, the reference to liberal positivism is troubling because the term has assumed a political cast. As Anthony Giddens (1974:ix) writes, "The word 'positivist,' like the word 'bourgeois,' has become more of a derogatory epithet than a useful descriptive concept, and consequently has been largely stripped of whatever agreed meaning it might once have had."

I want to make my own usage clear. By liberal positivism, I do not mean to refer to one or another formal or self-conscious philosophical school. To suggest that the conventional practice of scientific foreign policy studies occurs within a liberal positivistic discourse is not to indicate that it is founded on foreign policy analysts' contortions of philosophical reflection, let alone the careful reading of, say, Vienna School arguments. Nor is it to insinuate that scientific foreign policy studies are in the main "regime supportive," that they involve "mindless number crunching" or "brute empiricism," or that they are deserving of any of the other dismissive charges often implied by the word "positivism."

Instead, quite in keeping with modern sociological usage,[2] liberal positivism here refers to a kind of practical paradigm, if you will. It here refers to a structured set of more or less habitual interpretive dispositions, metaphors, and preconceptual commitments that social scientists learn through practice, that orient their interpretations of themselves and their actions, that limit their discourse, and that thereby circumscribe the range of collectively imaginable scientific possibility. By liberal positivism I mean to refer to habitual cognitive structures that can be grasped, not as consciously preconceived rules or as formal methodological doctrine, but in the objective coherence of the scientific practices that these structures generate.

In order to understand this "paradigm," it is useful to begin with the practical dispositions of positivism in general. Then it will be possible to understand liberal positivism as a specific form of positivist discourse worked out in response to the antinomies of positivist science in modern society.

Positivism in General

Perhaps the most general characteristic of positivistic scientific discourse is its commitment to the "received model" of *natural* science (Giddens, 1979:257). Positivist social science, it must be stressed, is not a copy of *actual* practice in the natural sciences. It is, instead, committed to the realization in social scientific discourse of a particular *model* of natural scientific practice: a widely shared and practically effective interpretation that implicates science's relation to nature and science's practical socal significance. One may say that positivist social science is committed to a "naturalistic model" of scientific practice.

This naturalistic model has many variants, but its main features can be sketched in terms of five commitments. It can be introduced, that is, in terms of five *interpretive dispositions* that together structure the scientific practice, including collective understanding of scientific possibilities, within a positivistic community (see Ashley, 1983a):

1. The disposition to comprehend and practice science as an enterprise aiming to grasp an external reality—a reality obeying certain fixed structures or causal relations that exist independent of the historical discourse in which science is actively engaged. Since these fixed structures and causal relations are, like natural objects, said to exist independent of human subjectivity, volition, and history (including the development of scientific knowledge), they are said to be objective. This disposition might be called the "externality of social reality" disposition.
2. The disposition to understand sought-after structures or causal relations as obeying a singular, contradiction-free logic of universal compass—as if all science anticipated an ascent to a vantage point from which all history resolves

itself into a single thematic unity. Reality is expected to appear, in other words, as if it were authored and harmoniously interpretable from a single, central viewpoint in time and space. This disposition might be called the "singularity of structure" disposition; it says that social reality obeys a unity of logical order, independent of history, that science aspires to uncover.

3. The disposition to grasp scientific method, and the knowledge it makes possible, as inherently apolitical and value-neutral. Since science and its method aspire to knowledge of extra-historical structures and relations that are independent of subjectivity, will, and human values, scientific knowledge and scientific method are inherently neutral with respect to the value-linked struggles of political life. Insofar as science takes a side, positivism is disposed to see science on the side of enlightenment and the march of human progress as over against darkness and the stifling influence of tradition, ideology, and myth. This is the "value neutrality" disposition. Thanks to scientific enlightenment, the story goes, women and men will discover their true values and interests, previously obscured by mystery and myth, and will transcend the false values, the false conflicts, perpetuated by prescientific understanding.

4. The disposition to understand, gauge, and evaluate science's contribution to human betterment primarily, if not exclusively, in terms of its production of technically useful knowledge, that is, knowledge that enhances human capacities to make predictions, orient efficient action, and exert control over an objective reality in the service of human values. Science finds its legitimacy, on this interpretation, primarily in technical terms, in terms of its enhancement of the efficiency of means in the service of pregiven ends. Only in an indirect, advisory sense can science speak to questions of practical interaction. Focusing as it does upon the grasping of an extra-subjective reality, a positivistically conceived science cannot comprehend social interaction as a potentially creative, potentially reflective process of mutual interpretation and consensus-seeking among plural subjects against the background of a community or tradition. This is the "technical cognitive interest" disposition.

5. The disposition to define and value the truth of scientific discourse, and to focus the exchange of scientific criticism and correction, primarily in terms of the correspondence of knowledge claims to a reality understood as external to scientific discourse itself. While positivistic discourse seeks consensus, in other words, it is predisposed to a mode of

discourse that would make consensus dependent primarily upon technical criteria of fit. It makes consensus derivative of fit between scientific discourse and an extra-scientific reality that is taken to be extrasubjective and, hence, incapable of discursive interaction with science itself. This might be called the "truth as correspondence" disposition.[3]

Such interpretive dispositions readily situate positivist science in relation to other modes and styles of thought and practice. Inspecting these dispositions, one can quickly catch glimpses of the Enlightenment anticipation of the universalization of reason, of the liberal expectation of harmony and progress, of the Industrial Revolutionary faith in science as a font of power over nature. One can glimpse, too, the distrust of tradition and corresponding readiness to devalue phenomenological interpretation. All in all, these glimpses suggest, positivist dispositions reflect a particular tradition or culture: they are distinctly *modern* in their attitudes.

Two Historical Antinomies

Still, for all the apparent coherence of these modern attitudes, the naturalistic inclinations of positivist science are not altogether unproblematic in the context of modern society. Two antinomies in particular merit notice: One is the antinomy of positivistic naturalism versus liberalism; the other is the antinomy of positivistic naturalism versus subjectivism. We need to pay particular attention to these two antinomies, not only because of the contradictions they reveal, but also because they help us to understand an additional interpretive disposition that distinguishes the strain of *liberal* positivism. They help us to understand the interpretive disposition established by virtue of liberal positivism's need to resolve the antinomies in practice. Let us consider each of these two antinomies in turn.

The first opposition, between *naturalism and liberalism,* can be understood with reference to their common roots in the struggles of bourgeois society. On the one hand, liberalism, as the philosophical voice of the bourgeoisie, grew up in opposition to and as the critique of institutionalized absolutist privilege. As such, it is oriented toward the legitimation and defense of the possessive individual and his essentially private (and market- or ballot-mediated) decisions as the ultimate register of social value and social authority—an authority prior to the state and from which, according to this philosophy, the state derives its authority. On the other hand, and at the same time, the commodification and urbanization of bourgeois life, together with the breakdown of traditional authority, did more than create the social space for the expansion of the institution of an autonomous "economy." It produced for the first time a form of social existence recognizable as the "masses"—society as a heap or aggregate of individuals. This set before the state problems of legitimation (to which modern nationalism is arguably a response) and unprecedented problems of social management and discipline. This also produced a condition wherein society as a whole, atomized and deprived of the tradition-based intersubjective foundations of practical interaction, could be analyzed naturalistically—as if it were governed by objective relations, independent of social consciousness and will. It was in answer to the political management problems of bourgeois society that positivistic social science evolved. It was the practical atomization of social life, set against the background of the Industrial Revolution and its mechanical metaphors, that made room for positivism and its naturalistic interpretations of social scientific practice.

Yet the contradiction is plain. If positivist social science, as a project and in its naturalistic rules of knowledge-constitution, sets out to enhance social prediction and control in the service of improved state management of mass society, the same project is potentially a threat to the liberal concept of society, with its privileging of individual freedom. With the growth of the modern state, this antinomy sharpened. Just this antinomy, for instance, was central to Weber's problematic of the basis in legitimate authority for rationalized bureaucratic power (Giddens, 1979: 146–48; see also Giddens, 1972). The same antinomy reappears in Popper's (1966) arguments centering on the "open society," including his fears of historicism as he understood it. As Weber and Popper sensed, there are totalitarian implications in viewing society, like nature, as the singular object of some singular set of contradiction-free laws to which a naturalistic social science supposedly gives privileged and extrademocratic access. Such a view, carried to its logical end, threatens to put the lie to the legitimating principles of liberal democracy.

How is such an antinomy to be resolved? One response, typified by Weber, was to urge the development and maintenance of an independent parliament capable of checking the power of a scientifically rational bureaucracy. Another response, typified by Popper, is addressed more directly to the scientific method itself. As

Popper understood the problem, only by interposing upon social science certain limiting principles—the principles of antihistoricism, piecemeal social engineering, methodological individualism, and the limited hermeneutics of situational rationality, to name four—can the concept of the open society be preserved against the anti-individualist tendencies present in science on the model of natural science. Of these, the commitment to methodological individualism is key. For Popper (1966, Vol. 2:98), methodological individualism amounted to the principle that "all social phenomena, and especially the functioning of all social institutions, should always be understood as resulting from the decisions, actions, attitudes, etc. of human individuals. ... [W]e should never be satisfied by an explanation in terms of so-called 'collectives.'" In other words, if it is the essentially private individual that is endangered by positivist science, then it is the subjectivity of just this individual, and his or her individual decisions, that must occupy the unchallenged and privileged center of positivist science. The individual is the true subject of history, on this account, and individual decisions must be the lens through which history is comprehended.

This disposition is reinforced and further elaborated by the habitually imposed resolution of the second antinomy, the antinomy of *naturalism and subjectivism*. This antinomy inheres in the fact that social life, which positivistic social science is disposed to approach as an *object* not unlike objects in the natural world, is evidently constituted by the actions and interactions of human *subjects* who themselves interpret their worlds, attach meaning to themselves and their circumstances, and evidently alter their practices in light of their interpretations. How can the objectivating dispositions of positivist science be reconciled with the subjective aspects of the social existence? How can social science make room for the question of meaning in social life—itself a matter of subjective interpretation—and still preserve science as an enterprise capable of producing calculable, objective results that enhance prediction and control? How can social science preserve its objectivity and detachment, given that scientists themselves—in the terms they use, their own horizons of understanding, and the social possibilities they can imagine—are potentially bound up in the normative structures that orient the attachment of social meaning, the signification of action, and even the production of social reality?

As it turns out, this second antinomy, like the first, finds its resolution in a commitment to individual decisions as the interpretive center of history. More specifically, it finds its resolution in an unequivocal commitment to technical rational decisions and actions as an essentially objective practical frame: a value-neutral framework, devoid of normative content and independent of culturally variable subjective structures. According to this resolution, technical rational decisionmaking constitutes the universally valid framework for the scientific interpretation of social action, a framework that can be adopted without compromising science's claim to objective detachment (see Ashley, 1984:248–54).

Technical rational action, it can be quickly observed, is means–ends rational action. It is a mode of action that presupposes an unproblematically given individual subject having unambiguously defined values or ends and having definite, uncontested boundaries separating it from its environment. It involves the individual subject's attempts to define problems in terms of a gap between actual and desirable conditions (where these conditions are external to the boundaries of the subject). And it involves the subject's attempts to manipulate and control aspects of its environment—means—in the interest of producing desirable outcomes—ends (Ashley, 1983b:474–76).

It can easily be seen that this commitment to the objectivity of technical rationality offers a resolution to the antinomy of naturalism versus subjectivism. Consider first of all the problem of maintaining a naturalistic social science—a science capable of generating predictable and controlled results—given that human action is subjective in character and depends upon the meanings that participants attach to their circumstances and actions. If, facing this problem, one can assume that all interpretation can come to rest with individual decisions, and if one can assume that individual choices proceed in the framework of technical rationality (as just outlined), then one can make an additional assumption that permits the scientist to dismiss the question of intersubjective meaning structures, the conditions of their social recognition, and the practices by which they evolve. One can say that from the scientifically objective vantage point of the individual decision-making subject, society *cannot* appear as a meaningful horizon of more or less continuous intersubjective interaction in which the subject's own boundaries, identifying structures, values, and competency to act are forever problematic, open to question, and always potentially transformed. Since the framework of technical rationality dictates that the subject must be an unproblematically given agent existing prior to and independent of society, one must regard society as a subjectless set of external constraints, a meaningless "second nature" on a par with the physical environment. In turn, this allows one to conclude that meaning enters social reality primarily through the autonomously generated values of individually acting subjects. Meaning enters, that is, through motivated technical rational decisions and action (see Giddens, 1974:5). Such a commitment, one can quickly see, allows an immediate reconciliation of naturalistic science with the question of meaningful social action. Since meaningful action is, on this view, merely motivated action, the interpretation of meaningful action and the causal analysis of objective relations are one and the same: with knowledge of a subject's pregiven ends, together with the supposedly meaningless social constraints that the subject confronts, the analyst can grasp the meaning of social action while at the same time rendering social action calculable, predictable, and susceptible to causal accounts.

Consider, too, the related problem of preserving scientific objectivity and detachment despite the possible entangling of scientists' norms and values with the norms and values at work in the social world examined. Again, the commitment to the essential objectivity of technical rational actions offers an answer. If the framework of technical rational action is inherently objective and value-neutral, then to the degree that scientific discourse itself can be confined to this action framework, its own objectivity and value-neutrality can be insured. Science's claim to objectivity and detachment can be preserved so long as two conditions are met. One is that scientific discourse is confined to the process by which the validity of scientific concepts and knowledge claims may be decided—a process wholly within the objective framework of technical rational action. The second condition is the exclusion from scientific discourse of the value-laden, meaning-expressive process by which scientists take interest in, generate, or come to recognize as valuable or significant the concepts, knowledge claims, or fields of inquiry. The objectivity of scientific discourse can be preserved, put succinctly, by excluding from its responsibility all questions that defy formulation and answering within the framework of technical rational action (Ashley, 1984:253).

Liberal Positivism

Taken together, the two antinomies and the resolutions associated with them point to an additional interpretive disposition of considerable significance, which, when added to the five dispositions discussed earlier, defines a particular strain of positivist thought, liberal positivism. In resolving the antinomy of naturalism versus liberalism, we have seen, positivism exhibits a commitment to methodological individualism. In resolving the antinomy of naturalism versus subjectivism, we have seen, positivism exhibits a commitment to the objectivity of technical rationality as an interpretive frame, both in the examination of social action and in asserting the objectivity of science itself. When the two commitments are taken together, *they describe a doubly reinforced disposition to interpret all history and all scientific practice through the lens of technical rational decisions on the parts of pregiven individual agents whose identities, values, and ends are independent of society.*

This interpretive disposition, present in the liberal positivist resolution of the two antinomies, is not an *explicit* model in the consciously deliberated sphere of theoretical discourse. Rather, among most liberal positivists, this interpretive disposition has assumed almost a *methodological* status. It is seen to be value-neutral, normatively empty, and devoid of theoretical content—an unspoken set of presuppositions equated with being scientific in international studies. Yet it is important to note that, in fact, the disposition bears considerable theoretical and normative content. It, in fact, commits liberal positivist social science to a specific *implicit* model of social reality—a model that profoundly limits the range of social possibilities that scientific discourse can imagine and the range of criticisms scientific discourse can entertain.

In brief, the implicit model is this: The autonomously motivated decisions of individual pregiven agents occupy the center and constitute the focal point of analysis, the interpretive point of entry and the coming-to-rest point of scientific explanation. The individual agents—including their wants, needs, interests, defining structures, boundaries, and self-understandings—are taken to be the true subjects of history, the true registers of social value. They are taken to have existences independent of the larger social whole, including one another, and society is regarded as an emergent property to be approached from the interpretive starting point of individual choice under constraints. Subjectivity, then, is essentially a psychological (that is, individualistic) matter. Action is seen as a matter of rational action, that is, technical rational action. By contrast, social structures are taken to be external to the individual agent, its wants, needs, and boundaries; and since they cannot be immediately changed to reflect the subjective dispositions of individual actors, they appear to be extrasubjective constraints. They are granted the status of objective structures. They are understood to appear before the agent as a kind of natural phenomenon, that is, as external limits existing independent of the knowledge and will of human beings. As for history, it is to be grasped as a serial development of technical rational decision episodes, their aggregate effects and emergent systemic properties, and the production of constraints on subsequent technical rational decisions.

The same implicit model can also be understood in terms of what it leaves out or denies. Most importantly, it excludes reflection on the problematic social constitution of the individual rational agents it puts at the center of its analysis. Reducing subjectivity to an atomized psychological relation, it disables all reflection on the historical processes and practices by which women and men participate in the production and transformation of normative social structures, organize their practices, and coordinate their investments of social resources. It disallows all reflection on the intensely political processes by which women and men struggle to produce, transform, or subvert the collectively recognized interpretive structures, categories, and narratives within which socially competent subjects find their meaning, secure recognition, assume their values, and are thus historically constituted and empowered to act in a socially effective manner.

LIBERAL POSITIVISM AND THE SCIENTIFIC STUDY OF FOREIGN POLICY

Such limitations should not be allowed to obscure the evident attractions of liberal positivist discourse for social scientists interested in examining and evaluating international political practice. On the face of things, the interpretive dispositions of liberal positivism would seem to promise a workable answer to the challenge of scientific foreign policy evaluation posed earlier. By committing themselves to these interpretive dispositions, scientists would seem to be able to undertake examinations of foreign policy that find practical meaning by virtue of their centering on the value-expressive decisions of individual technical rational subjects. The same commitments, once made, would seem to guarantee scientists' detachment and objectivity vis-à-vis the world they study. Scientists can, for instance, express their deeply felt social values in deciding the subject matter for their studies so long as these values are held to be prior to scientific discourse and so long as scientific discourse itself develops within the rubric of technical rational action.

It would be an understatement to suggest that this promise has not gone unnoticed among North American students of foreign policy. It would be far more accurate to say that for self-consciously scientific analysts of foreign policy, liberal positivist discourse seems to exhaust imagination as to what science could possibly be. It appears to be the only discourse worthy of the name "science."

This commitment to the interpretive dispositions of liberal positivism exerts a powerful discipline over analysts of foreign policy. To be scientific is, in this view, to conform to and express the interpretive dispositions of liberal positivism. It is to heed collectively recognized ideals by giving these interpretive dispositions decisive weight in shaping and limiting the development of scientific discourse. Conversely, to stray from those dispositions is to call into question one's own scientific credentials. To defy conspicuously these dispositions is to invite doubts as to one's worthiness as a continuing partner in the scientific enterprise.

This is a sweeping claim. Quite evidently, its merits as an interpretive hypothesis cannot be conclusively demonstrated in a few pages. It is possible, however, to offer a few examples of liberal positivism's disciplinary status: its status as the conventional discourse whose norms dscipline the practice of scientific foreign policy analysis.

The Naturalistic Bias
of Scientific Foreign Policy Studies

Consider, first of all and most generally, the naturalistic bias of positivist social science, and compare that with the naturalistic tendencies of most self-consciously scientific students of foreign policy. James N. Rosenau, perhaps the leading figure in North American foreign policy studies over the last two decades, is exemplary in this respect. Writing in 1979, Rosenau offered the following view:

> As a focus of study, the nation–state is no different from the atom or the single cell organism. Its patterns of behavior, idiosyncratic traits, and internal structure are as amenable to the process of

formulating and testing hypotheses as are the characteristics of the electron or the molecule.

To be sure, the behavior of atoms may be more easily assessed than that of nation–states, with the result that an enormous discrepancy exists between physics and foreign policy from a science-as-subject perspective. In terms of science-as-method, however, the two are essentially the same. Both require the analyst to specify units of analysis, to identify relevant variables, to operationalize key concepts, to frame testable propositions, to gather quantified data, to evaluate the patterns formed by the data, and to revise the propositions in light of the findings (Rosenau, 1980b:32).

Not all social scientists make so bold as Rosenau on this issue, to be sure. Yet the naturalistic bias asserts itself time and again. It asserts itself, for instance, in McGowan's (1976:218) references to scientists' philosophical commitment to a unity of scientific method. It is exhibited yet again in foreign policy analysts' readiness to model their enterprise on a metaphor to philosophers' and historians' reconstructions and standards of natural scientific practice (from the so-called covering law model to a disposition on behalf of hypothetico-deductive logic). And, perhaps most compellingly, the commitment to positivist naturalism is evident in foreign policy analysts' habitual exercise of the five interpretive dispositions of a naturalistic model of social science, as discussed earlier.

The first of these interpretive dispositions, it will be recalled, refers to the externality of the social reality addressed by social science in its knowledge claims. This disposition has done much to structure scientific discourse on foreign policy: in the course of its development, that discourse has found its direction in reflection of the tacit expectation that the collective task is to establish a reliable intersubjective consensus about patterns, regularities, laws, structures, or properties that exist external to, and hence independent of, the scientific discourse itself. The disposition is seldom made explicit, it is true. Yet it makes its presence felt in at least three ways:

1. The disposition is implicit in scientific analysts' physicalistic images of cumulation in theoretical knowledge. Harold Guetz-kow's (1950) often invoked image of "building bridges among islands of theory," for example, envisages a two-step process in which (1) scientists validly grasp aspects or sectors of social reality and then (2) uncover causal linkages or patterned

relations among them. Yet such a conception itself presupposes that the differentiation of social aspects or sectors to which "islands of theory" refer is not itself dependent upon science's complicity in the fragmentation of practical knowledge (e.g., the scientific ritualization of social divisions by way of maintaining disciplinary divisions of social scientific labors).

2. The disposition is implicit in statistical methods, with their presupposition of fixed population parameters generating observables.

3. Most generally, the disposition makes its presence felt in social scientists' systematic failure to question or criticize the role of their discourse—its presuppositions, normative structures, implicit values, and socially inscribed limits—in the historical constitution of the patterns, regularities, laws, structures, and properties they address as the objects of their inquiry. More pointedly, it makes its presence felt in the specific tendency to interpret such questioning and criticism, when it occurs, as so much philosophy, ideology critique, or metaphysical speculation, but never as a true part of scientific discourse.

The second disposition discussed earlier is the tendency to interpret social reality as singular in the logical order—the structures or lawful regularities—it obeys. Where this disposition prevails, scientific practice proceeds in anticipation of a unique vantage point from which all history, in all its diversity, resolves itself into a single contradiction-free thematic unity, as if authored from one rational and unambiguous point of view. This is the mythic standard of knowledge to which all aspire. It is the mythic standard to which Rosenau (1980c:23) refers when he writes that "To think theoretically one must be able to assume that human affairs are founded on an underlying order." Among scientific students of foreign policy, this disposition may not always seem immediately apparent. Scientific analysts who share liberal principles are, in fact, inclined publicly to disown expectations of determinism that this disposition might seem to imply. The fact remains, though, that in their aspiration to depict global life in terms "a general theory that encompasses middle-range theories and a host of generalizations" (McGowan and Shapiro, 1973:26), scientific foreign policy analysts bespeak a readiness to interpret the variety of international political life in terms of a universally applicable, logically consistent, and context-independent language. In their inclinations to believe, with Chittick and Jenkins (1976:282), that "comparative analysis is an essential part of the scientific method," they bespeak a readiness to approach international life as if its scientifically interesting aspects were necessarily comprehensible in terms of universally interconvertible terms and standards of comparison.

The third disposition involves the tendency to interpret scientific method, and the knowledge it makes possible, as inherently apolitical and value-neutral. The commitment is deeply held. Patrick McGowan's (1975:74) assessment, published over a decade ago, exemplifies this commitment:

> The private values of the researcher or the public values of his employer invariably influence his choice of problems to research. To the extent that his empirical findings relate to policy issues, they can have an impact on public values. If the student of foreign policy has a scientific orientation to his subject, he is aware of this role of values in research. Just because of this he adopts scientific procedures in order to reduce as far as possible the chance that his or anyone else's values will influence his findings. That this can or should be done is open to some dispute, but responsible scholarship which aims at establishing reliable knowledge must eschew the clamor for relevancy if this means allowing personal or public values to predetermine research results. Students of the problems involved also conclude that a scientific approach to human behavior can reduce to negligible levels the role of preferences and values in determining findings.

The fourth interpretive disposition associated with the naturalist tendencies of positivist science expresses the "technical cognitive interest," the dispositon to understand science's social value primarily in terms of its production of technically useful knowledge.[4] The aim and social justification of science, according to this disposition, is to produce reliable knowledge that disabuses actors of tradition-bound ideologies and myths, and that reliably informs them of the probable consequences of their actions so that they might perform efficiently, avoid objective obstacles, and avail themselves of objective means in the service of human ends. Such an interpretation is evident among scientific foreign policy analysts. It is expressed, for instance, in the shared inclination to develop causal explanations, especially causal explanations that locate manipulable independent variables. It is plainly at work in the following lines from Bruce Russett and Harvey Starr's (1981:35) excellent text:

> We must depend on many ways of knowing that are not scientific, since there are not enough resources to do all the

desirable science. Yet we must also know when to suspect what passes as ordinary knowledge, when to question it, and how to supplant or supplement it by scientific knowledge when needed. Social science should be directed at key points of inquiry where ordinary knowledge is suspected to be wrong and where the consequences of being wrong would be serious.

Because so much of what we know is ordinary knowledge, we must be wary of accepting it too confidently. People long ago were sure the world was flat. It is easy to become complacent about what we think we know. Dr. Benjamin Spock begins his world-renowned book, *Baby and Child Care,* with the words, "You know more than you think you do." Maybe so, but in world politics, the opposite is sometimes true: you know less than you think you do. Political decision makers take actions every day that determine the happiness and the lives of millions of people. They do not always know what the effects of their acts will be, nor do their advisors. While recognizing that action is necessary, it is important to retain a sense of humility about the knowledge base of our actions. In addition, it is essential to be very self-conscious about the basis, in logic and/or evidence, of the propositions that guide our acts and our advice.

The fifth interpretive disposition, it will be remembered, bears the name "truth as correspondence." This is the disposition to comprehend and value the truth of scientific discourse primarily in terms of its fit or correspondence to a reality regarded as an objective, external referent of that discourse. Among students of international politics, a perhaps extreme expression of this position is J. David Singer's (1969:65) statement that "knowledge cannot be said to exist—and certainly cannot be codified or accumulated—without data." Yet most scientific students of international political practice would agree with Charles McClelland's (1969:5) view: if the first step of a scientific approach is "the constructing of testable hypotheses," the "second step involves the task of showing whether a hypothesis fits observable facts." The sentiment of Jones and Singer (1972:3–4) would be widely applauded:

> Whether we seek to understand the past or anticipate the future, we need something more than vague recollections or a vivid imagination. We need evidence. Without evidence, there is little basis for selecting among the contending (and often equally plausible) models and explanations of the international politics we have experienced, and until we can adequately account for the past and present, our predictions of the future will remain mere conjecture.

The Sixth Interpretive Disposition:
Practice as Technical Rational Action

The examples so far all relate to the interpretive dispositions of positivist science in general. Of themselves, they do little to suggest that the scientific study of foreign policy conforms to the sixth disposition, an interpretive disposition expressly associated with the *liberal* strain of positivist method. This is the disposition to grasp all history and all social practice in terms of a particular subjective vantage point: the subjectivity of technical rational decisions on the part of pregiven individual actors whose identities, boundaries, values, and ends are all defined independent of society and its historical development. To what extent is the scientific study of foreign policy disciplined by a shared commitment to this interpretive disposition? To what extent is it bound to the implicit model of social practice (discussed earlier) generated by this disposition? The answer, in brief, is "to a very large extent." The scientific study of foreign policy has, indeed, obeyed this interpretative disposition and has, indeed, conformed to the model it implies.

That this is so can be seen, once again, by way of a number of examples:

The influential formulation by Snyder, Bruck, and Sapin (1962) typifies the interpretive disposition and explicates one possible variant of the implicit model. Their analytical scheme of a "decision-making" approach to international politics centers on the notion of "the state as actor in a situation." Justifying their position in terms of "analytical convenience" and not their preferences, the authors locate the nation–state as "the significant unit of political action," and as one of their "basic methodological choices" they define the state as its official decision-makers, i.e., "those acting in the name of the state." These decision-makers are the central subjects of Snyder, Bruck, and Sapin's analytic perspective—the subjective lens through which analysts would peer in their attempts to arrive at meaningful accountings of international politics. Action is defined in terms of actors, their goals, means, and situations. International politics is taken to consist of "planful" actions and interactions among multiple actors, each one of which defined in terms of its decision-makers, and each one of which relates to others as part of its situation.

The preface to Rosenau's (1969:xviii) reader, his widely assigned *International Politics and Foreign Policy,* described the

organization of the book and, with it, the organization of the field
as follows:

. . . [T]he book continues to be organized in such a way as to
concentrate on both the *actions* and the *interactions* of the
actors who comprise the international system . . . [M]ost of the
work in the field falls under either of these two foci. One group
of theorists and researchers are interested in discerning
regularities in the behavior of actors, in the common goals
that are sought, in the means and processes through which the
goal seeking behavior is sustained, and in the societal sources
of the goals and means selected. In other words, the members
of this group are concerned with the study of *foreign policy,*
and they tend to regard the condition of the international
system at any moment in time as stemming from the foreign
policy actions of nation–states. A second group of theorists and
researchers are mainly concerned with the patterns that recur
in the interactions of states, in the balances and imbalances
that develop under varying circumstances, in the formation of
coalitions and other factors that precipitate changes in the
international system, and in the development of supranational
institutions that might regulate one or another aspect of the
international system. Stated differently, adherents of this
approach are concerned with the study of *international
politics,* and they tend to view the condition of the international system at any moment in time as stemming from
properties of the system that require conforming behavior on
the part of its national components.

One of the persistent themes among self-consciously scientific analysts of international affairs—a theme explicitly
pronounced and implicitly replicated in the organization of
countless textbooks and graduate seminars—is that the field
can properly be comprehended in terms of discrete "levels of
analysis." J. Davi Singer's (1961) distinction among levels is
certainly illustrative. What is especially important to note is
that Singer's levels, like those of other authors, are not treated
as problematic: they are pre-given boundaries that define the
limits of modes of analysis. Implicitly, they take for granted,
and exclude from the sway of scientific analysis and criticism,
the historical production of the effective boundaries that
separate national from international, define actors in contra-
distinction to their environments, and, hence, distinguish his
analytic levels.

Among scientific analysts of foreign policy, one of the most
widely favored conceptions of the "international systemic" level
of analysis—regarded by many as exemplary—is the formulation
put forward by Kenneth Waltz (1979). As is well known, Waltz

specifically declares himself in reaction against "reductionist" models of international politics; and so, it might seem that foreign policy analysts, in approving Waltz's formulation, depart sharply from any alleged tendency to see the social whole as a property emerging from the rational decisions of individual actors. However, while it is true that Waltz's formulation is not built up from the assemblage of the *idiosyncratic* features of nation–states and their leaders, the fact remains that Waltz's formulation is founded on a "microeconomic" conception of state action that reinforces rather than challenges foreign policy analysts' disposition to interpret international political practice as rational action on the part of the individual actors. As I have elsewhere pointed out, Waltz's "structuralism" is characterized by its *failure* to call into question the (possibly systemic) constitution of states and their spokespersons as agencies competent to act (see Ashley 1984:240–42, 254–61).

McGowan (1975:53) speaks for many when he defines foreign policy behavior as "the official behavior of the authorities of states that aims to control the behavior of other authorities beyond the jurisdiction of the acting state for the purpose of adapting the national state in an optimal fashion to its external environment." For purposes of analysis, these words suggest, the scientific student of foreign policy leaves unexamined the historical strategies and normative structures that orient social practice, discipline opposition, defeat opposing ordering principles, secure the consensual basis and boundaries of rule, and thereby produce the state, its authoritative agents, and its effective jurisdiction as historically effective parties.

Among scientific analysts of foreign policy, perhaps the most valued and relied upon data types are events data, a fact that suggests two points. First, in view of the "who does what to whom and when" orientation that characterizes the coding of international events, events data analysis is predisposed to interpret international political practice as a series of context-independent acts (collapsible, for example, into an unambiguous categorical scheme or singular scale), undertaken by univocal actors, and directed unambiguously toward certain discrete targets. Second, events data analysis is disposed to render history as a series of action episodes, each one of which can be discretely defined and assigned its meaning, and the several of which describe history according to certain causal interconnections or rules of aggregation among these elements.[5]

In his famous "Pretheory" article, James N. Rosenau (1980a:119) lamented the fact that "foreign policy analysis is devoid of general theory." Yet his diagnosis, stated more fully, seems to reflect a commitment to the intepretive disposition to grasp social reality in terms of the technical rational choices of individual actors under constraints. "[F]oreign policy analysis lacks comprehensive systems of testable generalizations that treat societies as actors subject to stimuli which produce external responses," he writes. Later he adds that "The stimuli which produce external behavior must be processed by the value and decision-making systems of a society, so that it ought to be possible ... to link up varying types of responses with varying types of stimuli" (Rosenau 1980a:123).

In one of the most widely known critiques of the state-as-rational-actor conception, Graham Allison (1971:3–4, 5) has persuasively argued that "Professional analysts of foreign affairs ... think about problems of foreign and military policy in terms of largely implicit conceptual models that have significant consequences for the content of their thought." Suggesting that the "Rational Actor" Model ("Model I") needs "to be supplemented, if not supplanted, by frames of reference that focus on the governmental machine," Allison offers his Model II (organizational process) and Model III (bureaucratic politics). Of the latter two, strikingly, it has been the bureaucratic politics model that has captured the most attention in subsequent work. Yet, as described by Allison and as practiced by analysts learning from him, this model does not in fact dispense with the disposition to interpret foreign policy in terms of the actions and interactions of individual actors. What it does do, so to speak, is push down the level at which the individual actor, as a well-bounded, purposive, and technical rational entity, is located: from the level of the state as a whole, with its supposed national interests, to the level of the bureaucracy, with its bureaucratic interests. Consistent with liberal positivist interpretive dispositions, the larger whole, i.e., the state and its policies, are rendered as emergent properties of instrumental coaction (i.e., the metaphor to games and strategies) among individual technical rational subjects (in this case, bureaucracies).

As the wide acceptance of Allison suggests, it would be an error to contend that scientific students of foreign policy are committed to the *state* as the one kind of subject through which a meaningful comprehension of international politics can be accessed. Many echo the tendency, characteristic of internationalist liberals, to readily question the statist position: the position, often crudely equated with realism, that the state is necessarily and forever the principal actor on the international landscape. Many speak of the possible transformation of international politics and the demise of the nation–state as the principal actor. Yet an inspection of the discourse among contemporary scientific analysts suggests that such thinking, while questioning the state as the key actor, nevertheless perpetuates the disposition to interpret international reality in terms of the technical rational action and interaction of individual actors. Thus, much of the discourse centers, not on the social constitution of competent social agents ("actors" securing recognition, mobilizing social resources, and therefore capable of practically effective action), but on a contest among various classes of pre-given actors having different ends, wielding different instruments, and thus differentially capable of asserting their paramountcy in the shaping of global outcomes. Terrorists, tourists, transgovernmental bureaucrats, transnational groups, and, not least of all, multinational corporations—these are among the "new actors" presumably vying with state actors.

Many other examples could be cited, but the point is clear. In countless ways, the content and direction of theoretical discourse among scientific analysts of foreign policy is disciplined and circumscribed by habitual conformity to the interpretive dispositions of liberal positivist method. In particular, scientific foreign policy analysts exhibit a disposition to interpret all history and all practice from the point of view of technical rational decisions on the parts of pregiven individual actors whose identities, values, ends, and competencies to act are taken to be independent of society and independent of social practice. Given this disposition, the center and starting point of analysis must always be with the autonomously motivated decisions of pregiven agents—agents whose interests, defining structures, boundaries, and self-understandings are assumed to be independent of the historical practices that analysts seek to examine, understand, and evaluate. Given the same disposition, social structures and institutions, which appear as subjectless external constraints upon individual decisions, are taken to be the aggregate effects or (intended and unintended) consequences of decisions, actions, and interactions among individual agents who must ultimately relate to one another in essentially external, essentially technical terms. As for social science, its place in this implicitly theorized social order is unproblematic, and its task is clear. Approaching social order on the metaphor to natural scientific attitudes toward nature, the task of social science is taken to be the grasping of that singular set of fixed, universal, and objective regularities—regularities existing independent of the knowledge and intentionality of individual acting subjects—whose knowing will enhance human capacities to predict the consequences of their actions and, accordingly, to make decisions and employ means efficiently in the service of their values.

DIAGNOSIS:
THE IMPASSE IN THE SCIENTIFIC STUDY
OF FOREIGN POLICY

If it does little else, the discussion so far suggests that there are good reasons to question a longstanding opinion widely shared among scientific foreign policy analysts. This is the opinion—a recurring plaintive theme at least since Rosenau's original "Pre-theory" article—that "foreign policy analysis is devoid of general theory" (in Rosenau, 1980a:119). The opinion is certainly true if by "general theory" one means what positivist philosophers tend to mean, namely, a comprehensive set of explicit, testable generalizations or laws positing external causal relations among variables and thereby enhancing prediction and control.[6] In this sense, the scientific study of foreign policy fares no better than, say, Freudian psychoanalysis, whose claim to scientific status Karl Popper (1966) sought to deny on the grounds of its nonfalsifiability.[7] Yet if by "general theory" one means a set of structured and transposable interpretive dispositions—a "paradigm" for questioning, interpreting, and understanding human affairs—then the discussion so far indicates that another verdict is in order. Like psychoanalysis, the scientific study of foreign policy does not fare so badly.

Admittedly, the set of structured dispositions deployed by scientific foreign policy analysts may not be so rich or penetrating with respect to foreign policy as psychoanalysis might be claimed to be with respect to the human psyche. With its empiricist and technical–rationalist fixations, the scientific study of foreign policy is, after all, disposed toward the interpretation of surface where psychoanalysis tilts always toward the exploration of depth. Yet it must be said, too, that superficial theory is not the same thing as no theory. Anything but lacking in a theoretical consensus, scientific students of foreign policy have long shared a set of theoretical commitments bearing substantial empirical content.

We have already noted the reason for foreign policy analysts' disparagement of the theoretical richness of their enterprise. The empirical content of the scientific study of foreign policy does not, as it happens, reside in the realm of explicit theoretical knowledge claims. It is not to be found among consciously posed propositions— set in relief against recognized counterclaims and falsifying counterarguments—which are subjected to examination by way of deliberate scientific methods. Rather, the empirical content of the scientific study of foreign policy is unappreciated and unspoken because it resides in deeply held commitments that are regarded as methodological—commitments whose objectivity is unquestioned. It finds its home, that is, in the habitually obeyed interpretive dispositions of liberal positivism. As we have seen, these interpretive dispositions have a definite historical specificity: *they are born of struggles to work out specific understandings of social scientific practice under specific historical circumstances and in reaction to specific antinomies and normatively laden problematics of a liberal order.* Among self-consciously scientific foreign policy analysts, though, this is a history effaced. The timeless and universal adequacy of these dispositions is simply taken for granted. Accorded a methodological status and suspended beyond the critical reach of theoretical discourse, the dispositions seem to exhaust the interpretive imagination of science. Exerting a formidable discipline among self-consciously scientific analysts, they are simply taken for granted as necessary and essential elements of being scientific.

Implications

The point to be stressed, however, is not so much the "doxic" quality of these commitments,[8] but their implications for the scientific *evaluation* of foreign policy. Two general implications merit our attention. They correspond to the two opposed requisites of a scientific approach to foreign policy evaluation, as discussed earlier—the two requisites which, when poised in tension, describe the challenge for the scientific evaluation of foreign policy. On the one hand, it will be recalled, there is the requisite that specifically scientific approaches must satisfy: they must exhibit detachment and openness to criticism vis-à-vis the order and practices evaluated. On the other hand, there is the requisite that any approach to evaluation, scientific or not, must satisfy if it is to claim significance: it must secure recognition and establish meaning with respect to the real historical discourse and practical problematics of the historical subjects whose actions are evaluated.

Tradition-Bound Closure

The first general implication, which corresponds to the first of these requisites, can be succinctly stated. If it is true that the discourse of scientific students of foreign policy is bound up in a historically specific theory masked as a timeless method, then it must also be true that *the scientific study of foreign policy fails to satisfy the conditions of detachment and openness to criticism that distinguish scientific evaluation from an evaluation grounded in "tradition."*

Far from exhibiting a radical *detachment* from traditional values, expectations, and practical understandings, the scientific study of foreign policy takes over and replicates the values expectations and practical understandings of one particular tradition in history, the tradition of *modernity*. The scientific study of foreign policy unquestioningly accepts modernity's traditional understanding of social action, including science's role in the story of human progress, and it embeds this understanding in its method. Relying on this method, it seeks detachment, not from its own tradition of modernity, but vis-à-vis traditions that the progressive expansion of modernity would overturn. In this respect, one might note, the "great debate" between scientific and traditionalist approaches to the study of international politics was in fact a contest *between traditions*.

Likewise, far from exhibiting an *openness* to the questioning and correction of its theoretical content, the scientific study of foreign policy locates the most significant part of its theoretical content in a privileged method suspended outside of, and circumscribing, the critical reach of scientific discourse. In so doing, it discounts the critical vantage points afforded by opposed traditions—traditions rooted outside of, or in the criticism of, the tradition of modernity. It immunizes from scientific criticism the normative commitments of modern society, recasting these traditional commitments as objective necessities of life. And it imprisons scientific imagination, binding scientific discourse and the generation of scientifically grounded evaluations to modern society's normalized order.

The Lack of Practical Significance

The second implication, which corresponds to the second requisite, takes a bit longer to spell out. For in a way, it is a story of deceptive appearances. One might think that the scientific study of foreign policy, anchored as it is in the normative structures of modern society, would perform well with respect to the requisite of relevancy. After all, to the extent that the scientific study of foreign policy takes over and makes its own the interpretive dispositions of modern society, one might expect that it thereby secures its recognition and establishes its meaning in terms of the historical discourse and problematics of practically engaged participants. Depite its failure to meet the conditions of distance and openness to criticism—or perhaps *because* of this failure—one might expect the self-consciously scientific study of foreign policy to establish immediate practical relevance.

In fact, though, the record of the scientific evaluation of foreign policy is mixed in this regard. Yes, it secures some recognition in some eyes, for its liberal positivist dispositions do indeed normalize and naturalize the practical self-understandings of modern society and do indeed anticipate the universal objectification of just these understandings. To that extent, it serves the structured interest in the perpetuation of that order and the universalization of its ideology—an interest especially to be associated with the dominant in that order. But no, the scientific evaluation of foreign policy has not hitherto demonstrated a deep sensitivity to the political problematics—the practical dilemmas and power political struggles—involved in the perpetuation of the order it serves.

Precisely because its "theory-masked-as-method" is so thoroughly a captive of the tradition of modernity and its interpretive dispositions, the scientific study of foreign policy cannot adequately comprehend opposing traditions and modes of order with which modern society contests. It cannot comprehend them, that is, in their own terms, independent of the discursive structures of modernity. Opposing traditions and modes of order, if they are taken seriously at all, are reduced to mere reworkings of the interpretive dispositions of liberal positivism and the tradition of modernity it reflects. As a result—and it is an extremely important result—the richness of a genuinely *pluralistic* conception of political practice is sacrificed. *As a one-sided partisan of modernity, the scientific study of foreign policy cannot even begin to comprehend the struggle of modernity to perpetuate and expand its arc against the resistances mounted by a plurality of opposing traditions, modes of order, and ways of seeing, saying, and making the world.* It cannot conceive of international political practice as a continuing power political struggle among opposing traditions, of which modernity is only one tradition, albeit the most powerful.

This failure to comprehend modernity in political contest with opposing (actual and possible) traditions bears upon the question of relevance. For what it means is that the scientific study of foreign policy, bound up in liberal positivist dispositions, cannot come face to face with the multiple dimensions of politics in international life. It cannot grasp the layers of significance in which international political practice, including foreign policy, is played out: at once as *action* to achieve ends, as *performance* aspiring to elicit recognition of competence and virtuosity by playing off of habitually recognized interpretive dispositions of a traditional community, and as *political strategy,* set in opposition to counterstrategies, involving the political struggle to secure or creatively transform the tradition-bound interpretive dispositions upon which the historical efficacy of all social action depends:

> Comprehended as *action,* international political practice is behavior undertaken by subjects differentiated from their social and natural circumstances and oriented to the achievement of ends. Seen exclusively in these terms, the givenness of subjects or actors—be they possessive individuals, mullahs, firms, tribal chiefs, mobilized interest groups, or nation states—is simply presupposed. The social world may be regarded as "pluralistic" in the sense that there are multiple actors or subjects. But since the plurality of subjects is (unreflectively) defined by reference to the interpretive categories and practical terms of reference of a singular traditional order, this is a superficial pluralism.
>
> Comprehended as *performance,* international political practice additionally involves the social constitution of competent subjects—subjects socially recognized and empowered to act—through performative practices that secure social recognition of competence by playing off of the interpretive structures shared by participants in a tradition. Seen exclusively in these terms, the production of subjects (and their boundaries and ends) is now problematic: it depends upon performance in the context of tradition. However, the traditionally anchored interpretive structures in terms of which performance finds its meaning—and thanks to which subjects are recognized and empowered as competent agents—are still regarded as given and independent of politics.
>
> Comprehended as *political strategy,* international political practice still additionally involves the exercise of socially circumscribed latitude for action (1) to interpret creatively novel circumstances and opposing traditions within a structured set of interpretive dispositions, thereby to affirm the habitual reliance upon those structures, conserve a given traditional order in contradistinction to others, and maintain solidarity under conditions of novelty; or (2) to explore and expand the contradictions and transformational potential of traditional interpretive structures, thereby to expand latitude for socially empowered action and to make possible creative, perhaps revolutionary change of a traditional order. Seen now in these strategic terms, not only subjects but also the traditional interpretive dispositions off of which they play are regarded as problematic and

historical. Neither the singularity nor the fixity of traditional structures is taken for granted. Traditional structures that make possible the social constitution and empowerment of acting subjects are themselves set in the context of possible alternatives, and social action is understood to find much of its significance in terms of its implications for the reproduction, transformation, and interpenetration of traditional structures.

Caught up in the liberal positivist interpretive dispositions of modern society, the scientific study of foreign policy can comprehend international political practice only on the dimension of action, not as performance or political strategy in the senses given here. It cannot comprehend international political practice as it largely is: an open-ended, intensely political struggle to shape, perpetuate, and transform subjects and tradition-bound modes of collective action on a global scale. It offers at best a flattened, "one-dimensional" portrait of this struggle.

A "three-dimensional" analysis of foreign policy practice might be exemplified with reference to Ronald Reagan's "decision" to use military force in smashing the independence of Grenada. Only by collapsing history to an abstracted moment can one regard Reagan on the singular dimension of technical rational decision making and action under constraints. A two-dimensional view understands Reagan and his advisors to be performing as well as acting: they are exploring and expanding the latitude for action and empowering their own practices by engaging in performances that elicit public recognition and support because they play off of collectively shared interpretations of state action implicit in shared understandings of a common history. There is, for instance, a significant positive metaphorical play on the image of an "assertive" and "decisive" Franklin Roosevelt supportive of his military and boldly calculating the D-Day invasion to free Europe from totalitarianism. There is also a significant negative metaphorical play on the image of a timid Jimmy Carter indecisively pacing the Rose Garden during the Iranian hostage crisis. At the same time, Reagan and his advisors are not just making use of established metaphors, as a two-dimensional view might imply. On still a third dimension, they are actively in the business of establishing just these more "assertive" and militaristic images as the socially correct and powerful images to be brought to bear in understanding foreign policy, authorizing and criticizing statesmanship, and socially empowering state action. And they are disarming their political opposition by displacing other metaphors and their collectively sensed implications for the interpretation and practice of international politics—the metaphor to Vietnam, for instance, and the so-called "Vietnam syndrome." In the process of reinterpreting and redeploying the symbolic resources of society, they are literally transforming the state as a collective subject competent to act in history. As strategic political leaders, they are artfully exercising the symbolic resources of society within historically established material limits, and in so doing, they are participating in the social process of defining the state, the boundaries of permissible state action, and even the collectively recognized and socially supportable ends of statecraft.

This, of course, is a limited example. A reasonably complete analysis of the Grenada invasion would want to take into account a fourth dimension: how international political practices perpetuate or transform (unintended) social processes that in turn establish the historically effective material conditions with which action, performance, and political strategy must contend. In the case of the Reagan administration and the Grenada invasion, for instance, one would want to understand the administration's political strategic innovations, not in isolation, but as specific historical responses to a global crisis in relations of production and exchange—a crisis that opens the way for resistance on the part of subordinate peoples and necessitates the legitimation of coercive reaction on the part of the dominant.

Yet, however limited the example, the point comes through. The practice of international politics always takes place in multiple dimensions and within a horizon of plural frameworks for the production and interpretation of the world. As we readily sense, actors' boundaries, values, and competencies to act are never factually given conditions. Nor are the codes, precedents, images, and interpretive dispositions of people pregiven and secure foundations for social and political performance. They are forever contested, forever ambiguous, forever subject to multiple interpretation from multiple points of view. When women and men are called upon to act, we know that they must do more than merely grasp the appropriate means for the given ends under objective constraints. We sense that before they can act, they must somehow elicit the recognition of others as to their competence, and to do that, they must somehow have some practical understanding of others' interpretive dispositions as well as their own. When women and men are called upon to act creatively, we sense that they cannot simply follow the preexisting rules but must instead perform in such a way as to show how the symbolic resources of a relevant community can be creatively redeployed. And we know that social science, as a participant in the production of knowledge, does not stand apart from all of this, as a kind of objective onlooker. Inescapably, social science is implicated in the process of working and reworking, solemnizing and expanding, naturalizing and deconstructing the symbolic resources of society. It is implicated, not just in the analysis of action, but in the historical constitution and transformation of acting subjects and modes of conduct.

Yet liberal positivism must know none of this. As method, it disposes those in its sway to theorize an ideal world in which analysis can finally come to rest with actors who are given, with ends that are known, and with all ambiguity ultimately collapsible, thanks to science, into a singular set of objective understandings.

The Impasse:
Promise Frustrated

We thus approach an understanding of the impasse in the scientific evaluation and study of foreign policy. Bound up as it is within the modernist tradition, the scientific study of foreign policy manages to do the impossible: it fails to satisfy *both* requisites of a scientific approach to evaluation. It does not satisfy the condition of detachment and openness to criticism. It fails to speak to the multidimensional practical dilemmas and problematics of historically situated men and women.

This, however, is not yet an adequate depiction of the impasse. For there is a good deal more to the scientific study of foreign policy than its liberal positivisit commitments. Even the hastiest review of the deliberate discourse of scientific analysts suggests that, in countless ways, they are undertaking a conscious struggle to break with the epistemological limits of the current order. As early as 1969, for example, Rosenau expressed the view that "we have built solid conceptual jails around ourselves, and we have developed a convincing rationale for remaining incarcerated in them. Yet, even if the talents for effecting a jailbreak are lacking, at least possible escape routes can be identified. ..." (Rosenau, 1981a:26).

Rosenau's own writings in fact offer conspicuous evidence of the attempt to "plot a break." If one examines his writings overall, one finds that, taken together, we have the stuff of a strong indictment of the notion that the status of the state, the individual, the firm, the terrorist leader, or any other decision maker could ever be fixed, once and for all, as the starting point and end of scientific analysis. Those who view the state-as-actor as the starting point and end of international political life are the targets of Rosenau's fury. Instead, he emphasizes multiplying loyalties, shifting structures and foci of authority, changing cognitive structures and habits of thought, and even the transformation of roles. Boundaries, in his work, are never finally fixed, never impermeable, always subject to penetration. Novelty is always on the horizon. Asymmetries abound. The capacities of states to act, in his view, threaten to be overwhelmed by mounting interdependencies, consequent growing demands for political action, and simultaneous diminishment and diffusion of political authority. Directions and possibilities of political adaptation are open to question. Despite his ritual references to the search for regularities, the dominant image that comes through is of a striving to give voice to the pervasive fluidity and openness of international political life. The "eternal verities" of international politics, Rosenau understands, are not natural lawful truths. They are political creations and subject to change. In none of these respects is Rosenau alone in his contentions. In most, he speaks for a generation of scientific foreign policy analysts.

That this is so suggest that there is considerable promise in the scientific study of foreign policy. In their conscious theorizing, at least, scientific foreign policy analysts are inclined toward a more "multidimensional" understanding of international political practice. Their analyses question conventional categories of practice and call into question the self-satisfied understandings of states and other agents of international political life. In these ways and others, scientific analysts have exhibited promise of meeting the challenge of scientific foreign policy evaluation. More importantly, their explicit theoretical arguments, if taken seriously, would offer independent ground upon which to view, recognize, and criticize the limits of liberal positivist method.

The promise, though, is unrealized. At turn after turn, the normative force of liberal positivist dispositions—all the more powerful because these dispositions occupy the domain of unspoken, habitual commitments—subverts the liberative potential of analysts' explicit theory. They do so by disposing social scientists to take seriously, as science, only those aspects of theoretical argument that can be rendered consistent with liberal positivism's own "theory-masked-as-method" and to cast aside or neglect (as perhaps interesting but unscientific speculation) those arguments that resist reduction to liberal positivist understandings. Rosenau's own original "Pretheory" article offers an excellent

example. Extremely lengthy, the article contains extensive epistemological and conceptual commentary bearing on the national–
international distinction as well as a section on "the penetrated
political system." Yet just a few years later, what had "the Rosenau
Pretheory Article" come to signify in the minds of scientific
students of foreign policy? For most—as in the excerpt (Rosenau,
1975) reproduced in a volume edited by Coplin and Kegley—it had
come to mean essentially the abbreviated pretheory as it appeared
in Section 2, or the even more simplified version of Table 1. What
are filtered out are precisely those aspects of the article that
challenge the limits of liberal positivist interpretations. What are
remembered—and what are therefore significant for the cumulative *scientific* dialogue among scientific students of foreign policy—
are those elements that can be made consistent with liberal
positivism's habitually involved interpretive dispositions.

The impasse of the scientific evaluation of foreign policy thus
may be characterized with a tinge of irony. Scientific analysts of
foreign policy have, to date, failed the challenge discussed here. But
it is not for want of trying. It is not for want of intelligence,
intellectual courage, or even conceptual daring. It is because their
theoretical discourse is caught in the habits of liberal positivist
method and because, so trapped, they have been unable to read the
following words self-reflectively:

> The best way to understand ... oppressive habits is by using the
> liberating habit of scientific inquiry, which offers man perhaps
> the only route to the kind of understanding of his dilemma
> necessary for the development of radical and effective solutions.
> Unless account is taken of the persistence of habitual forms of
> organization and traditional modes of interaction, desired
> change cannot be effectively promoted and undesired change
> resisted (Rosenau, 1981b:200).

TOWARD AN ALTERNATIVE METHOD

However compelling such an argument might be in the abstract, its
persuasive force remains dependent upon the availability of an
alternative approach or framework that would not only displace
liberal positivism but also overcome its limits. My tasks in this
concluding section are to suggest that an alternative does indeed
exist, to highlight some of its distinguishing qualities, and to

indicate that it does hold out significant promise of answering the challenge for the scientific evaluation of foreign policy. This method, I must stress, is not without its own implicit theory, its own interpretive commitments. Like positivism, it is grounded in a specific historical experience, and like positivism, it projects that experience in its approach to the world. The difference—the *crucial* difference—is that this alternative framework acknowledges the inescapable historicity of any possible method, and it boldly incorporates critical reflection on this fact as part of its own method.

The framework I have in mind could be called by any number of names. One could call it a "critical" approach, after Jurgen Habermas and his notion of critical theory; for, like Habermas's critical social science, the present framework aspires not only to disclose recurring regularities but also to distinguish truly invariant regularities from tradition-produced regularities that are subject to change under conditions, and by way of practices, that might be specified. Alternatively, one might refer to the present framework as a "postmodern" approach; for, as in recent currents of French thought—Derrida and Foucault, for instance—it is animated in part by a reflection on special forms of reason, characteristic of modern experience, and the limits and contradictions of those forms. In the words of Gerard Raulet (1983:205), postmodernity aspires to understand that Western reason "has only been one narrative among others in history; a grand narrative, certainly, but one of many, which can now be followed by other narratives." As a third alternative, one might refer to the framework discussed here as "poststructuralist." For it learns from formalist and structuralist argument and the problem of the subject, and it takes quite seriously the phenomenological investigations of, say, Husserl and Merleau-Ponty. To give yet a fourth alternative, one might entitle the present framework a "linguistic" approach; for it learns from the so-called "linguistic turn" in philosophy, as exhibited by the diverse writings of Peirce, Dewey, Wittgenstein, Heidegger, and, one might add, Karl Deutsch (see Rorty, 1967, 1979). It invests considerable importance in the proposition that, as Terence Ball (1983:3) puts it, "our language does not merely mirror the world but is instead partially constitutive of it." In Karl-Otto Apel's (1972) phrase, the "*a priori* of communication" is the foundation of society. Finally, as yet a fifth alternative, one might label framework "dialectical," as in the usage of the term by Alker and Biersteker (1984), and others in their "Dialectics of World Order" Project; for the present purposes, and for reasons that will quickly become plain, I will refer to the framework simply as a *critical–dialogical* framework.

A critical–dialogical approach may be described in terms of a number of overlapping features:

> A critical–dialogical approach recognizes that social reality—its divisions, structures, objects, and subjects—is discursively constituted, that is, is produced by the interpretation-bound practices of historically situated men and women. It holds to a metatheoretical perspective in which women and men every day encounter the ambiguities of their worlds; interpret and reinterpret their conditions and their own practices by reference to socially recognized, habitual, but indeterminate schemes, structures, and myths; differentiate their experience and coordinate their production and empowerment of their worlds, themselves, and their self-understandings; and, at the same time, engage in an open-ended, intensely political, but not always openly politicized struggle, to create, reaffirm, call into question, or transform the interpretive structures off of which their practices play.
>
> A critical–dialogical perspective refuses to assume, on *a priori* metaphysical grounds, that any set of structured relations can be accorded the status of an objective "external reality"—a logic of history, a set of structures, some fixed laws, or some natural processes existing independent of human practice. This is not idealism. It instead amounts to a challenging (and a historicizing) of Cartesian dualisms between mind and body, subject and object, ideal and material. It wants not to take objectivity or materiality for granted as extra-historical, quasi-natural limits on society; it wants instead to grasp the historical and social production of objectivity and materiality.
>
> A critical–dialogical approach cannot be reduced to a technical matter of clarification, of sharpening representations, of symbolically appropriating an object world. It goes beyond the descriptive concern with "what" and the causal–explanatory concern with "why" to additionally pose the question of "how." How, under what conditions, and by way of what practices are social structures, produced, objectified, and hegemonically secured? How, under what conditions, and by way of what practices, might these structures by transformed? Reviving interest in these "how questions," it raises theoretical sights from an exclusive concern with the *opus operatum* of international political life to a focus upon the *modus operandi*.
>
> A critical–dialogical perspective refuses to assume the possibility of achieving a monothetic representation of social

reality, a reality that is necessarily pluralistic. It insists on openness to the possibility that the given order—despite its seeming objectivity, and however pluralistic it may seem in its immediate empirical expressions—sustains a mode of unity existing in opposition to alternative modes of order that are repressed or denied. From a critical–dialogical standpoint, all attempts to arrive at singular, contradiction-free representations must themselves be held to account as interpretive enterprises engaged in the power political struggle to produce the socially lived truth. They are part of an open-ended struggle between practical strategies producing the normalization and naturalization of given structures and practical strategies that uncover the historical arbitrariness and potentialities for change of social structures that might otherwise be taken for granted.

A critical–dialogical approach politicizes all truth-seeking activity, including social science, by asserting that there is no truth prior to power. It does not conceive of theorizing as an extra-historical, extra-political activity made possible by a true break with political practice. Theoretical practice is instead comprehended and subjected to criticism as political practice, a participant in the production, and potentially the transformation, of the order theorized. All theorizing, this perspective teaches, tends to objectify and externalize beyond the reach of practice—as quasi-natural, extra-historical limits—what are in fact transcendable products of practice. And this, the perspective further teaches, is not a lamentable mistake that can be avoided or overcome by an act of will. It is an inescapable part of the processes by which society produces and normalizes itself, legitimates or naturalizes social structures, empowers subjects, endorses modes of practice, circumscribes categories of social possibility, and disciplines action. This is what Bourdieu calls the "theorization effect," and it is an effect exhibited in varying degrees by all cultures.

A critical–dialogical approach dictates that theoretical activity become self-referential and self-critical. Aware of theory's own potential political significance in the production of objectified social structures, and posing the question of *how* social structures are produced and objectified, the critical–dialogical approach invokes a determination to reflect critically on the political significance and possibility conditions of its own attempts to arrive at objectivist conclusions. Whereas positivistic social science is distinguished by its closing off of just those avenues of scientific criticism that would expose its participation in the "theorization effect," a critical–dialogical approach is distinguished by its determination to avoid this kind of closure.

In presenting this listing of features, one caveat needs

immediately to be offered. Contrary to the insinuations of positivists of the right and left, this determination to reflect critically on the political aspects of theorizing cannot be dismissed as a matter of self-indulgence on the part of theorists yet to awaken to problems in "the real world," too preoccupied with scholastic disputes, or too timid to venture their own solutions. Rather, such a determination is a canon of methodological responsibility. It is a scientific responsibility whose grounding and practical significance become plain when scientists refuse the temptation to anchor their enterprise in the safe harbor of an uncritical, unhistorical, unrealistic, and scientifically indefensible commitment to a dichotomy of theory and practice. Refusing the metaphysical circumscription of scientific criticism, a critical–dialogical approach anticipates a science that, in comparison to positivism, is methodologically more demanding.

Viewed as a method, a critical–dialogical approach works toward the "cumulation" of knowledge only in a restricted sense of the term. It does not aim to build a store of confirmed hypotheses. Nor does it aim to arrive at a fixed model whose representational structures are intersubjectively comprehended and provisionally accepted. Nor, further, does it aspire to establish a paradigm and found a normal science; normalization, from its point of view, is a strategy of power that political scientists want to study, not an ideal they want blindly to practice. Least of all does it aim to subsume other models of opposed traditions within its own unquestioned framework. Rather, as a method, it disposes a program to openness, to the readiness to discover possibilities, not to closure, to the search for necessities.

The aim is to maintain openness and establish critical distance from one's own immediate tradition through an unceasing readiness for dialogical engagement with competing traditions or paradigms of practice. The aspiration is not to achieve "victory" over another tradition; it is not to deny or dismiss an opposing tradition from the point of view of one's own privileged standards. The intent, rather, is a kind of *mutual* liberation. One starts from the assumption that if a tradition is worth worrying about (if it is genuinely a live tradition and not just the idiosyncratic mumblings of a couple of social isolates), then no matter how wrongheaded or one-sided its universalizing claims may seem to be, the tradition is nonetheless valid from a particular point of view; it bespeaks a particular field of discourse, reflecting a particular background of experience, and actively engaged in the production of the world. The task of mutual criticism and synthesis is to engage opposing traditions in dialogue, questioning the limits of their comprehension, but also testing one's own. The test of cumulation, on this account, is not abstract and intellectualist, but practical and political. It is in the cotransformation of the traditions engaged; the production of a collective will.

This "dialogical" method is at the core, if you will, of a critical–dialogical approach, but I must hasten to add that it does not exhaust that approach. Rather, what this dialogical method provides is a background normative standard against which it becomes possible to grasp the practical performances and power political strategies by which parties can and do deploy and play with symbolic resources under material constraints to shape, reaffirm, and transform the subjects, objects, and modes of collective existence.

Two general observations about this approach need to be made. First, it is extremely important to note that a critical–dialogical approach, by virtue of its insistence on respect for the practical traditions it interprets, is continuously drawn to maintain a rich sensitivity to the practical commitments and tradition-bound struggles of participants. It is disposed and able to grasp those struggles on all dimensions, not just the dimension of rational action on the part of given subjects.

Second, it is no less important to note that, despite contrary pressures, a dialogical approach is nonetheless able to maintain detachment and openness to criticism. It is able to do so because, given its pluralism, it is forever disposed to doubt all pretenses to closure and to search out dialogues with alternative and opposing traditional vantage points, this to establish a basis for critical reflection on its own limits.

An example is in order. Consider two traditions, one unflaggingly statist in its orientation toward foreign policy and the other liberal internationalist. The two traditions are evidently opposed, the one seeing the state as forever the true subject of history, and the other viewing the state as a relation about to be surpassed or overwhelmed by the mounting demands of interdependent transnational subjects. Each of the two traditions thus sets out to interpret the world through the privileged lens of its own particular subjects, and what is at stake in the interpreting is not so much the story told but the relative adequacy of the traditions' respective subjects as collectively recognized subjects for the interpretation, organization, and practice of international life. Each tradition aspires, put differently, to establish the practical hegemony of its own subject—to make its own subject the consensually recognized subject of collective history. The relation is a contest, a struggle on multiple dimensions, an engagement at the level of political strategy.

Accordingly, representatives of each tradition perform interpretations that have the effect of normalizing, calling into question, or socially transforming alternative subjects and modes of collective action. Such relations rightly occupy a central place on the explicit theoretical agendas of scientific analysts of foreign policy. Could a liberal positivist approach grasp this multidimensional strategic engagement? No, because it is predisposed to reduce social interaction to a matter of individual rational action. Could a critical–dialogical approach exhibit a deep sensitivity to the full dimensions of this engagement? Yes, because a critical–dialogical approach replicates—it participates in—the very discursive processes by which this struggle is historically waged.

In short, as this example is meant to suggest, a critical–dialogical approach holds promise of answering both sides of the challenge of the scientific evaluation of foreign policy. It meets the condition of relevance, insofar as it is drawn toward direct engagement with the practical commitments and familiar struggles of women and men. Yet it also meets the condition of detachment and openness, for the approach dictates a ceaseless attempt to mine the reflective and self-critical potential encountered in engagement with opposing traditions. This is a sanguine conclusion. Will this promise be realized?

If trends in other fields are any indication, then the answer may well be yes. Clifford Geertz (1980:168) for instance, has recently written of the "blurring of genres" in the social sciences owing to the so-called "interpretive turn... In the social sciences," he writes, "or at least in those that have abandoned a reductionist conception of what they are about, the analogies are coming more and more from the contrivances of cultural performance than from those of physical manipulation—from theater, painting, grammar, literature, law, play." He adds that "the casting of social theory in terms more familiar to gamesters and aestheticians than to plumbers and engineers is well under way." The trends Geertz describes would seem to bode well for a shift among foreign policy analysts in the direction of a critical–dialogical approach.

Yet there is room for a less optimistic conclusion. The shift Geertz discusses is likely to be a sticky one as it pertains to the scientific study of international politics and foreign policy; for if we have already learned anything from this "intepretive turn," it is that socially inscribed habits exert a powerful discipline, and long-standing habits die hard.

NOTES

[1]See Habermas (1971b, 1979); Foucault (1980, 1979); Said (1978).
[2]See, e.g., Radnitzky (1973); Bernstein (1976); Shapiro (1981); and Alker (1982).
[3]On consensus versus correspondence theories of truth see Habermas (1973).
[4]The term "technical cognitive interest" is from Habermas (1975, 1971a). See also the discussion in Ashley (1981).
[5]On the "who does what to whom and when" orientation, see Kegley (1975:99). See also Azar and Ben-Dak (1975).
[6]This line is a close paraphrase from Rosenau (1980a:119).
[7]For a more recent treatment, see Grünbaum (1984).
[8]The term *doxa*, which appears in Plato, is used by Pierre Bourdieu (1977):93 to refer to a social condition wherein "there is a quasi-perfect correspondence between the objective order and the subjective principles of organization. ..." According to Bourdieu, under these conditions "the natural and social world appear self-evident."

REFERENCES

ALKER, H. R., Jr. (1982). "Logic, Dialectics, Politics: Some Recent Controversies." In H. Alker (ed.) *Dialectical Logics for the Political Sciences,* Vol. 7 of *Poznan Studies in the Philosophy of the Sciences and the Humanities.* Amsterdam, Holland: Rodopi. Pp. 65–94.

ALKER, H. R.. Jr., and T. BIERSTEKER (1984). "The Dialectics of World Order: Notes for a Future Archaeologist of International Savoir Faire." *International Studies Quarterly,* 28:121–42.

ALLISON, G. (1971). *Essence of Decision: Explaining the Cuban Missile Crisis.* Boston, Mass.: Little, Brown.

APEL, K. O. (1972). "The *A Priori* of Communication and the Foundation of Humanities." *Man and World,* 5:3–37.

ASHLEY, R. K. (1981). "Political Realism and Human Interests." *International Studies Quarterly,* 25:204–36.

ASHLEY, R. K. (1983a). "The Eye of Power: The Politics of World Modeling." *International Organization*, 37:495–535.

ASHLEY, R. K. (1983b). "Three Modes of Economism." *International Studies Quarterly*, 27:463–96.

ASHLEY, R. K. (1984). "The Poverty of Neorealism." *International Organization*, 38:225–86.

AZAR, E., and J. BEN-DAK (eds.) (1975). *Theory and Practice of Events Research*. New York and London: Gordon and Breach Science Publishers.

BALL, T. (1983). "The Linguistic Turn in Political Science." Paper presented at the annual meeting of the American Political Science Association, Chicago, Ill., September 1–4.

BERNSTEIN, R. (1976). *The Restructuring of Political and Social Theory*. New York: Harcourt, Brace, Jovanovich.

BOURDIEU, P. (1977). *Outline of a Theory of Practice,* translated by Richard Nice. London: Cambridge University Press.

CHITTICK, W., and J. JENKINS (1976). "Reconceptualizing the Sources of Foreign Policy Behavior." In J. Rosenau (ed.), *In Search of Global Patterns*. New York: Free Press. Pp. 281–91.

FOUCAULT, M. (1979). *Language, Counter-Memory, Practice*. Oxford: Blackwell.

FOUCAULT, M. (1980). *Power/Knowledge. Selected Interviews and Other Writings, 1972–1977*. New York: Pantheon.

GEERTZ, C. (1980). "Blurred Genres: The Refiguration of Social Thought." *American Scholar,* 49:165–79.

GIDDENS, A. (1972). *Politics and Sociology in the Thought of Max Weber*. London: Macmillan.

GIDDENS, A. (1974). *Positivism and Sociology*. London: Heinemann.

GIDDENS, A. (1979). *Central Problems in Social Theory*. Berkeley, Calif.: University of California Press.

GRÜNBAUM, A. (1984). *The Foundations of Psychoanalysis: A Philosophical Critique*. Berkeley, Calif.: University of California Press.

GUETZKOW, H. (1950). "Long-Range Research in International Relations." *American Perspective,* 4:421–40.

HABERMAS, J. (1971a). *Knowledge and Human Interests,* translated by Jeremy Shapiro. London: Heinemann.

HABERMAS, J. (1971b). *Towards a Rational Society,* translated by Jeremy Shapiro. Boston, Mass.: Beacon Press.

HABERMAS, J. (1973). "Wahrheitstheorien." In H. Fahrenbach (ed.), *Wirklichkeit und Reflexion.* Pfullingen, FRG: Neske. Pp. 66–105.

HABERMAS, J. (1975). "A Postscript to *Knowledge and Human Interests.*" *Philosophy of the Social Sciences,* 3:428–52.

HABERMAS, J. (1979). *Communication and the Evolution of Society,* translated by Thomas McCarthy. Boston, Mass.: Beacon Press.

JONES, S., and J. D. SINGER (1972). *Beyond Conjecture in International Politics: Abstracts of Data-Based Research.* Itasca, Ill.: F. E. Peacock.

KEGLEY, C. W. (1975). "The Generation and Use of Events Data." In C. Kegley, G. Raymond, R. Rood, and R. Skinner (eds.), *International Events and the Comparative Analysis of Foreign Policy.* Columbia, S.C.: University of South Carolina Press. Pp. 91–105.

McCLELLAND, C. (1969). "International Relations: Wisdom or Science?" In J. Rosenau (ed.), *International Politics and Foreign Policy,* revised ed. New York: Free Press. Pp. 3–5.

McGOWAN, P. (1975). "Meaningful Comparisons in the Study of Foreign Policy: A Methodological Discussion of Objectives, Techniques, and Research Designs." In C. Kegley et al. (eds.), *International Events and the Comparative Analysis of Foreign Policy.* Columbia, S.C.: University of South Carolina Press. Pp. 52–87.

McGOWAN, P. (1976). "The Future of Comparative Studies: An Evangelical Plea." In J. Rosenau (ed.), *In Search of Global Patterns.* New York: Free Press. Pp. 217–35.

McGOWAN, P., and H. SHAPIRO (1973). *The Comparative Study of Foreign Policy: A Survey of Scientific Findings.* Beverly Hills, Calif.: Sage Publications.

POPPER, K. (1966). *The Open Society and Its Enemies.* London: Routledge.

RADNITSKY, G. (1973). *Contemporary Schools of Metascience,* 3rd enlarged ed. Chicago, Ill.: Henry Regnery.

RAULET, G. (1983). "Structuralism and Post-Structuralism: An Interview with Michel Foucault." *Telos,* No. 55:195–211.

RORTY, R. (ed.) (1967). *The Linguistic Turn.* Chicago, Ill.: University of Chicago Press.

RORTY, R. (1979). *Philosophy and the Mirror of Nature.* Princeton, N.J.: Princeton University Press.

ROSENAU, J. (ed.) (1969). *International Politics and Foreign Policy.* New York: Free Press.

ROSENAU, J. (1975). "A Pre-Theory of Foreign Policy." In W. Coplin and C. Kegley (eds.), *Analyzing International Relations.* New York: Praeger. Pp. 37–48.

ROSENAU, J. (1980a). "Pre-Theories and Theories of Foreign Policy." In J. Rosenau, *The Scientific Study of Foreign Policy.* London: Frances Pinter; New York: Nichols. Pp. 115–69.

ROSENAU, J. (1980b). The Science. Introduction to Part 2 of J. Rosenau, *The Scientific Study of Foreign Policy.* Pp. 32–33.

ROSENAU, J. (1980c). "Thinking Theory Thoroughly." In J. Rosenau, *The Scientific Study of Foreign Policy.* Pp. 19–31.

ROSENAU, J. (1981a). "The Adaptive Actor Strategy." In J. Rosenau, *The Study of Political Adaptation.* London: Frances Pinter; New York: Nichols. Pp. 23–35.

ROSENAU, J. (1981b). "Adaptive Polities in an Interdependent World." In J. Rosenau, *The Study of Political Adaptation.* London: Frances Pinter; New York: Nichols. Pp. 199–218.

RUSSETT, B., and H. STARR (1981). *World Politics: The Menu for Choice.* San Francisco, Calif.: W. H. Freeman.

SAID, E. (1978). *Orientalism.* New York: Pantheon.

SHAPIRO, M. (1981). *Language and Political Understanding.* New Haven, Conn.: Yale University Press.

SINGER, J. D. (1961). "The Level of Analysis Problem in International

Relations." In K. Knorr and S. Verba (eds.), *The International System: Theoretical Essays*. Princeton, N.J.: Princeton University Press. Pp. 72–92.

SINGER, J. D. (1969). "The Behavioral Science Approach to International Relations: Payoff and Prospects." In J. Rosenau (ed.), *International Politics and Foreign Policy*. Pp. 65–69.

SNYDER, R., H. W. BRUCK and B. SAPIN (eds.) (1962). *Foreign Policy Decision-Making: An Approach to the Study of International Politics*. New York: Free Press.

WALTZ, K. N. (1979). *Theory of International Politics*. Reading, Mass.: Addison-Wesley.

10

Explaining and Evaluating Foreign Policy: A New Agenda for Comparative Foreign Policy

John A. Vasquez

There is a certain malaise within the scientific study of foreign policy. The controversy and excitement that surrounded the birth of comparative foreign policy and then the collection of event data has gradually given rise to disappointment that more has not been found (see Lentner, 1981). Even more disillusioning has been the resurgence of antiquantitative moods complete with all the epistemological flaws of earlier traditional analysis. It is clearly time to take stock—to see what has been accomplished, why there have been disappointments, what should be continued, and where we need to go.

The main charge against the scientific study of foreign policy has been that for all the attempts to analyze data and develop sophisticated statistical techniques, little advancement in learning has occurred. Indeed, one could argue that the two main insights on foreign policy in the last 15 years—bureaucratic politics and the role of misperception and images—have come from those who have eschewed quantitative analysis (Allison and Halperin, 1972; Jervis, 1976). This charge accurately captures a mood in certain quarters, but it is in part due to expecting too much in too short a time, as well as underestimating the intractability of the intellectual task.

However, it is hardly clear that the charge is correct. In the second half of the 1970s, there has been a virtual explosion of statistical findings. Most of these, however, consist of little pieces to various puzzles, in the absence of a grand theory; consequently they do not provide an overall understanding of foreign policy. That does not mean that no advancement in learning has occurred. While a review of these findings is beyond the scope of this chapter (see Vasquez, 1983: Chapters 4 and 8), it cannot be denied that we know more now than we did 20 years ago about crisis behavior (McClelland, 1968; C. Hermann, 1972; Snyder and Diesing, 1977), participation in foreign affairs (e.g. Rosenau and Hoggard, 1974; East, 1975), the role of personal characteristics in foreign policy making (Guetzkow and Valadez, 1981; M. Hermann, 1980; Etheredge, 1978), and even conflict behavior (Holsti, North, and Brody, 1968; Rummel, 1977; Leng, 1980; Wallace, 1982; Wilkenfeld et al., 1980). Likewise, there have been quantitative analyses of bureaucratic politics (e.g. Phillips and Crain, 1974), including arms races (Ward, 1984), and of perceptions and images (e.g. Axelrod, 1976) that have provided nonobvious findings and sharpened conceptualizations. Some things have been learned.

In addition, advancement has occurred in other ways. A great deal of the underbrush has been cleared away. New methodologies and techniques have been developed and are in place. Of greatest importance is the fundamental notion that explanations about foreign policy should be testable and tested and not just accepted because they seem insightful and can be cogently argued. Consequently, one of the major contributions of quantitative analysis has been to show that many of the things we thought were true are wrong. Among these are basic assumptions such as the realist notions that the nation–state can be conceived as a unitary rational actor, or that cooperation–conflict is unidimensional (see Vasquez and Mansbach, 1984; Vasquez, 1983:205–215; Rummel, 1972:98–100). Along with this, we have learned that the world is much more complex than we thought, and that this complexity is beginning to be reflected in our statistical findings (Russett, 1983). Finally, the scientific approach has provided conceptual advances. The concept of national interest has all but been abandoned as an explanatory concept. The simplistic and ambiguous tendencies of the concept of power have been elucidated. The tradition of explaining foreign policy primarily through idiographic national histories has been replaced by a more general and theoretical approach.

If all of this is true, why the criticism, why the malaise? To a certain extent, the criticism and malaise come from different quarters. One quarter consists of those who have either been outright hostile to the scientific enterprise and/or uncomfortable with quantitative analysis. To them, quantitative analysis is not worth the effort. It is hard work not only to do it, but to read it. They are much more comfortable sipping sherry in drawing rooms and being brilliant than they are collecting data or using computers to test hypotheses. To a certain extent, criticism from this quarter is a natural counterrevolution to the behavioral revolt and should be treated as such. Unfortunately, this counterrevolution is occurring at a time when many within the scientific camp are beginning to doubt the significance of normal science findings, are impatient with the slowness of the enterprise, have seen funding dry up, and are wondering whether their work will ever become policy-relevant. It is this malaise that poses the most serious threat to the scientific study of foreign policy. While some of this malaise is due to disappointment over the lack of a major breakthrough, a great deal has to do with the growing doubt that we are really explaining or getting at the heart of foreign policy and that many of our findings and explanations are tangential to actual foreign policy debates. It is to this source of the malaise that this chapter is addressed.

The positivist foundation upon which the scientific study of politics was based has had two negative effects. First, in the attempt to study foreign policy scientifically, the notion that one of the purposes of the discipline was to explain the substantive foreign policy of states—why they have a particular policy, how it would affect their behavior, where it came from, where it was going—was lost. Realists, like Morgenthau (1951) and even Wolfers (1962), saw it as part of their enterprise to explain (and then evaluate) the policies that nation–states brought to the global arena. The effort to be comparative, theoretical, and scientific diverted attention away from what was ultimately meant to be explained. Thus Snyder, Bruck, and Sapin (1954), in an attempt to avoid anthropomorphizing the nation–state, ended up studying decisions, which in turn gave rise to decision making and group dynamics as the main dependent variables. Rosenau's pretheory (1966) was devoted almost entirely to independent and intervening variables, so much so that when it came time to test it, no one was quite sure what the dependent variable was. Rosenau and Hoggard (1974) treated foreign policy as cooperation–conflict behavior, but in fact ended up examining participation, providing an example of the kinds of problems that can develop when insufficient attention is paid to conceptualizing the dependent variable. Not until the CREON project was the dependent variable given full attention (see C. Hermann, 1978). Here it was treated as a set of foreign policy

behaviors. Important information can be provided by this conception (see Callahan, Brady, and M. Hermann, 1982); however, the
behaviors of nation–states are not the same as the policies they
hold. Even those who sought to reintroduce a policy perspective
through the concept of issue position (Coplin, Mills, O'Leary, 1973;
Mansbach and Vasquez, 1981: Ch. 6) did not capture the holistic
notion of policy, but instead examined its atomistic components.
Clearly, operational concerns were primary in bringing about these
results. If the malaise is to be overcome, then a way of scientifically
studying substantive foreign policy in all its holistic richness must
be found.

Second, the positivistic emphasis on separating empirical and
normative analysis and the related belief that science is neutral
and irrelevant to value questions led to a rejection of highly
practical concepts,[1] like "the national interest," as too normative.
With the rejection of such concepts, the foreign policy scholar was
stripped of all tools with which to participate in foreign policy
debates as a scientist. In the absence of any corroborated theory of
foreign policy, he or she could not claim a special foreign policy role
for the profession. The scholar's views were reduced to matters of
opinion. As a result, the scientific study of foreign policy has not
been, to date, very policy-relevant. Occasionally, quantitative
scholars would consult on technical questions for which they had
answers or try to develop research projects with a policy focus. In
the process, the historical responsibility of intellectuals to provide a
critical perspective by which to view society (Lynd, 1939) was
abdicated. This has been due, in part, to an inability to conceptual-
ize substantive foreign policy in a way that will permit foreign
policy not only to be explained, but to be evaluated. To resolve this
problem, we must pay more attention to explaining foreign policy
in a way that speaks directly to evaluating the conduct of foreign
relations. This chapter argues that this challenge can be met by
developing a taxonomy of foreign policies. This will facilitate both
the explanation of general forms of behavior and the evaluation of
common practices.

EXPLAINING FOREIGN POLICY
SO THAT IT MAY BE EVALUATED

As Charles Hermann (1978:26) points out, we as scholars feel so
confident that we know what foreign policy is, that we have devoted

little time to explicitly defining it (see also Cohen and Harris, 1975). To a certain extent, the easiest way to define foreign policy is to point to what it is. Thus, containment was a policy of Truman, detente of Nixon and Kissinger, appeasement of Chamberlain. If this is accepted, it is clear that a *policy* is not the same as the *issue* that gives rise to the policy. For example, both containment and detente were policies on issues dividing the United States and the Soviet Union. Likewise, a policy is neither a set of goals and objectives nor a set of strategies and tactics, but rather a bundle of goals, objectives, strategy, and tactics, which may have various degrees of rationality, consistency, and consciousness depending on who makes and implements the policy (see Lindblom, 1968).[2]

In addition, it should be clear that a state has many foreign policies, not one. If for no other reason, a state has many foreign policies because it deals with many issues and has different relationships with different actors. It may also have several foreign policies on a single issue that may emphasize different aspects of the issue and in the process may contradict each other. This, of course, occurs primarily because what is regarded as the state is rarely a unitary actor (see Mansbach and Vasquez, 1981: Ch. 5). In addition, historical vestiges or inertia may cause former policies to linger as new ones are implemented. Finally, for any given policy there may be alternative or even rival policies that may be advocated by elites or significant policy influencers (see Coplin, 1974:74–82, on policy influences). Clearly, in the late 1930s in the United States there was a division between isolationists and internationalists on the issue of fascism. From the perspective of explanation, it is interesting to know why one policy rather than another emerged as dominant and why sometimes there is consensus and sometimes division.

While all of these distinctions are familiar to students of foreign policy and could serve as a basis for trying to identify foreign policies, a more precise definition would make the concept less ephemeral and would point toward an operationalization. Elsewhere I have presented a conceptualization of foreign policy based on the assumption that global politics consist of the raising and resolving of issues. Actors are seen as contending on these issues by developing proposals for the disposition of political stakes. Actors agree or disagree with these proposals by taking, either implicitly or explicitly, an *issue position* on each proposal. They then try to change each others's issue positions by sending positive and/or negative acts, which in turn leads them to develop attitudes of friendship and/or hostility toward one another. On the basis of this conceptualization, foreign policy can be defined as a set of interrelated issue positions on a set of interrelated proposed outcomes (Mansbach and Vasquez, 1981:189).

This definition suggests that foreign policies could be identified by first listing the issues on an agenda. Next, the proposals made by all the contending actors on each issue would be delineated. The foreign policy of an actor would be indicated by these interrelated issue positions.

Eventually, a quantitative description would develop issue position indicators as a way of reconstructing foreign policies. At this stage, that would be premature, because we would first want to see whether such an approach is worth the effort. The easiest way to do that would be to see whether comparative historical case studies make any theoretical sense.

A complete case study of U.S. foreign policy would delineate every issue (above a certain salience) and then reconstruct the foreign policies on each. More realistically, an analysis might be confined to the two or three most salient issues or to certain issue areas—national security, economics, human rights, and so on (see Coplin, 1974:86, and Hermann and Choate, 1982, for various substantive issue area typologies). Operating as a good diplomatic historian, we could reconstruct foreign policies judgmentally on the basis of government documents, memoirs, interviews, and so forth. Formal policies, such as containment, that had been named would be the easiest to reconstruct, but there is no need to assume that more informal policies, such as neoimperialism, could not be delineated.

Our evidence to date, however, suggests that the single country approach is not as effective as the dyadic approach (Rummel, 1972; Vasquez and Mansbach, 1984:415). Statistical efforts to retrodict the foreign policy behavior of a state have been less successful than efforts to retrodict foreign policy behavior between two states. This, of course, makes eminent sense since a foreign policy is made in the context of an ongoing relationship with another actor(s). Thus in making a list of an actor's foreign policies it is necessary not only to control for issue, but for the target(s) of the policy.

This approach would make the scientific study of foreign policy more historical, which is probably theoretically useful, since learning and structure, which may be critical variables, are best treated historically (see May, 1973; Jervis, 1976: Chapter 6; Galtung, 1971;). Methodologically, the approach would be useful because it would encourage the wedding of historiographical techniques and sources of evidence with social science procedures to overcome some of the problems with event data. In addition, it would make comparative foreign policy more authentically comparative, especially if regional or global issue area histories rather than solely national histories are written. Of course, much of this hard work has already been completed by diplomatic and Marxist historians. What we need to do is to sift through these histories with a more theoretical and general perspective. When that work is completed, the results might look something like Table 10.1, which lists some of the major U.S. foreign policies in the postwar era on the most salient issue in each administration. The list is illustrative of the kind of work being suggested and is not intended as definitive.

The policies in Table 10.1 are derived from a diplomatic perspective. In order to record the effects of internal decision making and general domestic political factors, it would be necessary to supplement the table with a list of the options considered and the potential rival policies. Options consist of elements within the existing policy that could have been adopted but were not, or elements that will be adopted if aspects of the present policy fail. The plan for an air strike during the 1962 Cuban missile crisis is an example of an option. Rival policies consist of any alternative solution to the problem at hand. They may involve a drastic change in the means, goals, issue position, and/or even the definition of the issue and situation. Although rival policies may be held by those who make the official foreign policy, typically they are advocated by policy influencers. During the beginning of the cold war, rival policies to containment were: F.D.R.'s four policemen proposal, Henry Wallace's accommodation policy toward the Soviet Union, traditional isolationism, idealism that sought to convert the U.N. into a world government, suggestions that there be a division of the world into spheres of influence, and right-wing calls for an anticommunist crusade to liberate Eastern Europe and topple the Bolshevik regime.[3]

If foreign policy histories like these were written for most actors on the most salient issues since the sixteenth century (or some other natural break—1648, 1815), then a complete description of the dependent variable—substantive foreign policy—would be made. How would it be possible to go beyond idiographic genetic explanation? By finding patterns. To that end we would want to know to what extent other actors (or, the same actor at different times) had similar policies—that is, policies that were detente-like,

Table 10.1

Recent Major U.S. Foreign Policies

Leadership	Issue	Target(s)	Policies
Franklin Roosevelt	Postwar political order	USSR, U.K., China, France, Italy, Germany, Japan	Grand Alliance, 4 Policemen, U.N.
Franklin Roosevelt	Economic order	"	Bretton-Woods System
Truman 1945–47	Postwar order	USSR, U.K.	Break down Grand Alliance
Truman 1947–53	Russian Communist dictatorship vs. U.S. Capitalist Democracy	USSR	Containment, Marshall Plan, Truman Doctrine, cold war, limited war
Eisenhower 1953	"	"	Flirtation with liberation; containment, cold war, massive retaliation, foreign aid
Eisenhower 1954–61	"	"	Containment, cold war, massive retaliation, covert intervention, foreign aid, compellance
Kennedy 1961–63	"	"	Containment, cold war, deterrence—Mutal Assured Destruction (MAD)—compellance, limited war, counterinsurgency, foreign aid
Johnson 1964–69	"	"	Containment, cold war, deterrence (MAD), limited war, counterinsurgency, foreign aid

Leadership	Issue	Target(s)	Policies
Nixon 1969–73	Russian Communist dictatorship vs. U.S. Capitalist Democracy	USSR	Switch from cold war to detente, Sino–American rapprochement, limited war, counterinsurgency, deterrence (MAD), containment, covert intervention
Ford 1973–77	"	"	Detente, deterrence (MAD), Sino–American rapprochement, containment, counterinsurgency rejected by Congress
Carter 1977–81	"	"	Detente, human rights, deterrence—move to counter-force from (MAD), covert intervention, boycott of USSR (partial return to cold war)
Carter 1977–81	North–South	Third World	Accommodationist stance toward Third-World concerns
Reagan 1981–	Russian Communist dictatorship vs. U.S. Capitalist Democracy	USSR	Abandonment of detente and human rights (rhetorical return to cold war), covert intervention, deterrence and counterforce, anti-Communism
	North–South	Third World	Defense of free enterprise, abandonment of accommodationist stance

containment-like, protectionist-like, mercantilist-like, and so forth. Out of this we would try to delineate by issue area the different *kinds* of foreign policies that seem to have existed.[4] My suspicion is that the number of truly different foreign policies in a single issue area is considerably fewer than we might think. We will probably be surprised by the extent to which history repeats itself.

A TAXONOMY OF FOREIGN POLICIES

Table 10.2 has some examples of these generic foreign policies in the security issue area. The middle column lists the major *kinds* of foreign policy in the security issue area that would probably be uncovered in a systematic historical review of world politics. Column three provides specific examples of each kind of policy. Most of the listed policies, like balance of power, take their names from participants in a particular historical period, but, as the examples illustrate, policies like these may be found in other periods involving other actors and other regions even if they employ a different name. Some of the policies, such as "penetration" or "accommodation," have labels applied to them by observers who have reconstructed the policy after the fact. Often these policies may be informal, and care must be taken that the observer not impose an order on the data that does not exist. Suffice it to say for now that since these *kinds* of policies appear to have historical referents that show them to be major and important policies in world politics, analysis of their causes and effects would not only seem possible but desirable.

Neutrality/nonalignment and isolationism are typical policies of states that are either relatively weak or whose interests are not sufficiently affected by an issue to warrant the risks and costs associated with participation. Neutrality/nonalignment is a policy where an actor refuses to take an issue position(s) on the major issue(s) dividing rivals. This policy may be specific to a particular issue and rivalry, as with the neutralist bloc of the 1950s and 1960s and subsequently the nonaligned nations vis-à-vis the cold war, or it could be more general, as with Switzerland's policy toward any European rivalry that threatens war. Isolationism, on the other hand, connotes nonparticipation in all the affairs, usually of a region, and not just on issues between two rivals. A state may be isolationist in one region, as the United States was toward Europe in the early part of its history, and very active in another region, as it was in its westward expansion.

Clientalism, as used in Table 10.2, refers to a set of policies between the weak and the strong. Three kinds—foreign aid, alliances, and penetration—can be distinguished by their techniques and the extent to which the stronger actor has limited goals. All three, however, involve the weak seeking something from the strong and the strong providing it in return for something from the weak.

Coercive diplomacy, balance of power, deterrence, containment, and spheres of influence are all policies that have dominated relations among equals in the modern nation–state system since 1648. While each of these policies tends to emphasize interest and reject moral constraints, employ and/or threaten force, and be concerned primarily with the struggle for power, there are differences that make them distinct (see Gaddis, 1982; George, Hall, and Simons, 1971; George and Smoke, 1974; Kaplan, 1957; Luard, 1976).

The policies of "accommodation," integration, regionalism, "concert of power," "regime creation," and world federalism reflect different kinds of efforts to reduce the struggle for power by peacefully resolving disputes. At the dyadic level, policies of accommodation, like detente, entente, and *Ostpolitik,* exemplify this tendency. Integration involves a more drastic agreement on procedures for resolving all kinds of political, economic, and social issues. The Schuman Plan for preventing war between Germany and France is an example of a successful integration policy, while the United Arab Republic illustrates a failed policy. At the global level, the policy of "regime creation" exemplifies this tendency. "Regime creation," which is a contemporary label, includes such historical efforts as the creation of international law, a system of courts, and various specialized international organizations such as the ICAO and ITU for regulating behavior, as well as more utopian organizations such as the League of Nations and the U.N. An actor may be said to have a foreign policy of "regime creation" if it is seeking to develop, abide by, or implement such regimes.

The history of foreign policy also reveals numerous messianic policies that have been guided by moral, religious, and/or ideological concerns. Observers will regard these efforts either as noble or as pernicious, depending on their attitude toward the underlying values of the policies. The policy of "cold war" is defined here as an unwillingness to engage in normal transactions because of moral

Table 10.2

A Taxonomy of Security Issue Area Foreign Policies

Families of foreign policy	Kinds of foreign policies (genus)	Historical examples (species)
Noninvolvement	Neutrality/ Nonalignment	Switzerland (Europe) 1914, India (toward U.S.A. and USSR) 1949–71, U.S. neutrality laws, interwar period
	Isolation	U.S.A. (toward Europe) 1789–1860, Japan (Europe–U.S.A. 1700s –1853
Clientelism	Foreign aid	U.S.A., USSR, China toward Third World (1950s–
	"Alliances between weak and strong"	Latin American countries that declared war against Germany in W.W.II (U.S. clients)
	"Penetration"	Finland, Germany, Japan (Clients U.S.S.R. and/or U.S. after W.W.II); covert intervention (Guatamala, Chile)
World order	"Accommoda-tion"	Detente, Ostpolitik, Entente, Appeasement
	Disarmament and arms control	Washington Conference 1921-1922, SALT
	Integration	Schuman Plan, U.A.R.
	Regionalism	EEC, OAU
	"Concert of power"	Concert of Europe, Collective Security
	"Regime creation"	World Court, League of Nations, WHO, Law of Sea
	World federalism	—

Families of foreign policy	Kinds of foreign policies (genus)	Historical examples (species)
Power politics	Coercive diplomacy	Gunboat diplomacy, big stick
	Balance of power	Bismarck, late 19th century
	Deterrence	Massive retaliation, Mutual Assured Destruction
	Containment	Truman Doctrine, Europe vs. Arabs & Turks (Middle Ages–17th century)
	Spheres of influence	Monroe Doctrine, Brezhnev Doctrine
Hegemony	National consolidation	Louis XIV Wars, Manifest Destiny, Zionism
	Irredentism	France (Alsace-Lorraine)
	Lebensraum	Germany and Japan, 1930s
	Imperialism	Spain, Portugal, Britain, France, 16th–20th centuries
	Empire	Rome
Messianism	Cold War	U.S.A.–USSR, 1947–1963, Sino–Soviet Dispute
	Idealism	Stimson Doctrine, Wilsonianism
	Revolution	Paine's Common Sense, Trotsky's Permanent Revolution, Lin Piao
	Counter revolution	The Counterreformation, U.S. Counterinsurgency 1950–
	Racism (including genocide)	Naziism, apartheid
	Jihad	Spread of Islam, crusades

disapproval of the other side. This relatively restrained policy can give rise to more active policies that seek to eliminate those who are seen to be in violation of some value or norm.

Finally, many foreign policies are concerned with establishing hegemony over territory and people. This can occur at the national, the regional, or the global level. The geographic scope, along with the goals of the expansion (reconquering territory, living space, economic control, political control) can be used to distinguish the different policies. As a group, these policies differ from those of coercive diplomacy, balance of power, and so on, in that they are much more expansionist and revisionist, while the others are primarily status-quo oriented.

While analysis should be concentrated on the generic policies in the second column, it may be possible to classify these policies into even broader categories. These are listed in column one. This level of classification implies that there may be "families of foreign policy," based on some shared characteristic(s) of goals and means, that produce a set of similar attitudes and behavior. Thus, while there are real differences between neutrality/nonalignment and isolationism, they do share characteristics that distinguish them as a group from the policies listed under power politics. Likewise, the policies classified as power politics (raison d'état, balance of power, deterrence, containment, and spheres of influence) are quite different from one another, but as a group are more similar to one another in goals, means, and attendant attitudes and behavior than they are to the policies classified as messianic. Whether such families of policies can be identified must await a systematic historical review, but the list seems sufficiently plausible to at least warrant undertaking this kind of research.

RESEARCH IMPLICATIONS

Once we delineate the different kinds of foreign policies that predominate, the utility of such a list could be assessed in two ways. First, does the list fit the evidence? Can each of the foreign policies of a period be classified as one of the generic foreign policies? Can the generic names be substituted for the historically specific names without too much violence? Can quantitative data on issue positions be analyzed through scaling or cluster techniques to delineate the different policies? Second, is this policy approach theoretically significant? As a dependent variable, is a classification of foreign policies something that, if adequately explained, would provide the knowledge we seek? Does such an approach get at the essence of substantive foreign policy, or is it like foreign policy decision making and foreign policy behavior—interesting variables in and of themselves, but not what we originally wanted to explain? More difficult to answer is: Does the conceptualization focus on that which is causally significant and obfuscate the unimportant, or does it focus on the irrelevant and obfuscate the significant? If it is the former, then it should produce propositions that pass empirical tests. Finally, can this conceptualization serve as an interesting independent and/or intervening variable? In short, these questions suggest that it is possible to assess the utility of this conceptualization by conducting an inventory of its causes and effects.

An answer to the first question, whether the list fits the evidence, can only be provided once the research is done. However, there is one piece of quantitative evidence and a recent suggestion on new uses of event data that can be mentioned to show how this approach can integrate traditional historical analysis and contemporary data analysis. In a very intriguing analysis, Rummel (1972:98–100, 111–12) factor-analyzed 19 indicators of U.S. behavior toward specific targets and uncovered six patterns of foreign policy behavior during 1955: West European cooperation, Anglo–U.S. cooperation, deterrence, cold war, negative sanctions, and (economic) aid. Deterrence, cold war, and aid tap obvious policies that were being followed by the United States in 1955. The other types seem to indicate more general behaviors rather than the effects of specific policies. However, "West European cooperation," which is a type of cooperation statistically distinct from Anglo–U.S. cooperation, reflects many of the effects of the Marshall Plan—movement of students and emigrants, treaties with those nations, military aid, and high level conferences (Rummel, 1972:98). The Rummel study is intriguing because it suggests that policies do leave behavioral patterns that can be used as an indirect way of delineating the existence of these policies. Suffice it to say for now that Rummel's analysis suggests one way of providing independent corroboration for historical reconstructions.

More explicit suggestions are provided by Callahan (in Callahan, Brady, and M. Hermann, 1982: Chapters 13 and 14), who argues that a foreign policy should produce a syndrome of behavior that is identifiable. This can be done by seeing whether various behavioral measures cluster in distinct ways. For example, in the CREON project (which measures foreign policy behavior in terms of scope of action, goal properties, instruments, commitment, affect, specificity, independence of action, and acceptance/rejection, among others), different foreign policies should produce different profiles of behavior.[5] Behavior profiles may be seen as the visible traces left by a policy. For this reason, they could be used as an indirect means of identifying foreign policy; however, it is probably more useful to treat these as behavioral effects of a policy and identify the policy either through historical reconstruction or quantitative analysis of issue positions.[6]

In order to make the case that such extensive comparative historical and quantitative research should be undertaken, the second question—exactly what kinds of theoretical insights and explanations are being promised—must be discussed more fully. First, it should be clear that this conceptualization of foreign policy does get at the substantive questions in which we are interested. Detente, deterrence, cold war, appeasement, integration, and foreign aid are identifiable policies that have played sufficiently important roles to warrant both explanation and evaluation.

Explanation and evaluation can be conducted by looking at the same kind of foreign policy in two countries or by examining the same policy at two different times in the same nation. An example of the former is Kjell Goldmann's (1982) analysis, which looks at the United States' detente policy and compares it with West Germany's *Ostpolitik* in an attempt to delineate factors making for foreign policy stability. Similarly, there have been efforts to compare different national policies of imperialism and colonialism, particularly the difference between the French and the British (see Crowder, 1968). An analysis that looked at the same policy at different times might compare Franklin D. Roosevelt's accommodationist stance toward the Soviet Union, Nixon–Kissinger's detente, and Carter's detente. Some empirical questions with important evaluative implications would be: what conditions make the policy feasible (able to be implemented) at one time and not another? Why does it appear to succeed at one time and fail at another? To a certain extent, Alexander George (1980) has addressed some of these questions in his examination of detente. Along with Richard Smoke, he asked similar questions when comparing deterrence policy in the Truman, Eisenhower, and Kennedy presidencies (George and Smoke, 1974). These examples should demonstrate that attempts to explain specific policies can be theoretically interesting and policy relevant. Conducting these studies on a more comparative, systematic, and generalizable basis would make them even more promising.

Second, following this research agenda should improve our knowledge of foreign policy in two areas. In the first area, we would like to know in more theoretical and, if possible, causal terms why certain *kinds* of foreign policies are adopted and other kinds rejected. Our current knowledge of this consists of only very narrow ideographic explanations typical of diplomatic history, or the very post hoc–deductive–impressionistic interest explanations of realists and marxists. It would be nice to see some comparative historical and quantitative research on this question. In this way we might come to understand the constellation of domestic and global factors that produce a certain kind of foreign policy.

Related to this is the question of foreign policy change (see Vasquez and Mansbach, 1983). Why are certain kinds of policies abandoned or replaced? Also, when one kind of policy fails, how does that affect its replacement? If Reagan is correct that detente is a failure, what comes next? Is it really possible to return to a cold war policy, or do domestic and global factors prohibit this? This raises the further question of whether policy sequences occur. Does the success or failure of one kind of policy automatically increase or decrease the probability of another kind of policy being adopted? Here questions of learning (Jervis, 1976) and precedents (May, 1973) become relevant. Are specific or certain kinds of foreign policy linked, and by what?

If research were successful in identifying "families of foreign policy," similar questions could be raised about them. It would be of theoretical interest to ask why an actor picked one policy within a family rather than another. In addition, we would want to know whether there are certain global and/or domestic structural conditions that favor certain families of policy over others in any particular time in global history or in the development of a relationship between two or more actors. Why are certain periods of history dominated by actors who pursue hegemony and others by actors who pursue policies of world order? Are the effects that different? Finally, how does an actor (or group of actors in a single historical period) combine the different kinds of policies? Are there representatives from more than one "family," and if so, are there certain families that naturally co-occur? For example, if power politics prevents hegemony, can it then give rise to world order? Or, if power politics fails and hegemony is imposed, does messianism follow? In this way the "family" classification would permit some of the old questions of philosophy of history to be raised in a more empirical and scientific manner.

A second area of inquiry has to do with the effects of a policy on competing actors. How do targets and others react to the policy? Are there any patterns? Do certain kinds of policies produce the same reactions (among the same kinds of actors), (in certain situations)? Are spiraling effects (hostile or cooperative) associated with certain kinds of policies? Do hard-line policies produce end results that are different from accommodationist policies, and if so, why? What are the effects of certain kinds of policies on allies or on the contention of other issues? Are certain kinds of policies (when controlling for the right variables) more apt than others to result in success, failure, or war? What are the short- and long-term global economic, political, social, and demographic consequences of certain kinds of policies? Little research has been conducted along these lines. The closest is the work of Leng (1980, and Chapter 3 in this volume) who compares the effects of realist and nonrealist strategies on the likelihood of war breaking out.

A related question is on the domestic effects of a foreign policy. How does adoption or rejection of a policy affect relationships within the decision-making elite and between the decision-making elite and policy influencers? Are there other political consequences? Do certain kinds of foreign policies encourage the government to enact certain kinds of domestic policies? Similarly, is there a linkage between certain kinds of foreign policies, their success or failure, domestic political reaction (e.g., hard liners vs. accommoda-tionists), and the domestic policy of a government? What are the short- and long-term economic consequences of certain kinds of foreign policies? In other words, do certain kinds of foreign policies produce certain kinds of domestic and global reactions, which then have amplifying effects? For many economic policies—protection-ism, beggar-thy-neighbor programs, high deficit spending—these effects are well known, if not well understood. For more purely political questions, little work has been done. Nevertheless, even as early a commentator as Thucydides saw such relationships, in his case a relationship among imperialism, war, and the decline of democracy. Although war is a behavior and not a policy, contempor-ary research on the domestic effects of war demonstrates how research on the effects of policy could be conducted and what theoretical utility and policy relevance this research is likely to have (see Stein, 1980).

The theoretical significance of these questions should be fairly clear at this point, but what is even more important is that all of these questions naturally lend themselves to a systematic evaluation of foreign policy. The accuracy of assumptions underlying the policies and the extent to which the consequences are those that were expected, desirable, and within an acceptable range of costs and risks can be evaluated. This can be done for specific historical policies as well as the broader categories of foreign policies. In addition, a comparison with other options or rival policies would permit a more prescriptive policy analysis to be conducted in a systematic and somewhat rigorous manner.

The use of a taxonomy of generic foreign policies and families of foreign policy also facilitates a more critical perspective. The relative merit of different families of foreign policies could be assessed by comparing their goals and their performance in different periods. Thus relatively similar situations could be identified; if in one situation a power politics policy was adopted, in another a messianic policy, and in a third a world order policy, then the effects of their different goals could be compared. A similar procedure could be employed to compare strategies, risks, and so on.

For too long those devoted to the scientific study of foreign policy in the United States have allowed their work to remain uncritical of the dominant trends within U.S. foreign policy. Research on different *kinds* of foreign policy can be critical and lend itself to "grand policy evaluation" in two ways. First, its empirical findings are likely to undercut the factual and theoretical justifications for policy. Secondly, its analysis of options, rivals, and other policies in history (such as world order) help liberate the imagination from the one-dimensional thinking so prevalent within the foreign policy establishment. In this last regard, the evaluation of historical foreign policies that were not based on the current power politics approach would help critics to move toward proposals that would be less utopian by facing and resolving some of the types of problems that arose in previous attempts to base foreign policy on a different approach.

The development of a taxonomy of foreign policies by issue area presents a new agenda for the comparative study of foreign policy. Its promise is that it will make foreign policy analysis more historical and more truly comparative and restore the evaluative component of the field, giving scholars a professional role to play either as policy influencers or as intellectual critics. This more substantive focus will make our work less alienated from the pressing needs of our societies for better guidance in foreign policy, while our commitment to science will make us aware of the dangers of accepting beliefs, images, and myths on some basis other than the evidence. In this way our research will not only create knowledge but help to shape how it will be used.

NOTES

[1]One may distinguish between systems of thought that are primarily concerned with practice from those that are concerned with scientific explanation. For the former, social theory comes out of the world and is developed as a way of guiding action in the world. For the latter, theory is supposed to be above the world rather than of it. Its primary purpose is to explain why things happen; any practical use is a side benefit. For similar distinctions, see the essay by Richard Ashley in the previous chapter, as well as Habermas (1971).

[2]An interesting problem that often separates pluralists and liberals from radicals is that the former often maintain that in order for a policy to exist, those who make it must be conscious of the policy and must be motivated to seek goals and objectives attributed to the policy. Clearly, containment and detente are foreign policies in this sense and are even more formalized in that they have *names*. Radicals as well as revisionist historians are willing to delineate functional foreign policies on the basis of behavioral consequences even if there are no conscious or consistent motives for that policy. Questions of U.S. neoimperalism often turn on this disagreement. Suffice it to say here that the degree to which a policy need be formal, conscious, and motivated is one end of a continuum that describes one kind of policy, which might be labeled *manifest policy* as opposed to *latent policy*.

[3]For a review of alternatives to containment within the government as well as an illustration of how scholars can derive options from the historical record, see Messer (1977).

[4]If a particular period of history, issue area, or foreign policy relationship between two or more actors were highly patterned, it might be possible to transform a list of *kinds* of foreign policy into a formal typology that is mutually exclusive and logically exhaustive. I have resisted taking this more deductive approach, because I think history is more open-ended and less patterned than is implied by such a procedure. Nevertheless, when the evidence for particular cases is consistent with typologies, the framework can be easily converted.

On the whole, we would probably be better off trying to create a taxonomy with specific examples of foreign policies (species) being grouped into generic kinds of foreign policy on the basis of shared characteristics (genus), and with these further grouped into families. An attempt at this is tried in Table 10.2. As in biology, classification will prove useful if it is employed as a heuristic device that may provide theoretical insight and suggest propositions, and not if scholars become preoccupied with the accuracy of the taxonomy itself.

[5]As the field becomes more sophisticated, and examines all the characteristics of foreign policy behavior, and stops reducing everything to cooperation–conflict, it will become feasible to construct profiles of this sort.

[6]Some critics have argued that a taxonomy of foreign policies would not be useful because a vast array of conflicting activities could be included in the generic

categories. This, of course, is an empirical question that cannot be answered until research is attempted. What is of interest is just how different will initiations by the actor and responses by the target be under the different policies. The empirical examination of such behavioral profiles would be one way of testing interpretations made in comparative historical case studies of generic policies. There is no a priori reason to presume that such research would find no difference in behavior patterns associated with the different policies if, as mentioned above, a sufficiently diverse number of behavioral indicators were employed.

REFERENCES

ALLISON, G., and M. HALPERIN (1972). "Bureaucratic Politics: A Paradigm and Some Policy Implications." *World Politics* 24 (Supplement):40–89.

AXELROD, R. (ed.) (1976). *Structure of Decision.* Princeton, N.J.: Princeton University Press.

CALLAHAN, P., L. BRADY, and M. HERMANN (eds.) (1982). *Describing Foreign Policy Behavior.* Beverly Hills, Calif.: Sage Publications.

COHEN, B. C., and S. A. HARRIS (1975). "Foreign Policy." In F. Greenstein and N. Polsby (eds.), *Policies and Policymaking,* Vol. 6 of *Handbook of Political Science.* Reading, Mass.: Addison-Wesley. Pp. 381–437.

COPLIN, W. D. (1974). *Introduction to International Politics,* 2nd ed. Chicago: Rand McNally.

COPLIN, W., S. MILLS, and M. O'LEARY (1973). "The PRINCE Concepts and the Study of Foreign Policy." In P. McGowan (ed.), *Sage International Yearbook of Foreign Policy Studies,* Volume 1. Beverly Hills, Calif.: Sage Publications. Pp. 73–103.

CROWDER, M. (1968). *West Africa under Colonial Rule.* Evanston, Ill.: Northwestern University Press.

EAST, M. A. (1975). "Explaining Foreign Policy Behavior Using National Attributes." Paper presented to the annual meeting of the American Political Science Association, September 2–5, San Francisco, Calif.

ETHEREDGE, L. S. (1978). *A World of Men: The Private Sources of American Foreign Policy.* Cambridge, Mass.: MIT Press.

GADDIS, J. (1982). *Strategies of Containment: A Critical Appraisal of*

Postwar American National Security Policy. New York: Oxford University Press.

GALTUNG, J. (1971). "A Structural Theory of Imperialism." *Journal of Peace Research*, 8/2:81–119.

GEORGE, A. L. (1980). "Domestic Constraints on Regime Change in U.S. Foreign Policy." In O. Holsti, R. Siverson, and A. George (eds.), *Change in the International System*. Boulder, Col: Westview. Pp. 233–62.

GEORGE, A., D. HALL, and W. SIMONS (1971). *The Limits of Coercive Diplomacy*. Boston, Mass.: Little, Brown.

GEORGE, A. L., and R. SMOKE (1974). *Deterrence in American Foreign Policy: Theory and Practice*. New York: Columbia University Press.

GOLDMANN, K. (1982). "Change and Stability in Foreign Policy: Detente as a Problem of Stabilization." *World Politics*, 34:230–66.

GUETZKOW, H., and J. VALADEZ (eds.) (1981). *Simulated International Processes*. Beverly Hills, Calif.: Sage Publications.

HABERMAS, J. (1971). *Knowledge and Human Interests*. London: Heinemann.

HERMANN, C. F. (ed.) (1972). *International Crises: Insights from Behavioral Research*. New York: Free Press.

HERMANN, C. F. (1978). "Foreign Policy Behavior: That Which Is to Be Explained." In M. East, S. Salmore, and C. Hermann (eds.), *Why Nations Act*. Beverly Hills, Calif.: Sage Publications. Pp. 25–47.

HERMANN, C. F., and R. A. COATE (1982). "Substantive Problem Areas." In P. Callahan, L. Brady, and M. Hermann (eds.), *Describing Foreign Policy*. Beverly Hills, Calif.: Sage Publications. Pp. 77–114.

HERMANN, M. G. (1980). "Explaining Foreign Policy Behavior Using the Personal Characteristics of Political Leaders." *International Studies Quarterly*, 24:7–46.

HOLSTI, O., R. NORTH, and R. BRODY (1968). "Perception and Action in the 1914 Crisis." In J. D. Singer (ed.), *Quantitative International Politics*. New York: The Free Press. Pp. 123–58.

JERVIS, R. (1976). *Perception and Misperception in International Politics.* Princeton, N.J.: Princeton University Press.

KAPLAN, M. (1957). *System and Process in International Politics.* New York: Wiley.

LENG, R. J. (1980). "Influence Strategies and Interstate Conflict." In J. D. Singer (ed.), *Correlates of War: II.* New York: Free Press. Pp. 125–57.

LENTNER, H. (1981). Review of J. Wilkenfeld et al., *Foreign Policy Behavior. American Political Science Review,* 75:756.

LINDBLOM, C. (1968). *The Policy-Making Process.* Englewood Cliffs, N.J.: Prentice-Hall.

LUARD, E. (1976). *Types of International Society.* New York: The Free Press.

LYND, R. S. (1939). *Knowledge for What?* Princeton, N.J.: Princeton University Press.

McCLELLAND, C. A. (1968). "Access to Berlin: The Quantity and Variety of Events, 1948–1963." In J. D. Singer (ed.), *Quantitative International Politics.* New York: Free Press. Pp. 159–87.

MANSBACH, R. W. and J. A. VASQUEZ (1981). *In Search of Theory: A New Paradigm for Global Politics.* New York: Columbia University Press.

MAY, E. R. (1973). *"Lessons" of the Past.* London: Oxford University Press.

MORGENTHAU, H. J. (1951). *In Defense of the National Interest.* New York: Knopf.

MESSER, R. L. (1977). "Paths Not Taken: The United States Department of State and Alternatives to Containment, 1945–1946." *Diplomatic History* 1:297–319.

PHILLIPS, W. R. and R. C. CRAIN (1974). "Dynamic Foreign Policy Interactions: Reciprocity and Uncertainty in Foreign Policy." In P. J. McGowan (ed.), *Sage International Yearbook of Foreign Policy Studies,* Vol. II. Pp. 227–66.

ROSENAU, J. N. (1966). "Pre-Theories and Theories of Foreign Policy." In

R. B. Farrell (ed.), *Approaches to Comparative and International Politics*. Evanston, Ill.: Northwestern University Press. Pp. 27–93.

ROSENAU, J. N., and G. D. HOGGARD (1974). "Foreign Policy Behavior in Dyadic Relationships: Testing a Pretheoretical Extension." In J. Rosenau (ed.), *Comparing Foreign Policies*. New York: Halsted/John Wiley and Sons. Pp. 117–49.

RUMMEL, R. J. (1972). "U.S. Foreign Relations: Conflict, Cooperation, and Attribute Distances." In B. Russett (ed.), *Peace, War, and Numbers*. Beverly Hills, Calif.: Sage Publications. Pp. 71–113.

RUMMEL, R. J. (1977). *Field Theory Evolving*. Beverly Hills, Calif.: Sage Publications.

RUSSETT, B. M. (1983). "International Interactions and Processes: The Internal vs. External Debate Revisited." In A. Finifter (ed.), *Political Science: The State of the Discipline*. Washington D.C.: The American Political Science Association. Pp. 541–68.

SNYDER, G. H., and P. DIESING (1977). *Conflict among Nations: Bargaining, Decision Making, and System Structure*. Princeton, N.J.: Princeton University Press.

SNYDER, R., H. BRUCK, and B. SAPIN (1954). *Decision-Making as an Approach to the Study of International Politics*. Princeton, N.J.: Foreign Policy Analysis Project, Princeton University.

STEIN, A. (1980). *The Nation at War*. Baltimore, Md.: Johns Hopkins University Press.

VASQUEZ, J. A. (1983). *The Power of Power Politics: A Critique*. New Brunswick: Rutgers University Press; London: Frances Pinter.

VASQUEZ, J. A., and R. W. MANSBACH (1983). "The Issue Cycle: Conceptualizing Long-Term Global Political Change." *International Organization*, 37:257–79.

VASQUEZ, J. A., and R. W. MANSBACH (1984). "The Role of Issues in Global Co-operation and Conflict." *British Journal of Political Science*, 14:411–33.

WALLACE, M. (1982). "Armaments and Escalation: Two Competing Hypotheses." *International Studies Quarterly*, 26:37–56.

WARD, M. D. (1984). "Differential Paths to Parity: A Study of the Contemporary Arms Race." *American Political Science Review,* 78:297–317.

WILKENFELD, J., G. HOPPLE, P. ROSSA, and S. ANDRIOLE (1980). *Foreign Policy Behavior.* Beverly Hills, Calif.: Sage Publications.

WOLFERS, A. (1962). *Discord and Collaboration.* Baltimore, Md.: Johns Hopkins Press.

INDEX

academics, 8, 12, 20

Acheson, Dean, 152–53

Afghanistan, 92, 101–2, 105, 109, 136, 146, 148–49

Africa, 123

alliances, 6, 8, 103, 104–6, 107, 115, 122, 215, 222

Allison, Graham, 181–82, 205

appeasement, 10, 46–47, 208–9, 220

Argentina, 102–3

arms control, 21–23, 29, 35, 59–60, 65–66, 67, 68, 86, 90–91

arms races, 6, 8, 10, 19–20, 21–23, 31–35, 55–56, 86, 88 (*see also* insecurity)

Austria–Hungary, 50, 78

balance of power, 6, 10–11, 40, 91, 214, 215, 218

bargaining, 6, 10, 39, 97–98, 107

Berlin crises, 50–52, 53, 54

Brezhnev, Leonid, 102

Bruck, H., 179, 207

bureaucratic politics, 9, 27, 43, 168–69, 181–83, 205–6

Callahan, Patrick, 219–20

Carter, Jimmy, 97, 102–3, 107, 113–15, 116–17, 119–31, 141, 143–44, 189, 212–13, 220

Central America, 7–8, 135

Central Intelligence Agency (C.I.A.), 142–43, 145, 147, 150

change, 8, 14, 145, 188–89, 156–96, 209–10

Chile, 145, 146, 149–50, 151, 153–54

China, 92, 143, 151

Clausewitz, Carl von, 24, 39, 77–80, 81, 86, 87–88

coercive diplomacy, 5, 6, 8, 44–48, 50–55, 56, 190, 215, 218 (*see also* sanctions, economic)

cold war, 8, 128–29, 152–53, 216–17, 219–20

commitment, 40–42, 45, 68–69, 102, 114, 129, 165

communism, 115, 116, 121, 122, 126, 127, 129–30, 136, 149, 151, 211

comparative foreign policy, 164, 171–72, 173–78, 180, 181–82, 183–88, 189–93, 199, 205–9, 210–11, 223–24

compromise, 47, 78

conflict: inter-state, 105, 126, 207; level of, 39–56, 68–69, 97, 98, 206

Conservatives, U.S., 115, 211

containment, 5–6, 208–9, 210, 211–14, 215, 218

cooperation, 44, 48, 51, 53–54, 98–101, 102, 107, 115, 117, 120, 124–25, 128–29, 131, 145, 206, 207, 209–10, 222

costs and benefits, 12, 14, 40, 41–42, 45, 55–56, 68–69, 86, 87, 91–92, 98, 101, 107, 108–9, 223

credibility, 40–42, 45–46, 51, 53–55, 89, 149

Cuba, 143–44, 146, 149, 150–51, 153–54

Cuban missile crisis, 48, 52–53, 54,
91–92, 211
crisis, 6, 10, 21–23, 35, 39–56, 189–
90, 206
critical perspective, 11, 13–14, 59–60,
159–64, 166, 172–74, 175–76,
185–86, 191, 192–94, 196, 197–
200, 208, 223–24
critical–dialogical framework, 164,
195–200

decision makers (*see* leaders)
decision-making process, 4–5, 39, 43,
169–70, 172–74, 179–80, 181–
82, 183, 189, 206, 207, 211,
218–19, 222
defense communities, 69, 73–76, 80–
86, 89–94
defense policy, 9, 19–35, 148–49 (*see
also* military expenditures)
democracy, 12, 78, 115, 116, 121,
122, 138–39, 141, 143–44,
145–47, 153–54, 160, 168–69
detente, 55–56, 97, 98–99, 102, 109,
208–9, 214, 220–21
deterrence, 6, 22, 23, 34, 55, 59–60,
65–67, 89, 215, 218, 219–20
Dewey, John, 11, 194
domestic politics and foreign policy,
8, 12, 46, 108, 114, 152, 211,
221–22
domino theory, 6, 140, 148–49
doves, 29, 79–80

economic factors in world politics, 9,
19, 91–92, 98–109, 115, 116,
121–22, 126, 140–41, 147–49,
152, 214, 222 (*see also*
sanctions, economic)
Egypt, 50

Eisenhower, Dwight D., 153, 212–13,
220
El Salvador, 137–38, 140–43, 145–46,
147, 149; 1932 revolt in, 140–
42
escalation, 6, 10, 21–23, 35, 41–42,
43, 44, 47–48, 52–54, 55–56,
68–69
Europe, Eastern, 10, 77–79, 81, 91–
92, 122–25, 127, 136, 147–49,
151, 211, 216–17
Europe, Western, 9, 59–60, 68–69,
77–79, 81, 102, 103, 105, 108,
148, 189, 216–17, 219
event data, 42, 99, 181, 205, 219

failure, 8, 9–10, 45, 50, 52, 53–54,
78, 90, 106–8, 114, 129, 175–
76, 215, 220–22
force, 40–41, 43, 45–46, 47–48, 49,
50–51, 52–54, 77, 139, 215
Ford, Gerald, 113, 212–13
foreign affairs, conduct of, 3–4, 207,
208 (*see also* practice)
foreign aid, 4, 9, 113, 115, 117,
121–22, 126, 137–38, 139,
141, 143, 153–54, 215,
219–20
foreign policy: conceptualization
of, 207–20; consequences
of, 3–5, 8–10, 12, 14, 45–48,
61, 140, 177–178, 220, 222–
23; evaluation of, 3–15, 159–
64, 173, 183, 185–88, 191,
192–93, 198–200, 207–9, 220,
222–24; explanation of, 13–14,
179–83, 187, 189–91, 195–96,
206–9, 218–19, 220–22; goals
of, 3–4, 9, 11, 13–14, 40–42,
49, 85–89, 113, 114, 117, 119,
129–30, 131, 137–38, 180,

208-9, 211, 218, 220, 223 (*see also* domestic politics and foreign policy; foreign affairs)

France, 50, 78, 104, 106-7, 139-40, 164, 215, 220

George, Alexander, 220
Germany, Federal Republic of, 103-4, 151, 162-63, 215, 220
Germany, Imperial, 50, 77-78
Goldmann, Kjell, 99, 220
Great Britain, 50, 106-7, 219, 220
Grenada, invasion of, 189-90
Guatemala, 143, 145, 146, 149, 151
Guetzkow, Harold, 175-76

Habermas, Jurgen, 194
hard-liners, 6, 10, 19, 29, 78-80, 222
hegemony, 12-13, 77, 88-92, 195-96, 198-200, 218, 221
Hermann, Charles, F., 335
history, 6, 7-8, 13-14, 141, 149, 159-64, 165-66, 167, 169, 171-76, 179, 180-81, 183-91, 193-94, 195-96, 197, 198-200, 206, 209, 210-17, 218-19, 221-22, 223-24
Hobbes, Thomas, 76-70
Honduras, 142-43, 146
hostility, 52, 67, 76, 78-80, 90, 91-92, 125, 144, 145, 209-10, 222
human rights, 10, 68, 113-31, 137-39, 141, 143, 147, 149-51, 210
Hungary, 136, 144, 148-49

idealism, 195, 211, 215

ideology, 8, 11, 13-14, 69, 75, 89-90, 91-92, 93, 126, 128-29, 161-62, 166, 175-76, 177-78, 186-87, 196, 215
images, 5, 6-7, 8, 189, 191-92, 205, 223-24
imperialism, 209, 210, 220, 222
India, 50
influence attempt, 42-43, 44, 51, 104, 209-10; defined, 43, 44
information, 12, 27-28, 127, 131, 153-54
insecurity, 19-20, 61, 69
intellectuals, 8, 11, 14, 208, 223-24 (*see also* academics)
Intelligence Quotient (IQ) tests, 7-8
interdependence, 98, 191-92, 198-200
international law, 102, 215
international organizations, 114, 117, 131 (*see also* nongovernmental organizations)
international relations inquiry, 4, 7, 12-13, 162-63; research in, 5-6, 7, 8, 164; theory in, 12-13, 74, 79-80, 84, 93, 164, 176-77, 183-87, 191, 192-93, 195-97, 198-200, 206, 208, 210-11, 218-19, 220-23 (*see also* scientific method and the study of politics)
Iran, 79-80, 143, 151, 189
isolationism, 209, 211
Israel, 50, 79-80
issues, 43, 48-49, 98-99, 107, 115, 117, 131, 208-14, 222, 223-24

Japan, 20, 92, 102, 104; dropping of A-bomb on, 64, 80
Johnson, Lyndon B., 212-13

Kennedy, John F., 52–53, 140, 148–
49, 212–13, 220
Kirkpatrick, Jeanne, 7, 137–38, 141,
143, 145
Kissinger Commission on Central
America, 7, 135, 144, 149–51
Kissinger, Henry, 9, 97, 98, 99–101,
109, 208–9
knowledge, 3–5, 8, 164, 167–68, 171–
74, 175, 176–79, 183, 191–93,
196, 205, 218–19, 221, 223–24;
cumulative, 9, 175–76, 179,
193, 197–98, 205–6
Korean war, 148–49, 151

Latin America, 7, 68, 115, 117, 120,
122, 137–38, 146, 149–51,
189–90
leaders, 3–4, 6, 11, 39, 40, 49–50,
52, 54, 59–60, 73, 75, 109,
136–37, 152, 189
learning, 7–8, 44, 46–47, 49–50, 52–
54, 55, 83, 109, 150–51, 165,
210–11, 221
liberalism, 11, 143–45, 160, 162–65,
167–69, 179, 182, 185, 198
linkage, 9, 97–102, 106–9, 221; defined, 98

McCarthyism, 127, 152
McClelland, Charles, 178
McGowan, Patrick, 175, 177, 181
Machiavelli, Niccolo, 39, 137
major powers, 43, 48–49, 51
Marxist analysis, 77, 210–11, 221
means and ends, 8–9, 11, 13–14,
85, 114, 148, 162–63, 166,
170, 177–78, 180, 183, 187–
88, 190–91, 211, 218
messianism, 215, 221, 223

military, the, 74–75, 78, 80, 81, 85,
86, 88–92 (see also defense
communities)
military expenditures, 6, 19–20, 32,
60, 107, 152, 153–54; problems
with measurement of, 23–29
modernity, 167, 186–88, 189, 191,
194
morality and politics, 7–8, 11–12, 14,
68, 83–85, 88–90, 92–94, 114–
15, 131, 135–54, 215 (see also
values and norms)
Morgenthau, Hans J., 5, 39–40, 137,
207
myth, 3–4, 7–8, 65, 166, 177–78,
195, 223–24

Napoleon Bonaparte, 78
national interest, 7, 40, 48–49, 53,
114–15, 135–54, 182, 206, 208
neutrality/nonalignment, 216–17,
218
Nicaragua, 136, 143–47, 149, 150–
51, 152
Nixon, Richard M., 79–80, 113, 136–
37, 208–9, 212–13
nongovernmental organizations, 10,
117–31
nuclear annihilation, 3–4, 59–60, 61–
63, 65, 67–68, 90, 92–93, 148
nuclear war, 7–9, 11, 20, 65–66, 67,
68–69, 126, 147–49, 150–51;
effects of, 61–65
nuclear weapons, 6, 19–20, 24, 59–
60, 68, 87, 150–51

objectivity, 159–63, 167, 168, 169–
72, 173, 177–78, 184–86, 191,
195–96, 198–200; and support

of status quo, 11, 13–14, 164, 165–66, 176–77, 196

Pakistan, 50, 102
Panama, 146–47
participation, 206, 207, 216–17; of major powers, 43, 48–49
peace, 102, 128–29; conditions of, 78, 114, 215
peace through strength, 6, 21–23, 35, 44
perceptions, 24, 52, 107, 135, 151, 205–6
Poland, 102, 104–5, 107–8, 109
policy relevance, 3–4, 14, 186–88, 191, 198–200, 207, 208, 222
Popper, Karl, 168–69, 184
positivism, 12–13, 162–66, 167, 168, 169, 171–74, 179, 182, 183–85, 186–88, 189, 191, 192–93, 197, 198–200, 207, 208
power, 6, 40–41, 43, 50–51, 53, 54–56, 68–69, 90, 116, 126, 136, 150, 151, 168–69, 197, 206; effect on behavior, 41–42, 44–46, 47, 48–50, 52–54, 55–56, 77–78, 98, 107, 109, 215 (*see also* status)
power politics, 5, 40, 195–96, 198, 215, 218, 221, 223
practice, 13–14, 39, 116, 159–68, 169, 173–75, 179, 181–82, 183–88, 189–91, 192–93, 195–200, 208–9, 223–24
prescription, 39, 41–42, 46, 47, 49–50, 53–54, 55–56, 223
prudence, 6, 40–41, 41–42, 47–48, 49–50, 52, 54
psychological factors in world politics, 41, 43, 49–50, 55, 73, 78–80, 172–74 (*see also* perceptions)
public opinion, 81–83, 135–37, 139–40, 149, 152, 153–54

quantitative analysis, 6, 205–7, 208, 219

rationality, 40, 41, 49–50, 55, 59–61, 67, 85, 86, 88–90, 93, 149, 152, 168–69, 172–74, 176, 181–82, 198–200, 206, 209 (*see also* technical rationality)
Reagan administration, 11, 97, 103–6, 153–54, 212–13; and gas pipeline, 9, 102, 103–9; and human rights, 10, 68, 115–17, 119–31, 143; and military expenditures, 6, 19–22, 23, 27, 30–31, 34–35, 65–66, 102, 117, 152; and nuclear strategy, 8, 59–62, 67; and revolution, 135, 137–38, 142–43, 189–90; and relations with Soviet Union, 30, 34–35, 51, 55–56, 59–60, 61–62, 67–69, 102, 104–5, 106, 107, 109, 117, 122, 212–13, 221 (*see also* United States)
realism, 10, 39–56, 68, 70, 206–7, 221, 222 (*see also* power politics)
reciprocity, 43, 46–48, 50–51, 52, 53–54, 99, 107
religion and politics, 77, 79–80, 102, 127, 215
resolve, 40, 41–42, 46, 47, 50, 51, 52, 54–55, 106
revisionist states, 21–23, 52
revolution, 7–8, 138–39, 141, 143–44, 147, 149, 188–89
Richardson, Lewis F., 32

risk, 3-4, 8, 10-11, 14, 20, 23, 40-42, 47, 48-49, 52-53, 54, 55-56, 61, 68-69, 223
rivalry, 67, 68-69, 151, 216-17
role, 41, 76, 191-92, 208
Roosevelt, Franklin D., 141, 189, 212-13, 220
Rosenau, James N., 174-75, 176, 180, 181-82, 184, 193, 207
Rummel, R. J., 98-99, 219
Russett, Bruce M., 99, 177-78

Sagan, Carl, 61-63
sanctions, economic, 9, 102-9, 115
Sapin, Burton, 179, 207
Schelling, Thomas C., 40-41
scientific method, 73, 80-81, 83, 87, 92-93, 160-62, 164-66, 167, 168-69, 171-72, 174-76, 184, 186, 192-93; and the study of politics, 3-4, 7-8, 9, 11, 13-14, 162-64, 170, 171-72, 173-79, 180-81, 182, 183-88, 189-93, 196, 197-200, 205-13, 210-11, 223 (see also comparative foreign policy, quantitative analysis)
Singer, J. David, 178, 180
South Africa, Republic of, 68, 120-21
Smoke, Richard, 220
Snyder, Richard C., 179, 207
Sparta, 85
spirals, 52, 61, 222
Star Wars (Strategic Defense Initiative), 19, 60, 65-66
state, the, 73, 75, 77, 161-62, 168-69, 181, 183, 189-90, 193, 198-205, 206, 209
status, 50, 55
status quo, 11, 21-23, 35, 52, 164, 218

strategy, 7-8, 10, 24, 39-56, 59-62, 65-66, 68-69, 73, 75-77, 79-80, 83-85, 86, 87-90, 91-94, 101, 105-9, 148-49, 153-54, 181, 188-90, 195-96, 197-200, 209, 222, 223
structure, 12-13, 74-75, 91-92, 159, 161, 164, 165-66, 172-74, 175-76, 180-81, 183, 187, 188-89, 191-92, 194, 195-96, 210-11
success, 4, 8, 9, 41, 42, 47, 49-51, 53, 54-55, 59-60, 78, 99, 108, 215, 220-22 (see also failure)
systems, 73-75, 78, 81-83, 91

technical rationality, 11, 12-14, 161-62, 164, 166-67, 169-74, 176-77, 179, 181-82, 183-85, 189, 196, 208
territory, 48, 90, 215, 218
threat, 40-42, 43, 45-47, 48, 49, 50-51, 52-54, 55, 89-90, 93, 115, 116, 126, 148-50, 151-52, 215
Thucydides, 39, 222
Tolstoy, Leo, 92
tradition, 159-60, 161-62, 166, 167-68, 177-78, 185-89, 191, 194, 197-200
traditionalists, 6, 205, 219
Truman, Harry S., 5, 208-9, 212-13, 220
Turkey, 52, 91

uncertainty, 34, 67, 68-69, 106, 145
Union of Soviet Socialist Republics, 10, 50, 81, 89-90, 91-92, 115, 125, 127, 129, 136, 144, 146, 148-49, 151, 211; military capability of, 21, 23, 29-31, 34, 107 (see also United States of America and Soviet Union)

United Nations, 102, 114, 116, 135,
- 139, 211
United States of America, 11, 81, 89–
90, 91–92, 113–15, 216–17;
foreign policies of, 209, 210–11,
219; and Latin America, 7, 115,
117, 120, 122, 135–54, 189–90;
military capability of, 19–20,
23, 29–31, 34, 116, 137, 150;
and Soviet Union, 6, 7–9, 19–
35, 41–42, 44, 49–56, 59–70,
73, 79, 86, 91–92, 97–109,
115, 117, 120, 122, 126, 147–
48, 150–51, 208–9, 211, 220
U.S. Congress, 20, 101, 107, 113,
116, 125, 142–43, 146

values and norms, 159–61, 162–63,
166, 169–74, 175–76, 177, 181,
183, 185–87, 190, 192–93, 198,
208, 215

Vietnam war, 7–8, 91–92, 136, 138–
40, 145–47, 148–49, 151, 152,
189

war, 5, 10–11, 12, 41, 55–56, 76–83,
87, 89–90, 99, 128–29, 148,
216–17; causes of, 4, 6, 21–23,
35, 41, 47–49, 53–54, 78, 222;
and democracy, 148–49, 152–
54, 222 (*see also* nuclear war)
Weber, Max, 168–69
world order, 215, 221, 223
World War I, 79, 80, 152
World War II, 68, 80–81, 85, 92, 144,
146, 148, 150–51, 152, 189,
209, 210, 211

Yugoslavia, 144, 151

ABOUT THE EDITOR AND CONTRIBUTORS

The Editor

John A. Vasquez is Associate Professor of Political Science at Rutgers University, New Brunswick, New Jersey, and a specialist in international relations theory. He is author of *The Power of Power Politics: A Critique,* coauthor of *In Search of Theory: A New Paradigm for Global Politics,* and editor of *Classics of International Relations*; he has published articles in *International Studies Quarterly, Journal of Peace Research, Journal of Politics, International Organization,* and *British Journal of Political Science,* among others. He was recently awarded a Fulbright research grant for his study on the steps to war.

The Contributors

Richard K. Ashley is Associate Professor of Political Science at Arizona State University, Tempe, Arizona, and coeditor of *International Studies Quarterly.* He is author of *The Political Economy of War and Peace* and has published articles in *International Organization, International Studies Quarterly,* and *Journal of Conflict Resolution.* His current work focuses on knowledge, practice, and system in international relations.

Louis René Beres is Professor of Political Science at Purdue University, Lafayette, Indiana. He is author of numerous books and articles on nuclear strategy and nuclear war, including most recently: *Reason and Realpolitik: U.S. Foreign Policy and World Order, Mimicking Sisyphus: America's Countervailing Nuclear Strategy,* and *Apocalypse: Nuclear Catastrophe in World Politics.* The *New York Times* has described Professor Beres' work as providing "one of the leading philosophical underpinnings" of the worldwide movement against nuclear war.

Russell J. Leng is Professor of Political Science and Chairman of the Division of Social Science at Middlebury College, Middlebury, Vermont. The findings reported in his chapter on crisis bargaining are drawn from his Behavioral Correlates of War project, a long-term effort to describe and analyze patterns of interstate conflict behavior, for which he was recently awarded a grant from the National Science Foundation. His research has been published in the leading journals of the field, including *American Political Science Review, Journal of Conflict Resolution, American Journal of Political Science,* and *International Studies Quarterly.*

Anatol Rapoport is Professor of Peace Studies at the University of Toronto, Canada, and formerly Director of the Institute for Advanced Studies, Vienna, Austria. Professor Rapoport has been hailed widely for his studies in game theory and has long served as gaming editor of *Journal of Conflict Resolution.* He has authored over 300 articles and books, including *Fights, Games and Debates; Strategy and Conscience*; and *Prisoner's Dilemma.*

Neil R. Richardson is Associate Professor of Political Science at the University of Wisconsin–Madison, Madison, Wisconsin. He is author of *Foreign Policy and Economic Dependence* and has published numerous studies including articles in *American Political Science Review, Journal of Politics, International Studies Quarterly,* and *Social Science Quarterly.* His main research area is international political economy.

E. Thomas Rowe is Associate Professor at The Graduate School of International Studies, University of Denver, Denver, Colorado. He taught previously at the University of Connecticut and at Virginia Polytechnic Institute and State University. His writings include a monograph on the United Nations, chapters in a number of books, and articles in several professional journals, including *Journal Conflict Resolution, International Organization,* and *International Studies Quarterly.*

Michael D. Wallace is Professor of Political Science at the University of British Columbia, Vancouver, British Columbia, Canada. He is author of *War and Rank Among Nations* and coeditor of *To Augur Well,* and he has written numerous articles on arms races and the causes of war, which have appeared in such journals as *Journal of Conflict Resolution, Journal of Peace Research, International Organization,* and *International Studies Quarterly.* In 1982 he was awarded the Karl Deutsch Peace Research Award in recognition of his outstanding work in that area. He is currently engaged in a research project on the risk of accidental nuclear war.

Howard Zinn is Professor of Political Science at Boston University, Boston, Massachusetts. Among his many books are *La Guardia in Congress,* which won the Albert Beveridge Prize of the American Historical Association, *The Politics of History,* and *A People's History of the United States.* He is coeditor of *The Pentagon Papers: Critical Essays.* Professor Zinn played a major role in both the civil rights and antiwar movements. He has written numerous articles in both popular and scholarly journals.